Surviving Stephen King

ALSO BY REBECCA FROST
AND FROM MCFARLAND

Media and the Murderer: Jack the Ripper, Steven Avery and an Enduring Formula for Notoriety (2020)

Words of a Monster: Analyzing the Writings of H.H. Holmes, America's First Serial Killer (2019)

The Ripper's Victims in Print: The Rhetoric of Portrayals Since 1929 (2018)

Surviving Stephen King

*Reactions to the
Supernatural in Works
by the Master of Horror*

REBECCA FROST

McFarland & Company, Inc., Publishers
Jefferson, North Carolina

LIBRARY OF CONGRESS CATALOGUING-IN-PUBLICATION DATA

Names: Frost, Rebecca, 1985– author.
Title: Surviving Stephen King : reactions to the supernatural in works by the master of horror / Rebecca Frost.
Description: Jefferson, North Carolina : McFarland & Company, Inc., Publishers, 2021 | Includes bibliographical references and index.
Identifiers: LCCN 2021044603 | ISBN 9781476684734 (paperback : acid free paper) ∞
ISBN 9781476643915 (ebook)
Subjects: LCSH: King, Stephen 1947– —Criticism and interpretation. | King, Stephen 1947– —Characters. | Supernatural in literature. | BISAC: LITERARY CRITICISM / Horror & Supernatural | LCGFT: Literary criticism.
Classification: LCC PS3561.I483 Z666 2021 | DDC 813/.54—dc23
LC record available at https://lccn.loc.gov/2021044603

BRITISH LIBRARY CATALOGUING DATA ARE AVAILABLE

**ISBN (print) 978-1-4766-8473-4
ISBN (ebook) 978-1-4766-4391-5**

© 2021 Rebecca Frost. All rights reserved

No part of this book may be reproduced or transmitted in any form or by any means, electronic or mechanical, including photocopying or recording, or by any information storage and retrieval system, without permission in writing from the publisher.

Front cover image © 2021 Shutterstock / Rob van Hal

Printed in the United States of America

*McFarland & Company, Inc., Publishers
Box 611, Jefferson, North Carolina 28640
www.mcfarlandpub.com*

To Patrick McAleer and Phil Simpson,
who were the first to ask for more.

Acknowledgments

I would like to thank Philip Simpson and Patrick McAleer, co-chairs of the PCA/ACA Stephen King area, for welcoming me with open arms in 2014. Thanks also go to my fellow presenters in the Stephen King area, whether we've only met once or we greet each other happily year after year.

I would also like to thank Lynne Walter, MSW; Russell Johnson, PhD; and Melissa Lovejoy for their brainstorming help early on in the project.

Thank you to my ever-encouraging constant supporters: Angela Badke; Tom Blessing; Zach Blessing; Isaac Flint; Stephanie Flint; Colleen Hix; Rae Hix; Jesse Koenig; Angela Musser; and Michelle Wright.

And finally, thank you to my parents, who once told me that *Pet Sematary* probably wasn't a good book for a precocious elementary schooler, no matter what her reading level, and to Eric, who has read exactly one Stephen King book but by this point could probably summarize them all.

Table of Contents

Acknowledgments   vi

Introduction: Man Against Monster   1

I—Explanation and Ritual:
Cultural Appropriation in King

1. The Burying Ground, the Wendigo, Whatever: Stolen Stories as Enlightenment   9
2. The Ritual of Chüd: Borrowed Solutions   32

II—My God Is Strong:
Christianity in the Face of the Unknown

3. The Power of Prayer: Christian Solutions to Supernatural Problems   59
4. Was It a Miracle? Light, Power and Belief   69
5. CARRIE WHITE IS BURNING FOR HER SINS: Christianity as a Weapon   84
6. ForJesussakeamen: The Danger of Performative Belief   104

III—Reality Is Thin Ice: Belief and Unbelief

7. Twisted, Silent Hulk: Destroying the Outer Shell   121
8. There Are Buicks Everywhere: Living with the Supernatural   140

Table of Contents

Conclusion: What It All Comes Down To: Standing and Being True   161

Chapter Notes   185

Bibliography   189

Index   191

Introduction

Man Against Monster

As the Master of Horror, Stephen King is known for putting his characters in difficult, and frequently deadly, situations. Although King does force some of his characters to face possible real-life menaces—a rabid dog in *Cujo* (1981), for example, or human serial killers in works like *Misery* (1987) or *A Good Marriage* (2010)—the vast majority of threats in his stories come in the form of the supernatural. King is known for beginning his tales in a world that seems to be very much like ours, centered around relatable, everyman sorts of characters who are then confronted with something that rationality and science cannot explain. They come face to face with, and often find themselves needing to defeat, the alien, supernatural, or otherwise nonhuman.

In most cases, this supernatural is indeed a direct threat, although frequently only against children or the childlike. It therefore falls to either children, or the childlike, to take up the fight. In part this is because they are the only ones to actually recognize the threat, but another aspect, as seen in King's recent book *The Outsider* (2018), is the adults' frequent refusal to recognize the monster, even when faced with its actions. As grownups, most of his characters lack either the imagination or the bravery to consider an explanation outside of what they perceive to be rational reality.

The various possible reactions and explanations such characters might have to the unknown clearly fascinate King, who has written variations on this theme in short stories, novellas, and novels his entire career. While some of those threats are resolved—or at least seem to be resolved—in a single work, others occupy multiple stories and might only be picked up years later. Although *It*, for example, was published in 1986 and ends with the villain Pennywise presumably defeated, in 2001's *Dreamcatcher* a return to the mythical town of Derry reveals that "Pennywise lives."[1] Likewise the events of *'Salem's Lot* (1975) are given both a preface and a sequel in short story form through "Jerusalem's Lot" and "One for the Road" (both collected in 1978 in *Night Shift*). Even if the events within a King novel seem to end with a victory for the protagonists, that victory can only be given the conditional "for now."

Much of the success seen by King's protagonists is not in the form of banishing evil entirely, but of causing it to relocate. Epics such as *The Stand* (uncut edition published 1990) and *Needful Things* (1991) already contain epilogues that indicate the villains—Randall Flagg and Leland Gaunt, respectively—resurface later, to try their luck with a different population. While King's protagonist group might have saved themselves, they have merely shifted the evil instead of destroying it. Yet when the threat is thought to have been destroyed completely, such as in *Christine* (1983), the final chapter frequently reveals that whatever method was used only delayed the inevitable, and the protagonists are once again in danger.

The problem so many King characters face is that there are no resources for dealing with the issues confronting them. Living in late twentieth- or early twenty-first-century America, they have access to horror movies but no grounded rituals by which to remove the monster. The first barrier they must overcome is in actually admitting that the threat is inhuman and not a vagrant, or a man in a clown costume, or some previously undisclosed Army project. Even when the core group of characters is able to reach an agreement and rely on each other, they are frequently blocked from asking for help from anyone outside of their trusted gang. At times this is because the threat has literally blocked them off from the outside world, such as in *Desperation* (1996) and its companion novel *The Regulators* (1996), but frequently the unbelievability of the explanation for what has been happening in the given small town is blockade enough.

The threat thus isolates as part of its danger, leaving a small group of people with little or no background in the occult, the monstrous, or the alien to negotiate both defining the menace and therefore finding its weakness. Frequently this discussion centers around questions of power, both as to where the supernatural gets its power and where the human protagonists might find some of their own, as young Ben Hanscom ponders in *It*: "What, exactly, *was* power, anyway?"[2] For Ben, as for so many other characters, the question comes as he examines the threat and seeks Its true form so that he and his friends can discover Its weakness. By defining where and how It gets Its power, the children—and then their adult selves—are able to battle It and at least give themselves the illusion of victory. The Losers' Club is just one group who find themselves seeking an explanation of the evil in order to prepare themselves to do battle with it.

Introduction 3

The ways and means by which King's human characters do—or do not—end up defining their inhuman adversaries vary from story to story, although both these explanations and the characters' methods of confronting the evil can be divided into general categories. King's characters, largely white American males, frequently reach beyond their own experiences and ancestral history in order to define and attempt to defeat these supernatural threats. In other words, they can choose to rely on cultural appropriation of rituals or so-called mythical figures in order to define the threat and identify its seat of power.

The second option is for characters to turn to Christian religion for solace or power of their own. Lapsed Catholics make frequent appearances in King's novels, as do characters who misuse their faith as a club to beat others—notably the figure of Big Jim Rennie in *Under the Dome* (2009)—but there are those who hear the voice of God speaking prophecy, and those who either witness or work miracles, like *Desperation*'s boy-Christ David Carver or *The Green Mile*'s (1996) John Coffey, whose initials are a clear giveaway. The protagonists in the short story "The Mangler" (collected in *Night Shift* 1978) even attempt to perform an exorcism, in spite of neither being trained as a priest.

Yet other characters, when faced with an inexplicable threat, follow the path of *Christine*'s Dennis Guilder and do their best to destroy the physical object as completely as possible. For Guilder, this means smashing the possessed car using a much larger and heavier vehicle. The surviving characters in *'Salem's Lot* have a similar idea when they return to set the vampire-infested town on fire. Because destroying the physical when it comes to a human threat eliminates the human, it seems that destroying the physical embodiment of a threat, no matter what form it takes, should do likewise.

The final approach King characters take to the supernatural and inexplicable is to simply accept it. This can have relatively benign results, such as are seen in *From a Buick 8* (2002) or can result in the deaths of the main characters when they find no way to fight back and are ultimately beaten down, as in "The Raft" (collected in *Skeleton Crew* 1985) or "Trucks" (collected in *Night Shift*). In the first, the protagonist cannot see a way to avoid the mysterious deadly oil slick and chooses to jump into it rather than continue to fight for his life. In the second, the vehicles—taking after Christine instead of the Buick 8—kill a number of the characters, forcing the remaining few to give in and bend to their will. For the characters who adopt this approach, this is simply their new life now; or, barring that, their choice of a death.

When divided this way, there is no clear single path for King's characters to choose in order to assure their—at least temporary—triumph.

While Christianity is generally not a safe bet for characters' survival, the endings of the various stories that fall into—or across—the other categories run the gamut from utter destruction, and therefore failure, to a presumed prolonged success. In these, there is no epilogue depicting that the evil has simply made a geographical relocation, and thus far no follow-up narratives indicating the same. There must, then, be another layer of consideration for what contributes to the characters' chances of success or failure.

It is one that King himself has placed in his novels more than once using his authorial voice, and a belief that is strong enough to be the title of his longest novel. In *It*, King exhorts his characters—and also his readers—to "*be true, be brave, stand*"[3] (italics in original). Repeatedly in *The Stand*, King's protagonists consider the importance of firmly setting their feet and holding a position, as opposed to freefalling in the wake of the plague. The final mention, often repurposed as a motivational quote, reads, "The place where you made your stand never mattered. Only that you were there ... and still on your feet"[4] (ellipsis in original). While previous instances of this repetition to stand and be true focused on those on the "good" side of the final battle, this last comes in antagonist Randall Flagg's future resurgence in a classic King epilogue that indicates success was not final. King's *Dark Tower* series, where Flagg may or may not face his actual final defeat, has its hero Roland frequently exhorting his companions to stand and be true.

This sentiment, though, runs through all the various character reactions to the unknown and inexplicable: if the reaction, at least in part, comes from the character taking a stand and reaching down inside him- or herself in response to the threat, then it is far more likely that the danger will not return. Attempting to counter the unknown using elements of the unknown, either from an outside culture or a religion that has lapsed or was never a part of the character's life, heightens the chances of the evil returning, or even of making the situation worse. King takes an especially negative view toward Christianity, although characters such as David Carver are allowed survival, if not an entirely happy ending. Even David's connection to Christianity, though, draws on his own past experience and functions to ground him more deeply in himself, rather than show him reaching out and beyond his, or his ancestors', experience.

The uplifting message—and difficult challenge—which runs through King's works is that, no matter what shape a threat takes or how powerful it may be, the greatest chance of success comes in being true to oneself. This means his characters need to rely on their own past experiences and their own interpretations of the supernatural or alien, looking inward rather than outward. It is not, however, an easy task, especially when characters are confronted with such overwhelmingly powerful inhuman threats.

Explaining the Inexplicable

This book examines King's works along these categories to make the argument that, no matter which approach his characters use when faced with the supernatural, at the core, their success is dependent upon whether or not they can be true to themselves and stand. The first section, "Explanation and Ritual: Cultural Appropriation in King," looks at the narratives in which his characters rely on Indigenous, Native, or other non–Eurocentric belief in order to confront the threat. It is divided into two chapters: "The Burying Ground, the Wendigo, Whatever: Stolen Stories as Enlightenment" in which the characters rely on non–Eurocentric beliefs and stories in order to explain the nature of the threat, and "The Ritual of Chüd: Borrowed Solutions," which looks at the instances in which King's usually-white American characters of European ancestry rely on non–European cultural rituals or narratives in order to defeat the given threat. Even though it seems that there would be overlap between cultural appropriation as the explanation, and cultural appropriation as the solution, this is in fact not often the case. It is even possible for one culture to be mined during the explanation and another used—or perhaps misused—during the final confrontation.

The next section, "My God Is Strong: Christianity in the Face of the Unknown," considers the ways King's characters make use of, or refer to, Christianity when confronted with the unknown. The first chapter, "The Power of Prayer: Christian Solutions to Supernatural Problems," examines the narratives where Christian practices, references, or trappings are used in an attempt to resolve the threat. The next, "Was It a Miracle? Light, Power and Belief," takes a closer look at the variations in which Christianity is treated as a direct opposite of the threat, becoming more "white magic" than the actual Bible-based religion. The third, "CARRIE WHITE IS BURNING FOR HER SINS: Christianity as a Weapon," looks at the narratives which have Christianity itself as the cause of the issue, or where Christian beliefs or practices in fact make the situation worse. The final chapter of this section, "ForJesussakeamen: The Danger of Performative Belief," discusses the ways Christianity itself is presented as a failure within some of King's narratives—not only as a failure in the current fight against evil, but also a failure in the everyday business of life.

The third section, "Reality Is Thin Ice: Belief and Unbelief," is devoted to non-religious and non-ritual reactions to supernatural threats. The first chapter, "Twisted, Silent Hulk: Destroying the Outer Shell," delves into the stories where the physical embodiment of the threat is destroyed by the protagonists, as completely as they can manage it. And lastly, the chapter "There Are Buicks Everywhere: Living with the Supernatural" examines common themes in the narratives in which the protagonists' reactions to the unnatural is seemingly apathetic acceptance and integration into their lives as a "new normal."

The conclusion, "What It All Comes Down To: Standing and Being True," pulls all of these themes together to examine them on a new level: whether the characters in question draw upon their own experiences and own sense of self, compared to whether or not they succeed, if only for their own time and location. The permanent defeat of evil may be an impossibility in King's narratives, but success—and survival—are tricky enough to achieve, even given the protagonist groups and their ability to rely on one another instead of facing the evil alone.

I
Explanation and Ritual
Cultural Appropriation in King

The vast majority of Stephen King's novels, novellas, and short stories take place in what is meant to be the real world of late twentieth or early twenty-first century America. The examples given in this book focus specifically on these kinds of stories: those in which an everyday, average person with no prior experience with the supernatural, paranormal, or extraterrestrial is forced to confront a situation that is inexplicable within what we think of as natural law. This has the narrative aspect of isolating the main character or a small group of characters within either the situation itself, or in their belief that something supernatural is indeed happening. Although some of King's other stories, like the *Dark Tower* series, intertwine worlds in which magic is expected and accepted with people from our own non-magical world, those stories are not the main focus of this book. Here we will concentrate on inexplicable events that happen in our own "real" world—generally in America, and then mostly in Maine—and not tales that take place in other worlds, including the future.

King prefers exploring these sorts of situations in which someone to whom the reader can relate is forced to confront a situation that the reader will find absolutely foreign. With so many stories and extensive casts in many of his books, the reactions these people have are varied indeed. What his characters tend to have in common, though, is both Americanness and whiteness.

Dominant American culture has its roots in Europe and, especially in the late twentieth and early twenty-first century, does not place its understanding in legends. Fairy tales and similar beliefs are dismissed as being for children and clearly fantastical, with a reliance on science and logic required in all explanations. Perhaps science cannot explain how a bumblebee is able to fly, but biology can dissect it all the same. Children are criticized for an overabundance of imagination and even fiction is divided into categories of realistic or not. A serial killer might actually stalk a reader, but not in her dreams.

Americans with so-called "Western" or European roots, then, may find themselves bereft of spiritual guidance or a deep connection to their ancestors' beliefs because they have been so belittled. Stories of magic have been relegated to the Disney corporation and the domain of Hollywood. Any spirituality or mysticism thus comes from marginalized cultures. Smudging with white sage, for example, is rooted in Indigenous culture—and then only in specific regions and peoples—and practices such as mindfulness or meditation are not part of mainstream Western thought. When such traditions become "mainstream," however, they are diluted, removed from their culture of origin, and packaged for dominant white America. Only fairly recently has this appropriation been flagged as problematic within the dominant culture as well as the marginalized cultures from which elements have been stolen.

When King presents his characters with threats that do not fit into their concepts of rational explanation, then, they have little in their own histories and cultures to fall back on for clarification or solution. This is especially true when King's characters are not churchgoers and therefore have a complete void when it comes to belief in a higher power or anything beyond the reach of their five senses. Is it any wonder, then, that they are forced to reach outside of their own knowledge bases and experiences in order to find ways to define and then confront the supernatural threats that have suddenly sprung up in their previously ordered and explicable lives?

1

The Burying Ground, the Wendigo, Whatever
Stolen Stories as Enlightenment

"Cultural appropriation" is most often used to describe the adoption of Indigenous practices or beliefs by non–Indigenous peoples. Frequently this means white people using dreamcatchers, claiming spirit animals, receiving "Indian names" from a "shaman," smudging with sage, or building "wigwams" or "sweat lodges." Such practices are taken piecemeal from the cultures in which they hold sacred meaning and performed by outsiders who seem to think they look cool or that it will somehow help on their own spiritual journeys. They are somehow more meaningful for being "Other" and new, although they have been sanitized or gutted by the transition to Pinterest and popular blogs.

The settling of the land that has come to be called America involved the violent removal of both the Indigenous peoples and their practices. Up until 1978 it was illegal for Indigenous peoples to practice their own spirituality, although many of these elements have now been co-opted by the dominant culture for matters like tattoos and spiritual awakenings. While the original settlers and colonists from Europe denied Indigenous peoples the right to speak their own languages, wear their own clothes, or practice their own beliefs, the continued disparity between dominant and marginalized cultures constantly centers European practices while treating any others as "exotic" and "mystical." The horror genre has, of course, made full use of the separation of cultures and the "spirituality" of Indigenous cultures in its explanations for supernatural occurrences.

American culture of the twentieth- and twenty-first century is meant to be modern and therefore defined by a base in science and rationality. Tales of the supernatural that have their roots in Europe are called fairy tales or legends and dismissed as the efforts of our ancestors to explain what we, as modern thinkers, write off as wild tales, madness, drunkenness, or natural phenomena. In order to explain a true supernatural occurrence in late twentieth- or early twenty-first-century America, horror writers frequently reach outside of this "rational" thought and look to curses bestowed by non-white peoples on the frequently-white main characters. The idea of supernatural events occurring because white people have desecrated an "old Indian burial ground" infiltrated the horror genre during the 1970s and 1980s and became a shorthand explanation for any number of terrible experiences inflicted on the script's main characters.

King, who has frequently admitted that his interests lie in placing everyday characters in unusual situations and seeing how they react, rather than explaining the cause of those situations, has not been immune to this shorthand. Indeed, the "old Indian burying ground" is the entire explanation of the mysterious powers shown in *Pet Sematary*, although his use of non-white cultural explanations for the situations facing his characters does extend beyond the old standby. In seeking to understand the problems they find themselves in, King's characters at times choose to look outside of their own home cultures in order to find an explanation, whether or not it helps them to defeat the threat by the end of the book.

Pet Sematary and the Wendigo

In *Pet Sematary*, elderly neighbor Jud Crandall tells newcomer Louis Creed about the strange piece of stony ground in the wood behind his property. After a truck kills young Ellie Creed's cat, Winston Churchill, Jud takes Louis on a strange journey. First the men must confidently climb a deadfall of branches without looking to see where they put their feet. Hesitation is a threat at any point in the journey, since Jud also instructs Louis to ignore any sounds he might hear as they cross swampy ground, stepping confidently from hummock to hummock in the mist. At the top of an old set of stairs, Jud tells Louis to dig a grave for Church and to keep back rocks—the ground is full of them—with which to build a cairn when he is done.

Louis follows both Jud and these instructions without fully understanding what he is doing. He is home alone since his wife has taken their two children to her parents' for Thanksgiving, and Louis does not report the cat's death at Jud's instructions, but also because he does not want his young daughter to worry. The subject of death is a difficult one in the Creed household, since although Louis is a physician whose first day at his new job resulted in his witnessing the death of a college

1. The Burying Ground, the Wendigo, Whatever   11

student, his wife, Rachel, refuses to broach it because of her own childhood trauma.

When the cat returns after his strange burial, Louis at first tries to convince himself to maintain a rational explanation. At first he attempts to argue that the cat was not, in fact, dead, and that although he might be a fine physician, he would have been a shoddy veterinarian. Memories of how the cat's head lolled on a broken neck, as well as how Louis had to work to peel him up from the frosty ground, quickly foil this justification. He also manages to talk himself out of thinking that he buried someone else's cat in the strange stony soil, or that the cat who returns is not, in fact, Church. Confronted with the fact that his daughter's cat was once dead and is now walking around the home place, Louis turns to Jud for an explanation.

At this point in the book, Louis has been positioned as a man who has a relatively healthy working relationship with death. His wife might face the subject with irrational fear and resist Louis answering Ellie's questions about it, but Louis is a doctor. He has been to medical school. Although the book includes paraphrased segments of the story of the resurrection of Lazarus, the Creed family is not religious. If something goes on after death, it is in an incorporeal form, and even if a dead cat could be revived with quick medical intervention, Church was cold and frozen to the ground. There is simply no explanation that aligns with Louis' previous experience of the world, and perhaps this is why he accepts the fuzzy one Jud offers.

As Louis was burying Church, he got the vague story that this was an old Micmac burying ground, which had "gone sour," and that the Micmacs explained the strange sights and sounds in the woods as being related to a Wendigo.[1] Louis was only vaguely familiar with what a Wendigo was, and Jud himself says later on he believes the Micmacs simply made up the whole thing. He explains that, during long winters, sometimes tribes had to resort to cannibalism in order to survive, and therefore invented the spirit of the Wendigo in order to explain the disappearance of the people who were killed and eaten. Jud further tells Louis that he believes the ground was soured because they then buried the bones of the consumed people there.

In the course of the book, Louis never looks up the Wendigo on his own. Even though he has just witnessed something inexplicable, he accepts Jud's version: that the Wendigo itself does not exist and is a story purely to help groups allay their own guilt over murder and cannibalism. He certainly does not question that the Micmac would commit cannibalism in the first place. Apparently it seems logical to him that any people living in Maine could find themselves short on food in the winter and be driven to an act that, after all, he may have been taught Indigenous peoples did not consider to be taboo.

There must, however, be something special about the fact that it is meant to be an old Micmac burying ground and not simply an old cemetery. Graveyards might be creepy, but they are nowhere near as powerful in the American psyche as "Indian burial grounds." White men cannot lay curses—although Billy Halleck of *Thinner* certainly does his best—but Micmacs are deemed capable. The curse may even have been accidental instead of intentional, born either of their apparently completely fictional Wendigo or their cannibalistic tendencies.

While the Wendigo is indeed a part of Algonquian history, and the Mi'kmaq people—the preferred spelling—belong to the Algonquin language group, Jud's explanation of the Wendigo, like the use of "an old Indian burying ground," seems more based on American horror movies than actual Indigenous culture. The Wendigo is frequently associated with greed, including cannibalism, and is never satisfied. After having eaten one person, the Wendigo must continually search for more, always hungry. In some traditions, the Wendigo's spirit possess people, and in others, greedy humans can themselves turn into Wendigos. Because the Wendigo is widespread through speakers of the Algonquin language family, there is variation across the regions and tribal groups. Indigenous depictions of the Wendigo, however, limit the destruction either to the spirit or the person possessed. Although the Wendigo brings greed in many forms and can turn otherwise innocent people into a Wendigo, Jud's explanation does not in fact rely on Micmac tradition.

King's, and therefore Jud's, understanding of the Wendigo is based on popular horror's perception of the Wendigo as introduced by the non–Indigenous Algernon Blackwood in the early twentieth century.[2] Horror's frequent use of Indigenous peoples and traditions as the basis for the inexplicable was already clearly established by the time *Pet Sematary* was published, as was the idea that displaced Indigenous populations would clearly seek vengeance on the white people who ousted them. Jud—and now Louis—are not the first white men to feel the call of the Micmac burying ground, although Jud tells Louis that "the Micmacs told Stanny B.'s grandda about the burying ground"[3] themselves. According to the tale as filtered through the generations and then through Jud, the telling was apparently meant as a sharing of information and not as a means of cursing Stanny B.'s grandfather and anyone else who heard it … although Jud himself seems reluctant to consider knowledge of the place to be a curse.

The journey the men must make in order to reach the burying ground is also not explained by Jud's "Wendigo" or "sour ground" tale. If

1. The Burying Ground, the Wendigo, Whatever

the ground is sour because it was where the Micmacs buried the bones of their own victims of cannibalism—and the Wendigo does not exist in any form but lies—then somehow that ground has also been protected. Louis himself could not have climbed the deadfall and gotten past the first barrier without Jud's help, much less found his way through the misty swamp and up the mysterious stairs. Jud has perhaps grabbed on to the Wendigo explanation because of its associations with hunger and greed: once a man knows about the place with the stony ground and the destroyed cairns, it preys on him until he uses it and passes the knowledge along. It could be that the place itself feels this hunger and needs such stories in order to keep it sated.

Neither Jud nor Louis cares much about the explanation for *why* the phenomenon works because each has proof that it does, at least to a point. It is enough for Louis to see that Church has come back, albeit changed, and Jud rationalizes that the strange new behavior Ellie sees in her cat will help her begin to cope. When Church dies again—presumably permanently this time—it should therefore be easier for her, as it was for Jud and his own childhood dog.

Whatever the explanation for the burying ground, the narrative of *Pet Sematary* does not position it as a problem or threat that needs to be fixed. Instead, it—the Wendigo or the sour soil—functions as the solution to the plot's central catastrophe. Just as Church was run over in the road and able to be brought back through this strange trip over the deadfall, Louis' toddler son, Gage, is also killed by a truck. Since the solution to an untimely death has already been handed to him by Jud, Louis makes his decision to pack up his remaining family members and send them off to Chicago so that he can once again carry a small body through the strange swamp and dig a hole to be topped with a cairn. Church's death served to introduce this solution, and Jud's explanation of a Wendigo and an old Micmac burying ground is inconsequential.

If Louis had instead wanted to destroy the burying ground or somehow deactivate its power, then the explanation would have mattered. He would have had to properly identify the source of power in order to determine whether he could defeat it. Many stories of the Wendigo do indeed come with lessons on how to turn the monstrous back into the human or banish the evil spirit. If, then, the Micmacs of the book had known that a Wendigo had been the cause of the sour ground, they would have had ways of dealing with it and resolving the issue instead of simply abandoning the location. Neither Jud nor Louis questions why they chose to pass on the story to a white man instead of making the amends necessary to heal the soil. Even if, as Jud suggests, the Wendigo was a made-up figure to cover up acts of cannibalism, surely the Micmac who accidentally cursed the ground by burying the bones of their cannibalized dead would have been able to atone for these acts.

Unless—although none of the characters consider this—the curse was purposeful and directed.

Because the Micmac abandoned that land, the only men Jud knows who have crossed the deadfall and buried their dead in that soil are settlers. Their actions—Louis' actions, especially when he buries the body of his son in the stony ground—are an affront to nature. Louis fails to confine himself to "the limitations of reality"[4] because he has found a magical place beyond understanding and beyond explanation. When Jud invokes the Micmacs, he is referring to a group of people either dead or fled. Neither Jud nor Louis seeks out any surviving member of the tribe—if there are any in the book's world—to ask for more information. They simply accept the vague notion of the Wendigo because each man knows that, at least to an extent, the burying ground works.

In the case of this novel, though, because neither Jud nor Louis wants to destroy the supernatural place of pseudo-miracle, the explanation need not be fleshed out beyond a few broad strokes invoking Indigenous peoples and their beliefs. It seems that King needed *some* sort of explanation for the supernatural events at the center of his novel, and the Micmac were convenient. Most of his readers would not themselves be Indigenous, and white audiences of horror, especially in the 1970s and 1980s, had been primed to accept "old Indian burial ground" as a valid explanation for inexplicable plot events.

The Wendigo, and therefore the Micmac, are explanation without understanding. Jud simply needs to give Louis *some* sort of clarification for his returned cat, thereby planting the seeds for what Louis will choose to do after his son's death. Jud later returns with a further explanation for Louis in which he tells the younger man that at least one person *has* been buried in the mysterious place beyond the deadfall, and that the consequences were less than favorable. Louis, clinging to his physician's logic even at the end, when his hair has gone white and he is meant to have gone mad, argues to himself that the place did not work properly on Gage because it had been so long since the boy died. With his newly-dead wife in his arms, Louis crosses the deadfall once again and buries her without tools, ruining his hands as well as his sanity. Whether Rachel Creed returns as more or less human than her son is left up to the reader's imagination.

There is no attempt to destroy the mysterious burying grounds in spite of the many warnings the characters receive. Heidi Stregell argues that Louis fully believes "in the furious Wendigo"[5] even when he refuses to have faith in Christ's resurrection, and this conviction pushes him past warnings both mundane and supernatural. The burying ground even reaches out itself, not just in the form of Gage, who silences both Jud and Rachel, but with a more mysterious force in an attempt to prevent Rachel from returning home in the first place. The burying ground, whatever powers it, tries to protect itself in ways that Louis not only does not understand—they are ways he had not anticipated, and ways he no longer cares about in his grief.

The true horror in *Pet Sematary* is not in the burying ground, no matter what its power, nor in what Tony Magistrale calls "the Wendigo vampire."[6] The book spends so long following the everyday lives of the Creed family in their new home in Maine in order to position the reader to feel the full impact of young Gage's death. The horror comes in the form of Louis himself, a formerly scientifically-minded physician who now believes that he can overcome the power of death. The explanation for how this happens—the Micmacs and their Wendigo—is secondary to the fact that it *can* happen. The Wendigo itself is never confronted, and no attempt is made to destroy it or the burying ground. In his grief and horror, Louis seeks only to *use* the power, in spite of its great expense, instead of to curtail or change it.

It: Indian Braves (and a Bravette)

The supernatural horror in *It*—where the supernatural element is indeed intentionally dangerous and malicious—is not itself related to Indigenous peoples or connected to Indigenous beliefs. The seven main characters, known collectively as the Losers' Club, first battle It in 1958 when they are eleven years old, and then return in 1985 to supposedly finish the job and kill It completely. Because they, unlike Louis, *do* want to destroy the supernatural element, they seek to understand what It actually is in order to identify both Its power and Its weakness.

Understanding of It differs depending on which characters are asked to explain what is happening in the small town of Derry, Maine, and why so many children are disappearing completely or turning up dead. The adults, including the police, believe that a vagrant must be killing the children. It cannot, of course, be one of Derry's own upstanding citizens. As more disappearances and murders occur, some amend this assessment to be perhaps two vagrants, one who preys on little boys and the other who goes after girls, but clearly the murderer must be human.

When King's narration follows the children who are threatened—and at times killed—by It, the answer is less clear. One boy, Eddie

Corcoran, is marked as a disappearance because his body was never found. The adults' explanation is that his stepfather must have murdered him, the way he murdered Eddie's younger brother Dorsey, or that Eddie must have just grown sick of the beatings and run away. Eddie, however, is shown to have seen first his dead brother and then a monster resembling the movie version of the Creature from the Black Lagoon. Eddie first insists to himself that his vision cannot be real and then, as It kills him, he continues to beat at Its back, searching for the zipper in the costume he *knows* has to be there.⁷

The Losers themselves encounter It in various forms, some of them culled from Saturday matinees, like the mummy and the teenage werewolf. Some are from the kids' own personal fears: Mike Hanlon sees a gigantic bird, pulled from the time when, as a baby, a normal-sized bird pecked at him. Bill Denbrough, like Eddie Cocoran, sees his dead brother, Bill in a moving photograph. It can also become multiple things, such as the drowned children that frightened Stan Uris, or even nonhuman, as in the blood that belched up from the drain in Beverly Marsh's bathroom.

When the Losers begin to tell each other about their encounters with such threats, they also start to understand that each of these forms is in fact the same creature. Only one of the children, Richie Tozier, has managed to force himself to believe that his own encounter, in which Derry's enormous plastic Paul Bunyan came to life and attempted to kill him with his enormous ax, was nothing more than a dream. The other six all understand that what they saw was real, and dangerous—but also come to learn that grownups *cannot* see It. Beverly is especially traumatized when her father ignores the blood-spattered bathroom, but the other children can see the gore.

By sharing their stories, and by looking through Mike Hanlon's father's album of the history of Derry, the Losers come to understand that It can take many forms; It preys on children and cannot be seen by adults; and that It has already been in Derry for centuries. Because they *are* all children, around eleven years old, they want to ask some adults for help, but quickly realize that they cannot. Adults would not believe them, especially since they cannot see what the children can. The seven therefore realize that, if something is to be done about It, they must do it themselves.

The fact that many of Its forms come from the children's own fears, and that these fears have been nourished by the movies the Losers love, spurs them on to think of solutions that also come from those movies. A werewolf on film, for example, can be stopped by silver bullets. The children decided that making bullets themselves would be too tricky, but they manage to make two silver ball bearings from one of Ben's silver dollars, and they give Beverly the slingshot. The power of belief emerges strongly during this battle between the seven Losers and the teenage werewolf form of It: although Beverly misses It with her first shot, and wounds it gravely with the second, It only flees when all seven pretend that she has a third hidden in the cup of the slingshot. Their belief—in the silver and in the imaginary third ball bearing—unites them against It.

But, because they want to destroy It, and perhaps because in their youth they have a curiosity Louis Creed lacks, the Losers also want to understand what It is. They have seen It under various guises and façades, and they learn that It is limited by the same rules that govern Its current face—a werewolf can be horribly injured by silver bullets, but the same defense would not work against a leper—but there are still deeper questions. The Losers want answers, and a number of events fall in line, guided by the force of good that acts in opposition to Its force of destruction, in order to provide them with the means to learn more.

Once all seven Losers have assembled, they perform a literal and ceremonial groundbreaking for their clubhouse. Instead of a tree house, as they originally wanted, Ben Hanscom instructs them in the creation of an underground hideout. The children work for days to dig out a hole in the soil in their favorite place to play, even though they have repeatedly been warned against going into the Barrens—and even though It is closer there. They shore up the sides of the hole to prevent cave-ins and cover the top with scavenged wood and squares of sod in order to make their hideout virtually invisible. This ends up working so well that, later on, one of the bullies sits directly on top of the cap while two of the Losers hide below, and their hideout is not discovered until the kids emerge.

This underground clubhouse, though, also serves another purpose. Ben Hanscom, current and future architect, tells the others about a book called *Ghosts of the Great Plains* in which he came across "the Smoke-Hole Ceremony." When the unspecified "Indians" were faced with a decision that needed special consideration, they would dig a hole in the ground and cover the top with branches. The Losers covered their clubhouse with planks, but the basic setup is the same. Ben then explains how "Indians" would light a fire down in the hole, piling on green branches, and the men would sit and wait. If the smoke became overwhelming, they would leave the smoke hole, and the few remaining men would have a vision. A vision that, Ben informed his friends, was usually correct.

The parallels are too great even for eleven-year-olds to overlook, and Richie thinks that, if they asked Ben how he came across that particular story, he would say that *"the book practically jumped into his hand"*[8] (italics in original). All summer the Losers have felt some sort of force guiding them and bringing them together, and they collectively refuse to believe that Ben reading this book and finding this story, especially since he has already helped them build their underground clubhouse, is a coincidence.

There is a temporary delay when the boys attempt to make Beverly stay up top, both because it is a ceremony for "braves" and because someone should remain literally clear-headed in case anyone below comes to grief. A small miracle occurs after Beverly tears out seven matches and lights one, holding out the other ends for each boy to take. The one who pulls the burned match will stay behind. When Bev opens her hand to look at the last match, all seven are miraculously unburned, and all seven children go down into the clubhouse.

Unlike *Pet Sematary*'s reference to the Micmac and the use of the word "Wendigo," there is nothing about the Losers' experience to tie it to a specific set of beliefs. The "Smoke Hole Ceremony" is given proper noun status, but there is no indication that it might have been named something else in the book Ben found, in a language other than English. Although Bill has previously struggled to pronounce French words in their search to explain what It is and where It came from, the Smoke Hole Ceremony is entirely removed from its original place and its original language. This ceremony comes from somewhere in the Great Plains, whereas Jud's explanation to Louis was at least based in the peoples who had once lived on the same land. The Losers' search for meaning has led them not only to an Indigenous ceremony, but to a ceremony that has no indication of ever being practiced in Maine before.

Concerns about cultural appropriation were clearly not as prominent in the 1950s when children played "Cowboys and Indians" and consumed all sorts of media in which the brave white man had an Indigenous sidekick to help him as he triumphed over the various hardships of life in the Old West. Children could also not be expected to recognize the fact that the Smoke Hole Ceremony in the book was not meant for them. Since it had already been printed and disseminated to audiences beyond the peoples for whom it was practiced, the Smoke Hole Ceremony had undergone the same sort of changes as the Wendigo: told now for a broader audience, it was already adapted for settler consumption and colored by European perception of how Indigenous peoples should act.

For the Losers, it felt as though they were being directed to participate in a Smoke Hole Ceremony of their own. Some outside force, later revealed to be the Turtle, was pointing them toward making their clubhouse and filling it with smoke from green branches. While the book Ben found suggested that the ceremony usually told participants the correct answer of what to do, however, this was not the case with the Losers. The two who remained down long enough to have the vision, Mike and Richie, did not in fact receive information on what the Losers should do next. What they witnessed was Its arrival, long ago, into the place that would in time become Derry and the Barrens. When they are pulled up out of the clubhouse and able to speak, they can tell the others that It is not only supernatural, but alien. However, this does not give the children a clear indication of what to do next.

The Smoke Hole Ceremony, then, does not work for the Losers the way Ben's book explained it did for the Plains people. The Losers are too excited over the fact that two of their number *did* have a vision to fully critique this fact. The knowledge that the creature they are fighting is alien indeed has little effect on their plans, since they continue to be uncertain and unsure of what to do next. After the Smoke Hole Ceremony and the trip to fight the teenage werewolf, the Losers enter into a stagnant period of simply waiting. It is the creature Itself, working through Derry and the children's bullies, that finally forces them to act.

The Smoke Hole is not included in the 1990 miniseries. This is partly due to the cost of filming a sequence that transports two of the children back to Derry primeval, and partly because the technology available for such visual effects might not have made the proper impact even if it had been in the budget. The miniseries, however, does not suffer a narrative gap because of this lack. Viewers do not need to watch along with Mike and Richie as It arrives from beyond the atmosphere in order to understand that It is not human, and that It has been here a long time. Confirmation that It is indeed an inhuman monster and very much Other might help the children in their quest to kill It, but otherwise the Smoke Hole Ceremony plays no role in their ultimate attack on, and defeat of, It. The ritual used by the Losers during this actual confrontation is discussed in the next chapter.

The purpose, then, of this borrowed ritual is not entirely clear. It functions to provide the Losers with the thought that, while It opposes them, there is some force of good working on their side. The creation of their underground clubhouse, followed by Ben's discovery of the Smoke Hole Ceremony in his library book, provides a supernatural experience that does not deliberately seek to harm the children. Although both Mike and Richie are sick from the smoke and emerge from the clubhouse with ripped jeans and bloody knees, they are also exalted and high on adrenaline from their time-traveling vision. The experience is a moral boost, if not an intellectually enlightening one.

Unlike Louis Creed, the Losers are hoping to destroy the supernatural. While Louis accepts the explanation of the Micmac burying ground and the Wendigo-as-legend, content to create his own horror through mere use of the place without further investigation, the Losers seek meaning and definition through their use of the Smoke Hole Ceremony. Even though it does not do what Ben explains it should—provide guidance on how they should proceed—the use of the clubhouse as a means to contain the smoke allows two of the Losers to share a vision and bring this new information back to the others.

The selection of Mike Hanlon, the only Black member of the Losers, and Richie Tozier, generally regulated to comic relief, as the recipients of this knowledge might be more important than either the "Ceremony" or the knowledge itself. Before they go down into the smoky clubhouse, Richie finds himself thinking that it will be Bill Denbrough who has the vision, since "Big Bill" is their leader. Bill also lost his younger brother, Georgie, to It and therefore has the most personal investment in finding Its lair and destroying It completely. Although all of the Losers have known some of the kids who have gone missing, and all of them have been threatened by It, Bill becomes their leader through a combination of charisma and personal strength born from his brother's death.

Mike and Richie have their own roles in the group throughout the span of the book, and by the time of the Smoke Hole Ceremony Mike has already functioned as the Losers' historian by sharing his father's old album with the others. He will grow up to be the town librarian, being the only Loser to stay in Derry, and it is his call that causes the others' memories to start returning. He is the group archivist, researching historical events of the town, and the group memory-keeper, retaining the events of 1958 even when the others forgot. The Smoke Hole Ceremony provides Mike with a first-hand explanation for how and when It originally came to Derry, long before it *was* Derry.

Although Richie will play a major role in the group's encounter with It in 1985, at the time of the Smoke Hole Ceremony he has not had a chance to use his "Voices" for anything but to amuse and annoy the Losers. He will grow up to work on the radio and hone his skill so that, when he pretends to be a celebrity such as Humphrey Bogart, listeners will in fact be able to identify the person he is impersonating, but in 1958 most of Richie's attempts to sound like someone else still very much sound like Richie. During the events of 1958 he will be able to produce an Irish Cop Voice that seems to cause It some pain, but Richie still mainly qualifies as class clown and very much sees himself as Bill's subordinate.

When Mike and Richie are the last ones left in the clubhouse and therefore the only two of the Losers to see It arrive on Earth, this positions them as having been chosen by the good Other and indicates their importance to the group. The knowledge they gain is itself overwhelming—not only is It alien, but apparently immortal—and not entirely helpful, since the Losers have not been given any directions on how to proceed, but if knowledge is power, the Losers have still moved a step forward. They are thus able to identify It not only as not human, but also as not of this Earth, perhaps releasing them from any lingering doubts about whether or not they should—or could—kill It.

Other Sources for Cultural Appropriation

Although cultural appropriation is frequently referenced in instances where people of European ancestry co-opt bits and pieces of Indigenous culture, it is applicable in any case where the dominant culture engages in practices or language that belong to a marginalized culture. This removes the activity, item, or story from its home culture and the traditions that both led to it and continue to support it. The declaration of something as a "spirit animal," for example, when the speaker does not engage in the spiritual practices from which the term derives robs the notion of its power and cheapens the phrase. Frequently cultural appropriation occurs when the marginalized culture has been actively suppressed and the peoples who hold those beliefs have been denied the ability to practice them. This makes it a further insult when the dominant culture flaunts its own perverted practice.

King's works reflect this when his characters use cultural appropriation as a handy, yet shallow, explanation for something that they do not comprehend. The "old Indian burial ground," for example, becomes an acceptable shorthand and needs no further explanation. King's characters, as well as his readers, accept the surface reasoning and gamely charge forward to the narrative's climax. It is accepted as a trope, a sort of closed unit that can be plopped in to get the business of understanding the threat out of the way so the characters can move on to either using it or destroying it.

Indigenous traditions and culture are not the only sites of cultural appropriation. Other peoples have been—and continue to be—marginalized and denigrated as a group while dominant culture compartmentalizes its perceptions of what can be gained from the Others. These marginalized groups and traditions can be tolerated in certain circumstances, as long as the Others recognize and keep their place as "good" Others, and their beliefs and traditions can certainly be mined when the supernatural threatens King's main characters.

Thinner and the Gypsy Curse

In *Thinner*, originally published under King's pseudonym of Richard Bachman in 1984, lawyer Billy Halleck finds himself on the receiving end of a "Gypsy curse" after being acquitted of vehicular manslaughter. The curse is laid on him by the father of the woman he killed, an old man named Taduz Lemke. Lemke approached Halleck after his trial and touched his face, saying the single word, "Thinner." Halleck, who has been overweight, starts to see the numbers on the scale go down in spite of his lack of a lifestyle change. Each chapter is in fact headed with his weight, firmly centering the narrative around the amount of pull gravity has on one Billy Halleck.

Halleck is a white man of the upper middle class, a lawyer living in comfort with his wife and daughter who still sneers a bit at those in a slightly higher tax bracket while enjoying his own creature comforts. He and his wife's feelings about Lemke's group of Gypsies is displayed in a flashback to a scene where they came to the town common and started putting on displays of juggling and knife-throwing. Halleck's daughter is intrigued, perhaps more by the good-looking young man holding the juggling clubs than the act itself, but Halleck's hackles lower when he sees how his daughter reacts to the young man's smile: "the young man's handsomeness had been spoiled for her"[9] by his lack of perfect dental work. The teenager's interest falls apart at this single perceived flaw.

The Hallecks, then, are clearly positioned as being formed by their class as well as their whiteness. Billy himself recalls hearing of the power of the Gypsies when he was a child, and although the term is capitalized, he does not realize that "Gypsy" is, in fact, a slur. Later he refers to their language as Rom, and King even records the Rom spoken between Lemke and the others although Halleck himself does not speak it. The language used in the book is actually Swedish,[10] further complicating matters by equating two non–English languages under the assumption that most American readers would not know the difference. They are simply speaking among themselves in front of the white man in a language they know he will not understand, so the language itself apparently does not matter.

Halleck also shows his position as a white American man of the latter twentieth century in his obsession with another of Lemke's descendants—not the great-grandson who entranced his daughter until his smile displayed missing teeth, but his great-granddaughter, Angelina. Billy's wife notices the way his eyes follow the beautiful young woman, especially sticking on her kick-pleated skirt as she displays her skill with a slingshot. A later encounter during which Angelina complains about deadlines for submitting assignments for her correspondence course feels like a very pointed slap to Billy's perception of the young woman as nothing more than a sensual vessel for men's fantasies—especially white men's fantasies.

Angelina is seen through Billy's eyes as knowingly flaunting her "exotic" Gypsy beauty and using it to ensnare men, and both she and her brother are frequently described using animal metaphors. They are Other, and thus inhuman, even if Angelina is a beautiful Other. She, unlike her brother, does not lose her sexual appeal when she smiles, and the trope deepens when Angelina is shown to be fiercer than even her curse-laying great-grandfather. She does not agree with Lemke's eventual decision to transfer the curse, and she is personally responsible for the death of the one person willing to help Halleck.

As Halleck starts to lose weight, this physical transformation is first greeted with congratulations by those who know him. The rate of weight loss, however, quickly becomes alarming, although it takes Halleck some time to notice the extent of the changes. One day in court he starts to stand up to object and nearly loses his pants. Upon closer inspection, he realizes that he has slowly begun using tighter holes on his belt, apparently without noticing, until he needs to hurriedly punch another one so he can get through the rest of the day. Being a sensible man of the twentieth century, however, Halleck makes an appointment with his doctor and even allows himself to be checked into a special clinic for a while, certain that this unexplained development must be due to cancer even though he remembers Lemke's statement of "Thinner."

Billy's wife and doctor are both convinced that he is suffering under a rare form of involuntary anorexia and refuse to listen to any other possible explanation. Halleck, however, learns that he was not the only one Lemke visited. Both the police officer who reported to the scene of the accident and the judge who let his friend Halleck off with an acquittal have visited the doctor with their own strange physical changes, which the doctor—the same as Billy's—dismisses as post-adolescent acne and psoriasis. Billy sees the police officer, whose skin seems to be nothing more than a mess of open and running sores, and he learns from the judge's wife that he was in fact slowly becoming covered in scales and turning into what might have been a crocodile. Although the policeman lived alone and therefore could keep his condition from being publicly known, the judge's wife is not able to tell Halleck the story while sober. She, like Halleck, is shaken by this irrational turn of events.

Halleck's wife and doctor represent the rational response to a supernatural event. Each is convinced that this is a mental condition and that Billy, therefore, needs serious help. His refusal to stay in the clinic and let the experts continue to try one solution after another, as well as his decision to leave home and attempt to track Lemke down, cause his wife to sign a committal notice. His insistence that his weight loss, as well as the other men's skin conditions, is caused by a Gypsy curse is illogical and, according to her, insane, as is his idea of confronting Lemke. What Halleck needs is a hospital.

He, however, becomes utterly convinced that Lemke has laid a curse on him. In spite of his drastic weight loss and the fact that he can no longer be seen in public without attracting stares, Halleck first follows the path of the Gypsies and then confronts them in person. He does not come away from this encounter unscathed, thanks to Angelina and her slingshot, but Halleck knows he cannot turn to his family for help. Instead he calls up a man he met through his work at the law firm—a man Halleck knows to have his own questionable past. Sure enough, Richie "The Hammer" Ginelli is able to get Halleck medical help at his hotel, no questions asked, and Ginelli even shows up himself to take stock of the situation.

It is not clear whether or not Ginelli himself believes in the curse. When Halleck asks him if he is superstitious, the final answer is no—that Ginelli only believes in guns and money—but this only comes after his acknowledgment that the female members of his family certainly were.[11] Ginelli does see Halleck's drastic weight loss, and he volunteers to help do what Halleck has threatened: to lay his own white man's curse on the Gypsies, still insisting that Lemke remove the one he placed on Halleck. This "white man's curse" and Ginelli's ultimate role in the book are further discussed in the next chapter.

When Halleck eventually returns home, he offers his wife a rational explanation for his actions that does not involve Lemke's curse as having been real. Playing on the involuntary anorexia diagnosis, Halleck tells his wife that clearly the curse was only in his mind. When he was finally able to see the old man again and speak to him about the idea of the curse, sanity and reason prevailed. Halleck tells his wife that, once he realized the curse was only inside his mind, he began to gain weight again, and that his sanity has likewise returned. His wife and his doctor were, of course, right after all.

This is a necessary lie about the explanation of Halleck's weight loss, tied up with the given solution for it. As a sensible lawyer situated in his own time and place, the explanation that Halleck felt so much guilt about killing Lemke's daughter—especially since he himself is comfortably positioned in a body and life that is not frequently rejected or ousted from public locations—that he *imagined* the curse to be real is far less threatening to others in his same position than the idea that a curse

1. The Burying Ground, the Wendigo, Whatever 25

actually *could* exist. Anyone who took Billy's side, whether or not they actually believed in the curse, was killed for their concern, so clearly it was safer to staunchly insist that the issue was all in Billy's head.

Halleck equates his wife's refusal to believe in the curse with her refusal to take responsibility for her part in the accident. For the first and only time in their marriage, she had reached over to pleasure him sexually while he was driving. Billy believes that, had his attention been completely on driving instead of what she was doing to him, he would have been able to stop in time before hitting the woman. This is part of his own guilt: the belief that he could, and *should*, have been able to prevent the woman's death completely. This information was not made public, and whatever else his powers, Lemke seems unable to read minds or discern truth because it is only Billy who is cursed. As he loses more and more weight, he begins to hate his wife for, in his eyes, not suffering at all.

The fact that belief in the curse, or at least belief that Billy needed to gain some closure through confronting Lemke, got people killed does not seem to weigh much on Billy's conscience. One of the men, hired by Ginelli, is a complete stranger, and at that point Ginelli's own excitement about the pursuit carries Billy along. Later, after Ginelli himself first disappears and is then discovered dead, Billy is too focused on his own act of revenge to feel much responsibility. After all, Ginelli had already been living a dangerous, mob-connected lifestyle, and it would have been something else had he not personally decided to help Billy. At that point Billy is too focused on getting revenge on his wife to feel guilt about Ginelli's death—or to ponder whether revenge is its own form of curse.

Once again, the explanation for the supernatural fate that befalls a character is taken from outside of that character's home culture and personal experience. Because he visually identifies both the woman he killed and the man who touches him as Gypsies, Billy falls back on the childhood knowledge that Gypsies can indeed hand out curses. The fact that others he meets in his quest to find Lemke also find the old man to be somehow mysterious and powerful just boosts this opinion. This ancient Gypsy man, who has lived for more than a century, is in possession of supernatural powers, likely born of the fact that he is indeed Gypsy, and therefore the power is ancient, mysterious, and beyond the full comprehension of a man such as Billy Halleck. A white man who finds himself under a Gypsy curse, however, apparently does not need to understand it—or even necessarily the reasoning behind why he was cursed in the first place—to attempt to do something about it. Halleck's final response to Lemke is discussed in the next chapter.

The Outsider: El Cuco

These references to marginalized cultures are not only limited to King's works of the twentieth century. One of his more recent books, *The Outsider*, starts off as a police procedural. The narrative jumps between witness statements and the arrest of the man at the center of those statements: English teacher and Little League coach Terry Maitland. According to the statements, Maitland is the man responsible for the gruesome murder of eleven-year-old Frankie Peterson, who was tortured sexually and also likely partially eaten before he died. Police Detective Ralph Anderson and district attorney Bill Samuels even have DNA and fingerprint evidence implicating Maitland, leading to a very public arrest. Maitland's continued insistence that he was not even in Flint City that day falls on deaf ears in the wake of this evidence.

Men employed by lawyers on both sides of the case work to break down Maitland's alibi. He was out of town in Cap City on the day of the murder, in the company of other English teachers and present at a talk given by author Harlan Coben at a time that would not have made it possible for him to return home and murder Frankie Peterson. In spite of the evidence the police have that places Maitland on the scene, more piles up in favor of Maitland's innocence. He is seen on camera asking Coben a question after his talk, and his fingerprints are also found in Cap City on a book he handled. The police, Anderson among them, are confronted with the fact that this might not be an open-and-shut case, although they cannot explain how this could happen.

The DNA evidence discovered on Frankie Peterson's body is not faked, and yet they cannot see how the fingerprints would be, either. It might have been possible for someone who looked like Maitland—the witness statements clearly identify him by sight—to perhaps plant his blood, but they cannot come up with an explanation for the fingerprints. The situation is further complicated when Frankie Peterson's older brother shoots and kills Maitland on his way to court. Peterson's brother is subsequently shot and killed by Anderson. When the detective watches the news footage, he realizes that one very distinct member of the crowd he remembered seeing that morning does not, in fact, show up on any of the cameras.

Anderson starts having doubts about the case, largely due to the cold reception he receives from Maitland's widow and an odd story about her younger daughter's encounter with a man who had "straws for eyes."[12] The second is less concerning, especially since Marcy Maitland insists that no man could have gotten inside her daughters' bedroom. At the time of the arrest Anderson had responded largely in anger.

1. The Burying Ground, the Wendigo, Whatever   27

Terry Maitland had apparently been discovered as a child molester who, lacking sons of his own, coached Little League in order to size up his victims, whom he not only raped and murdered, but also partially consumed. The viciousness and brutality of the crime, as well as the fact that Anderson's son once had Maitland as a coach, led him to decide on a public arrest. Although Anderson was not one of the men to go in and arrest Maitland in front of the crowd, he does feel nagging guilt about that decision, as well as having Maitland brought to the courthouse via the front entrance when clearly Anderson was not the only person in town to be emotionally wrought by the case. The continuing destruction of the Peterson family through the older brother's death, the mother's heart attack, and the father's suicide attempt just adds to Anderson's despair.

Luckily for Anderson, he has the contact information of one Kermit William "Bill" Hodges, the retired detective at the center of King's *Mr. Mercedes* trilogy. Although Bill himself is now dead from the pancreatic cancer diagnosis he received in the third book, Bill's partner, Holly Gibney, is both available and intrigued. Further, Holly has something that Anderson does not: a willingness to believe in the supernatural because of her own experience with Brady Hartsfield. Although *Mr. Mercedes* itself read like a police procedural, the way *The Outsider* begins, by the time Brady returns to center stage in *End of Watch*, he has developed the supernatural ability to take over the minds and bodies of people in semi-hypnotic states. When Holly, Bill, and their friend Jerome finally kill Brady Hartsfield, he is at that time inhabiting the body of a respected surgeon. A combination of the beating Holly gave Brady's head at the end of the first book and the experimental medications that surgeon had been giving him led to Brady's mind control powers and, in that scenario, Bill had to drag Holly along the road to belief. This time, though, Holly is open to alternative explanations that seem to defy the real, rational world.

Following a combination of tips, Holly traces Maitland's last visit to his father in Dayton, Ohio, and discovers that one of the men working at the elder Maitland's care institution had himself been arrested for a brutal murder of two young girls. That man committed suicide before he could be brought to trial, but the occurrence of such a similar crime does not strike Holly as coincidence. When she arrives in Oklahoma to present her findings to Anderson, Maitland's widow, and a handful of others, Holly is as confident as she can get in her explanation.

The murderer of the two girls in Ohio is the same one who killed Frankie Peterson. When Maitland visited his father for the last time, he ran into the man who was shortly to be accused of murder and came away with a scratch on his hand. One of the witnesses on the night of Frankie Peterson's murder, Claude Bolton, reported having his hand scratched when he shook hands with Maitland. Holly announces that Bolton needs to be found and watched carefully, because he is the next victim.

Holly shows clips from an old Spanish-language movie *Rosita Luchadora e Amigas Conocen El Cuco* in which Rosita and her fellow female wrestlers solve a very similar murder: although viewers watch a very distinctive-looking man kidnap a child, when he is put on trial, he protests his innocence. During the execution scene, the man looks out from the gallows and sees someone pull back a hood to reveal his own face. He tries to warn the others, but the trap is sprung. Later Rosita and her fellow lady-wrestlers confront the real murderer whose face is a misshapen lump—and who has beams of light emerging from his eyes. Mrs. Maitland recognizes that this must be what her daughter had been describing when she panicked about a strange man being in her bedroom.

Holly explains that, according to legend, *El Cuco* lives on the blood and fat of children, eating them to a far greater extent than was seen in Frankie Peterson. She goes on to argue that "in the world—our *real* world—he could survive not just on those things, but on people who think"[13] entirely rationally and refuse to accept that he does, in fact, exist. Holly has already internally made the jump from seeing the supernatural monster in her movie and using the movie as her explanation for what Anderson and the others are currently witnessing.

One of Anderson's allies, a police detective named Yune Sablo, recognizes not only the movie Holly shows but the legend of El Cuco itself. It is, in fact, a story that Sablo had already thought of, although he could not properly remember the name of the monster involved. For Sablo, though, the legend comes from his own roots. Unlike Holly—and Anderson, and the rest of this small group looking for answers—Sablo is not white. For him, the story of El Cuco comes from his grandmother and his past.

Holly's version of the legend has already been adapted for the movie in which a team of female wrestlers acts as masked superheroes. She explains that *las luchadoras* starred in more than fifty films, all of which were based on Iberian stories and beliefs. Although El Cuco is her touchpoint to prove that this group in Flint City is not the first to be confronted with such a creature, Holly also quickly shifts her language and refers to the specific being they are following as "The Outsider."

El Cuco, then, becomes to Holly what the Wendigo was to Jud Crandall and Louis Creed: a handy shorthand explanation for something they do not entirely understand. Where Jud and Louis have their own experiences with burying pets—and people—in the stony ground on which to really base their assumptions, Holly has the hard evidence discovered in the investigation of Frankie Peterson's murder. This is not just the appearance of fingerprints around the same time, miles apart, but also the strange barn where fingerprints seemed to be a weird fading pattern that may or may not have been Maitland's; the clothes he was seen wearing by all of those eyewitnesses the night of the murder; and some strange goo-like substance that makes straw turn black and decay. Holly quickly mates this evidence with the vague information provided by her movie and decides that the Outsider went into the barn to leave its Maitland clothes behind. The fingerprints are strange and blurred because it has already begun to change into Bolton, whose DNA the Outsider sampled the night of the murder, and the strange substance must be exuded during the change.

Young Gracie Maitland's description of the thing in her bedroom having straws for eyes is the only solid connection to the El Cuco myth, especially as Holly saw in her movie. Otherwise the group might as well have decided they were working with a shapeshifter, sticking to the English terms or perhaps reaching back through European myths and fairytales for their explanation. This shapeshifter apparently needs the DNA of the next person it wishes to impersonate, as seen by the scratches and encounters in both Dayton and Flint City, but this explanation is not provided in the movie clips Holly shows or given in her description. It is instead reasoned out of the evidence provided by the very literal-minded police.

The movie likewise does not provide any specific information on how El Cuco must be destroyed, if its destruction differs from that of a "normal" human being. In fact, as Holly well knows and fears, showing the movie might get her laughed out of the room. Making the very clear connection between the evidence the men have presented to her and this flashy, dubbed film could very easily work against her. Attempting to tell a room of mostly white men that they are in fact confronting a creature from old Iberian tales is risky, even if Holly has decided that it is necessary.

Why, then, show the movie? Why not just make the argument that the evidence could support a shapeshifting creature? Why use the term "El Cuco" at all?

Unlike the Losers, Holly seems uncomfortable describing their adversary simply as "It" and building its characteristics from the ground up. She has already been established as a character who likes old and sometimes obscure movies and, with the human brain's tendency to make connections, if she had ever seen *Rosita Luchadora e Amigas Conocen El Cuco* and heard Gracie Matiland's description of the man she either saw or dreamed, would have put the two together. Again, it is the "straws for eyes" observation that clearly connects the two.

Likely what Holly means to show them is that they are not in fact facing an entirely new threat. There is a name that can be assigned to it, even if she quickly switches from Spanish to a more general English term, and legends about it that go back centuries. They are also thus not entirely alone in facing it. Others have before them, enough for the legend of El Cuco to be turned into one of a popular series of movies. The Outsider is not something with absolutely no connection to past human experience, even if it has only been at home in a culture that most of the people in the room do not share.

Holly has the most trouble convincing Anderson, even though she also believes that their success or failure hangs entirely on *his* belief. She later tries to turn El Cuco entirely into something Anderson can relate to, considering his own past and training: "Wasn't Ted Bundy just a version of *El Cuco*, a shape-shifter with one face for the people he knew and another for women he killed?"[14] She argues that, if Anderson can believe in a Bundy sort of monster, *El Cuco* is hardly any different, without recognizing the very vital difference: the Bundy argument does indeed come from Anderson's past, including the lessons and experiences he has already internalized. When she asks him to consider *El Cuco*, once again using the Spanish instead of her adopted choice of "the Outsider," she is pointing him outward, beyond his own lived experience and the culture in which he has grown to be himself. In the end, Holly convinces the others to leave off the conditional and to fully believe in the Outsider for just one day—hopefully long enough to defeat it.

Definitions, Not Solutions

Just because King's characters define the supernatural threat using culturally appropriated terms does not, however, mean that they also then use that explanation in order to confront and hopefully defeat the threat. Louis Creed, for example, feels no desire to get rid of the Pet Sematary, and his actions show that he in fact hopes to control it. When both the cat and his son come back "different" and have to be killed, Louis does not give up or think that, perhaps, no one else should ever be buried there. Instead, he rationalizes that little Gage had been dead for too long, and that his newly-dead wife therefore has a better chance of actually returning to him. The condition of Rachel Creed after her burial is left to the reader's imagination as the book ends before Louis even turns around to see what, exactly, has entered his house and called him "Darling."

The Losers in *It* do indeed want to destroy the inhuman thing that has been killing Derry's children, but the knowledge they gain from their version of the Smoke Hole Ceremony plays no role in their attack. Similarly, although Holly Gibney uses El Cuco in her explanation of the supernatural serial killer to various members of Flint City law enforcement, the movie she shows them merely helps to caution them in their pursuit of the shapeshifter. There is nothing special about how the Outsider dies. It is even an attack that Holly herself has used before. Only Billy Halleck uses his knowledge of Gypsy curses in his attempt to get Lemke to lift the one laid upon him. Since that "knowledge" is produced from his position in the dominant culture, it is therefore tainted, and Halleck pollutes it further in his response.

In other narratives, though, other King characters reach for culturally appropriated solutions to their problems even if they have not defined those threats through a culturally appropriated lens. When confronted with the inexplicable, many then turn to mystical, barely-understood means of attempting to banish the threat—as always, with mixed results.

2

The Ritual of Chüd

Borrowed Solutions

The use of cultural appropriation to explain the presence of a supernatural threat in a Stephen King story does not always lead to a solution drawn from that same culture. In fact, it is more common for a culturally appropriated solution to have little or nothing to do with the explanation of the threat being confronted. El Cuco from *The Outsider*, for example, is not eliminated utilizing information from the myth Holly Gibney presents to others as her clarification of the abilities of the monster they are facing. Indeed, the movie upon which she draws for the myth itself would indicate that they needed a number of female Mexican wrestlers in elaborate costumes in order to defeat the Outsider. Holly is the only female of their group, which is largely comprised of white Americans. The solution for the problem of the Outsider thus does not fall into this essay.

Similarly, although the secrets of the burying ground beyond the deadfall in *Pet Sematary* seem to be hinged upon the Micmacs and the Wendigo, none of the characters in that book seek to actually destroy it. Instead, Louis Creed continues to try to use the supernatural ability of the place for his own benefit. *Pet Sematary* also does not fall into this essay.

It and *Thinner* both made appearances in the previous essay and are also discussed in this one, but with cultural shifts between the explanation for the supernatural and the means by which to confront it.

The further examples provided here—the dreamcatcher in the novel of the same name; the psychopomps in *The Dark Half*; and the demon ritual of "Sometimes They Come Back"—show characters whose explanations for what is happening do not involve the taking or molding of other cultures, but who do rely on beliefs that are very much new to them during the climax of the narratives. Although they are able to dismiss the threat as either extraterrestrial or not important in the moment, they grasp for a response that feels as mystical and inexplicable to them as the threat does.

The Losers and Himalayan Holy-Men

During the intercut childhood and adult narratives in *It*, the use of the Smoke Hole Ceremony as an attempt to discover what to do next and functioning as an explanation of what It actually is comes only once, in 1958. The adult Losers recall the event and remind each other of it during their long evening together in the library, going around the room and sharing important events of the summer in an attempt to prepare for once again descending into Derry's sewers. As children, the Losers gained the knowledge that It was both ancient and not of this earth. As adults, they are reminded of this information, as well as the encouragement that, while It was working against them, there were indeed forces working on the side of the children that summer, too. The battle was not simply seven children—and now six adults—against one unnamable evil, but seven children who heard the voice of the Turtle, its own cosmic force.

It is not the Smoke Hole Ceremony, nor even Ben Hanscom's library book *Ghosts of the Great Plains*, that provides the Losers with their method of confronting It. The ceremony that repeats on both timelines, once when they were children and once as an even smaller number of adults, is called the Ritual of Chüd.

This information comes from a library book Bill Denbrough found when he was attempting to put a name to a monster with so many faces. Bill explains to his friends that the idea of such a shapeshifter has many names—Glamour from the Gaelic; a manitou according to the Plains Indians; various terms from Europe; and, most importantly to the group, *tallus* or *taelus* for the Himalayans.[1] With the Smoke Hole Ceremony still in the future, the Losers do not look to see what the Plains Indians may have done in the case of a manitou, and Bill's book might not have said. When one of the others asks if it gave any ways to fight such a shapeshifter, Bill tells them that a "Himalayan holy-man"[2] could engage the *taelus* in the Ritual of Chüd. Bill explains that the book says both the holy-man and the monster have to stick their tongues out and bite in, binding themselves to each other. They would each then take turns telling jokes, and the first to laugh was the ultimate loser. Presumably, if the monster laughed first, it would be defeated, or perhaps even entirely destroyed.

Like many of King's characters when confronted with the

supernatural, the Losers are forced to move ahead with very little information at their disposal. It does not occur to them to wonder what sort of training a Himalayan holy-man would have to undergo to earn that title, and how it might help him face such a creature. Once Bill explains this abbreviated version of the Ritual of Chüd, no one asks him how to defeat either a Glamour or a manitou. Presumably they, veterans of the Saturday afternoon matinee, are already acquainted with ways to defeat vampires and werewolves, and although the Losers use silver slugs against Its werewolf form, the fact that the Ritual of Chüd might be the only "foreign" response Bill remembers means that the group decides to participate.

Bill, as the leader, is the one to engage It during their initial confrontation in 1958. While the others simply see Bill standing there, staring at the spider-like shape It wears at home, the description indicates that Bill does indeed bite for Its tongue, and that the Ritual begins. It takes place "In the Void" as Bill seems to see himself being hurtled through space, past the shell of a giant Turtle who speaks to him in 1958, apologizing for creating the universe, and who dies before their second encounter in 1985. The description of Bill's travels, apparently away from Earth and to the very edge of our known existence, makes it sound as though Its tongue is the bungee cord tethering him to reality, while at the same time pulling him away from it. It means to push Bill past this border and into what It calls the deadlights.

While the tongue element of the Ritual's description remains, Bill does not tell jokes or attempt to make It laugh. He is first an angry boy, confronting his brother's murderer, and then an angry man, mourning not just Georgie but one of the original Losers who had completed suicide rather than return to Derry to confront It a second time. Bill first only yells at It, biting in harder with the teeth of his mind, and then brings It to Its metaphorical knees by properly reciting a tongue twister he had never been able to manage before because of his stutter. Even though he seems to remember the "gross" part about biting into each other's tongues, Bill has forgotten or ignored the only other element he relayed from his own library book.

In 1958, Bill's grasp on Its tongue, if not on the Ritual, is secure. He manages to hurt It terribly and to get It to pull him back to his physical body, running on instinct more than knowledge simply because they have so little of it. Even though he used his book to give the shapeshifting creature various names and tie It in to many possible histories and mythologies, Bill is forced to feel his way forward one step at a time. Even the great Turtle is little help, telling him *"once you get into cosmological shit like this, you got to throw away the instruction manual."*[3]

Since Bill barely read the instruction manual, this is perhaps the best advice he can receive. If the Turtle had told him to follow the Ritual of Chüd exactly in order to defeat It, he would have been completely lost.

Unfortunately for Bill and the others, especially Stan Uris and Eddie Kaspbrak, he does not listen to the other, more concrete advice from the Turtle: that he should kill It now, while It is weakened. Bill, returned to his body and jubilant at the mewling, limping, retreating spider-shape, decides that It is already dying and needs no more assistance from the Losers on that front. Even though he has the knowledge, shared by Mike and Richie, that It is ancient and alien, and the advice from the cosmological and inexplicable Turtle who vomited up the universe, the Losers allow It to retreat deeper into Its lair and then, after more trials, emerge aboveground, victorious. All seven, however, promise to return if It ever does.

Twenty-seven years later, following the schedule that Mike Hanlon has since tracked, the murders begin again. Even though the Ritual of Chüd was not entirely successful last time—It was wounded, and Its murderous cycle curtailed, but It was not destroyed—the remaining Losers venture into the tunnels under Derry in order to confront It again, and again they plan to enact the Ritual of Chüd.

Even though the six adult Losers had shared many stories of the summer of 1958, none of them had, at that point, remembered what had actually happened during their previous confrontation. Only Bill had engaged It in 1958, metaphorically biting into Its tongue and eventually reciting a single tongue twister instead of a series of jokes, but the same thing cannot be repeated twice. In 1985, Bill is launched into the void of space, past the now-empty shell of the dead Turtle, and he misses his grip on Its tongue. The others, once again merely standing by while this battle of wills rages, can only guess that things are going wrong. Since none of them have a complete understanding of either the Ritual of Chüd or what happened between Bill and It the last time, Bill included, they are unsure of how to help.

Richie Tozier steps in, using not a tongue twister but calling on one of his now-professional Voices to catch Its attention. Both Bill in 1958 and Richie in 1985 therefore use speech to hurt and subdue It. Bill had practiced that one specific tongue twister because he believed in his secret heart of hearts that, if he could say it perfectly, his mother would come out of her grief and praise him. For Bill, the words he spoke had deep personal meaning, and his success in saying them correctly just that once might not have been within his mother's hearing, but it was justice against the monster that killed Georgie and caused her grief in the first place. For Bill, his talismanic phrase held deep personal meaning and was very much grounded in the anger and grief of the past few months since Georgie's death, directed against the creature who murdered his brother.

Richie's use of his Voices and wild laughter against It is not as clear-cut. As an only child, Richie of course knew of the murders and was acquainted with some of the dead children, but there was nothing personal to direct him so clearly against It. He was not a happy child, but that was true of most of the Losers. Richie's sharp tongue and manic energy often got him in trouble at school, and his parents, although likewise quick-witted, are also distant and disengaged. When Richie's glasses get broken because of a bully, his mother even refuses to hear what her son is telling her, insisting that it was his own clumsiness and lack of respect for his belongings that caused the damage. Even some of his classmates find Richie simply too weird.

His Voices, honed for the radio during college, were Richie's retreat as a child. Uncomfortable with sincerity or vulnerability, he is seen using his various—and at the time terrible—Voices to petition his father for money to go to the movies, or to ask Beverly along as a date to the same. He is thus able to both hide behind the personalities suggested by the Voices while at the same time attempting to express his deeper inner truth: his love of horror movies and lack of fiduciary planning, both of which make him feel defensive in front of his parents, or his attraction to Bev, perhaps worsened by her teasing acceptance of his casual invitation by clearly labeling it a "date." As a child, Richie only manages a good, impressive Voice when attempting to subdue It, the way Bill speaks without a stutter during the Ritual of Chüd on a phrase he was not able to say in any other situation.

Since the boy—and then the men—who engage with It during this so-called ritual are not themselves by any stretch of the imagination Himalayan, Bill's discovery of the Ritual of Chüd provides them with a vague notion at best. He relays to the group that the challenger has to bite the monster's tongue, which is indicated as happening during the sequences "In the Void," and that the monster should bite back. Although Bill and later Richie both have the sensation of biting into Its tongue, neither indicates that It seems to have also bitten. Further, although Bill also tells the others that both parties should enter into a turn-by-turn telling of jokes that might mimic flyting, what actually happens seems to be more of a challenge of wills. Further, unlike flyting, there is no audience from which to elicit laughter.

Once again, the information one of the Losers has found in a library book regarding the rituals of a culture outside of anything the Losers themselves have experienced provides the setup for an encounter with the fantastic, although it does not work out exactly as the book indicates. Bill is perhaps lucky that he somehow innately knows how to grip Its tongue, although he was not prepared for the experience that followed. The Smoke Hole Ceremony likewise provided the Losers with more information about their adversary, but not with the next step forward. Like many of King's characters, once confronted with the supernatural, the Losers are left to stumble forward one step at a time, metaphorically feeling their way in the dark. Even if Bill and the others had sought more information about the Ritual of Chüd or other ways to confront a Glamour or manitou, it seems that anything they discovered would likewise have been only partially true and perhaps not at all helpful. In the end, Bill and then Richie have to reach inside themselves for the acts of speech that make each of them feel powerful.

The Curse of the White Men from Town

In *Thinner*, Billy Halleck is presented as having only a few vague notions about Gypsies beyond their denigrated station in society that leads to an itinerant lifestyle full of rousting and annoyed locals. He is a slave to the white man's lust for young Gypsy girls and fully comfortable forgetting that they exist at all except for when they cross his path. As a child he learned that Gypsies are capable of handing out curses and now, as an adult, he finds himself the subject of one. Although Halleck later hears the Gypsies speaking to each other in a language he refers to as "Rom," the curse itself is in English: "Thinner." Halleck, after coming to the understanding that this is indeed real and not a psychological form of anorexia, sets out to track down the man who cast this curse and demand that he take it back.

Halleck seems to see himself as brave when he defies the wishes of both his wife and his doctor in order to set off on this quest. The other two men who were given curses of their own did no such thing. While one went to the Mayo Clinic and the other hid himself at home so as not to be seen, both completed suicide. From Halleck's point of view, they have decided to take the coward's way out instead of facing the problem head-on.

What Halleck himself lacks, aside from a proper understanding of Gypsy curses, is the capability of shouldering his own portion of blame. Halleck hit and killed a woman when he was driving his car, and no amount of rationalization—that she was jaywalking, or that his wife was distracting him at the time—can undo this. Halleck also knew that the judge should have recused himself from overseeing the trial of a friend, and the police officer in question did not so much as give Halleck a breathalyzer test: oversights that led to their own curses and therefore their suicides. The other men take ownership of their decisions and, in their own way, accept the curses that follow. Halleck is the only one stubborn—or perhaps stupid—enough to fight it.

When he finally tracks down the man who cursed him, Halleck makes his own threat: that, if Lemke refuses to remove the curse of thinness, he will lay one of his own: "The curse of the white men from town."[4] Halleck says, perhaps rightly, that white men do indeed know how to curse, although it is difficult to tell if he has added considerations of centuries of white supremacy to back his statement. Coming from such a thin and clearly troubled man, the "white men's curse" seems pitiful, with nothing to back it. The curse Lemke laid on Halleck, although it was in English, is real enough to work, but Halleck's threat seems laughable. What sort of curse could a white lawyer from an upper-middle-class neighborhood summon?

Halleck's ignorance is further shown in his repeated insistence that Lemke simply remove the curse. Even when beaten in the end, Lemke stands by his original declaration: that cannot be done. A curse cannot be removed—only transferred. What Halleck continues to demand, then, is impossible, although he does not know it. In the end he accepts Lemke's declaration that it must be transferred, although Halleck himself has done no research to confirm this. Between Halleck's continuing anger at his wife for what he perceives as her failure to accept her role in the accident, as well as the way his "white men's curse" has gone, he does not believe Lemke would lie to him. The admittance that the curse must be transferred is, in fact, Lemke's surrender.

The irony is that, while Halleck had no idea what he actually meant at the time he was speaking his own curse, events unfolded leading to that surrender. Before he leaves the Gypsies the night of their confrontation, Halleck is injured by Lemke's great-granddaughter, the beautiful and fierce Angelina, and he calls up an old acquaintance for help. Ginelli, with his shady connections, sends a doctor to Halleck's hotel and then arrives himself. The curse of the white men from town ends up being enacted by an Italian man from the city as Ginelli takes it upon himself to exact revenge for his old friend. Without Ginelli, Halleck would never have been able to enact the curse of the white man from town. Both Ginelli and a man he hires as his accomplice end up dying, but Halleck's curse succeeds when Lemke agrees to help Halleck transfer the "thinner" curse.

The difficult part is determining what Halleck actually had in mind when he speaks his curse. Throughout the book it is clear that he understands at least some of his own privilege as a white man, and the ways in which that privilege is maintained and enacted through violence against the Other. He has a working understanding of the way laws are interpreted differently or enforced more stringently when it comes to the Gypsies over men such as himself. Halleck does not explicitly compare the way he was able to get acquitted of manslaughter to the way the Gypsies were moved along from the town common in spite of the vast difference in level of offense, but he has made enough internal observations to show he is, on some level, aware of his whiteness. This does not mean that he hopes to work toward equality for all men, however, as shown by other internal observations when Lemke's great-grandson—gap-toothed brother of the beautiful Angelina—attempts to fight back because he has not yet grasped the immutability of his place.

What Halleck refuses to see is how a curse is the only recourse Lemke has at his disposal.

The law, of course, is not on the side of the Gypsies and has in fact worked to be sure that no one is held responsible for the death of Susanna Lemke. She was only a Gypsy, not a woman from town, and her death is preferable to town people than her continued life. Her family, including her father, was left with no justice and no response other than Lemke's curse. When Halleck shows up in their camp, having tracked them down and demanding that Lemke remove the curse, Halleck has lost sight of the fact that there is no equality between them. He tries to argue for his own daughter, but Linda is a white teenager who gets to be a cheerleader and live in a big house in a place that would not move her along for loitering in public. In his own selfishness and refusal to accept his own starring role in Susanna Lemke's death, Halleck refuses to see how anyone other than his daughter might also be suffering.

The unfairness in Halleck's mind hardly even touches on the concept of manslaughter: his wife chose a supremely wrong time to give him a hand job in the car, but, in Halleck's eyes, Lemke has made the egregious error of failing to properly parse out the blame. Halleck would *never* have killed Susanna Lemke without his wife's interference, and therefore it does not matter that he was in the driver's seat when his car ran her over. What matters is that his wife is not losing weight or suffering an extreme skin condition. Halleck, with his intense belief in the curse, only absently notices how much more his wife has been smoking, and he sees her comments about his physical condition as unnecessary nagging. Further, Susanna Lemke occupies no space in his concerns. The injustice does not begin with her death, but with Taduz Lemke's curse. For Halleck, as for so many other white men from town, Susanna does not interest him at all.

The suffering of fourteen-year-old Linda Halleck from her father's impending death is meant to not only be comparable to, but to override, any suffering Lemke, his family, or his friends have undergone. The injustice is not that a woman died and no one had to face consequences for it, but that Halleck himself is now answering through a curse his wife refuses to understand. He refuses to acknowledge her own suffering on a conscious level and is determined to cause some of his own. When Halleck inflicted his curse of "the white men from town," and when Ginelli terrorized and threatened Lemke's group, Lemke's surrender is not in removal of the curse but in a transfer, and Halleck does not have to think twice about who should take it.

Lemke agrees to meet Halleck in a public park, just the two of them, and he brings with him a strawberry pie. Lemke manipulates the wound in Halleck's hand, thereby removing the curse from Halleck's body and putting it in the pie. His last recommendation is that Halleck should eat it himself and be done with it—really to take responsibility for his actions instead of pushing blame off on his wife—but Halleck has already begun planning. And strawberry pie is, in fact, his wife's favorite.

Just as he believed in the curse itself, Halleck believes that it can be transferred. Lemke's continued insistence that it could not be removed did not make sense to him but, once he holds the now-cursed pie, Halleck fully believes: whoever eats this will suffer as he had so recently been suffering. The only difference is that it is Halleck and not Lemke who gets to lay the blame. Returning home after days of being away—and only after he demands that his wife call off the detectives and rescind the order for him to be forced into medical treatment—Halleck presents the pie as a gift and begs off from having his own slice, leaving his wife to eat some of it out of his sight. This would also be apparently of her own free will, although she does not know what actually resides within the strawberry pie, and the act is a parallel to Halleck's own habit of overeating that led Lemke to choose his curse in the first place.

Halleck's entire, utter belief in the curse is revealed the next morning when a number of clues leads him to intuit that Linda has come home in the middle of the night and had a piece of pie for herself. He does not wait until she wakes up to ask her if that is the meaning of the two forks and the two plates, or if his wife perhaps was the one to go back for a second slice herself and use new dishes. Halleck, now shocked to the core by human vagaries and free will, believes that he has cursed his daughter—the only innocent in the house—and begins to eat the pie himself.

The fate of all three Hallecks, however, remains uncertain. Lemke informed him, and therefore readers, that all of the pie must be eaten, and that the act must be completed in a timely manner lest the curse revert to Halleck, but his suggestion is that only one person should consume it: Halleck himself. There is no indication about what might happen if multiple people split the pie, and thus the curse, between them. Even if Halleck eats the remaining three-quarters, his wife and his daughter will each have ingested one-eighth. This is a normal serving of pie instead of a gluttonous amount, but when Lemke explained that a curse could be transferred, he did not tell Halleck if it could somehow be shared. If the entire curse meant that Halleck lost weight at speed until he would presumably die from it, does one eighth of the curse only remove one eighth of a person's vital weight, or slow that loss down to one eighth of the speed and ultimately result in death, anyway?

Halleck is, of course, too blinded by thoughts of revenge against his wife to consider any of these questions. He had been anticipating that Linda would stay with her aunt a while longer, during which time he would presumably convince his wife to eat every last slice of pie herself. His plan, as it has been all along, is to force his wife to take the consequences since he believes she has failed to take responsibility. Just as he could not see how the accident was affecting his family—or how it affected the Lemkes—Halleck could not see the transfer of the curse going wrong, either, even though he fully believed in it. This might not be a case of a white man *failing* to manipulate a culturally appropriated belief, but it certainly does not unfold the way Halleck himself had planned. Whether Lemke, who claimed to have the sight, anticipated or intended the destruction of the Halleck family is not revealed.

Dreamcatcher: Person, Place, Thing

The plot of *Dreamcatcher*, like many of King's books, is complicated. On the one hand it is the story of four boys who grew up as good friends and have stayed close as adults, coming together each fall in order to spend a week hunting together. An intersecting storyline tells of General Abraham Kurtz and his second, Owen Underhill, as they first confront and then attempt to neutralize a literal extraterrestrial invasion in the woods of northern Maine. A third part of the story, largely told through flashbacks and keeping its subject unnamed for as long as possible, examines the apparent power of one Douglas "Duddits" Cavell and his role both in the boys' past and the race to save the human race from the alien invasion. Duddits has Down Syndrome and a measure of telepathy that has impacted both his parents and the four boys who used to hang out with him when they were teenagers.

Those boys, now men—Joe "Beaver" Clarendon, Pete Moore, Henry Devlin, and Gary "Jonesy" Jones—find themselves in the woods at Beaver's camp during November 2001. This unfortunately places them within the Jefferson Tract at the same time the alien ship lands, bringing Kurtz and the rest of his men to first destroy the ship and then enforce containment of what is varyingly called "Ripley" or "the byrus." This shows up as a reddish-gold fungus, thriving on warm surfaces and dying quickly on cold ones, preferring to infest human hosts. The byrus provides a level of telepathy among those who are near it, but this is strongest with those who are infected. Anyone unlucky enough to have ingested the byrus incubates a parasite known as a "shit weasel" or a byrum. These creatures, meant to be symbiotic instead of parasitic, grow in both human and animal intestines, causing large amounts of gas while eating their hosts from the inside out. Although the aliens quickly learn that these creatures do not behave properly and end up killing their hosts, one surviving alien, dubbed Mr. Gray, believes it has a way to ensure that the next batch of implants will take.

The end result is a multi-level chase across New England in the midst of a blizzard. At its head is Mr. Gray, who has managed to take control of Jonesy's body. Jonesy has himself been insulated against Mr. Gray thanks to both his childhood interactions with Duddits and his experience that previous spring recovering from being struck by a car. Mr. Gray also has a small collie with him who is incubating one of the shit weasels, which he intends to drop into the pumping station of a reservoir that serves Boston. If Mr. Gray succeeds, then the byrum will infect everyone who drinks that water.

In the second group, Jonesy's surviving friend, Henry, travels with Owen Underhill, who has defected from Kurtz's mission. These two make a small detour on their way after Mr. Gray in order to pick up Duddits, who is dying from cancer but still inwardly powerful. Following them and coming up last is Kurtz and a much smaller number of men under his command. One of these men is himself suffering from a byrum, allowing him to maintain mental contact with the one inside the collie even when the surface byrus on the other men's skin dies and flakes off. Henry and Owen want to stop "Typhoid Jonesy" from spreading the infection, while Kurtz is more concerned with getting personal revenge on the man who has now twice defied him.

Jonesy knows that, with his and Mr. Gray's head start, something needs to happen in order to slow them down if the others have any chance at stopping him. Imprisoned inside his own head, Jonesy is nevertheless able to hold a conversation with Duddits from a room in which a large, colorful dreamcatcher hangs. This dreamcatcher is a double

2. The Ritual of Chüd   43

of the one that used to hang in Beaver's camp, before it was recently destroyed, and when Jonesy hears Duddits' voice, it comes from the dreamcatcher.

The camp itself, inherited from and presumably initially decorated by Beaver's father, was simple and rustic, mainly consisting of a single large room. That room held a Navajo rug, a Micmac woven wall hanging, and the dreamcatcher itself, a colorful "bit of weaving which hung from the center rafter."[5] While both the rug and the weaving are identified with tribal names, the dreamcatcher is not. Although it originated in Ojibwe culture, the dreamcatcher has since been appropriated as a symbol for pan-Indianness without any such specific associations. Even Jonesy, when thinking that it looks like a spider's web, does not recognize the cultural association of the dreamcatcher with that exact object. Indeed, since he has already observed the rug as Navajo and the wall hanging as Micmac, if Jonesy had a particular history associated with the dreamcatcher, it seems he would have already mentioned it.

Jonesy, his friends, and therefore Duddits associate that specific dreamcatcher—their dreamcatcher—with the camp and therefore their friendship. When Duddits leaves home for the last time to help Henry and Owen with their quest, one of the things his mother gives him is a smaller dreamcatcher that Beaver had given Duddits as a present. Owen asks Duddits about it, and he is granted a telepathic vision of the main room at the now-destroyed camp, dominated by the large and colorful dreamcatcher, even though Duddits himself had never been there. He had presumably seen the room in his friends' heads and, in the same way it stands out years later during the camp's final November, the dreamcatcher simply dominates the scene.

In Jonesy's prison in his mind, then, the dreamcatcher continues to represent his friends, two of them now dead and Duddits dying. He hears Duddits' voice coming through the dreamcatcher, although it is unaccented. Throughout the book, when Duddits speaks out loud, his words are written in phonetics, concentrating on the open vowel sounds and frequently dropping consonants. When his voice comes through the dreamcatcher, Jonesy hears him speak perfectly clearly, and when the time arrives for them to save the day, both Jonesy and Henry have to somehow run along the dreamcatcher. This takes them back in time until they seem to be the age they were when they first met Duddits and allows them to confront Mr. Gray in a space that really only exists in Jonesy's mind.

The dreamcatcher thus becomes not only a thing made of string and a symbol for friendship, but also somehow an actual place while at the same time being Duddits himself. Owen Underhill, the outsider who has nevertheless come with Henry to take Duddits from his home and to his death, is the one who states it plainly, albeit telepathically, to Duddits and Duddits alone: "*You're the dreamcatcher, aren't you? Their dreamcatcher. You always were.*"[6] The question, though, is what Owen and the others mean by all this.

Traditionally a dreamcatcher is used as a protective charm against any evil that might be around, and not just bad dreams. They were given to children and frequently placed on cradleboards, always made of natural materials meant to decay with time. Traditional dreamcatchers were also much smaller than the one at the Clarendons' hunting camp, which was presumably purchased prior to the Indian Arts and Crafts Act of 1990. Dreamcatchers are medicine, and medicine, when used by the wrong people or in the wrong way, can be harmful or even deadly. Neither Beaver nor his father, nor any of the characters in *Dreamcatcher*, are identified as anything but white.

Duddits is himself mystical and inexplicable, with his telepathy and other abilities—such as tracking a lost teenage girl or Mr. Gray—meant to be inextricable from his Down syndrome. His mother is described as having her own small amount of telepathy, presumably from her long contact with her magical son. Here again, though, is something that King's characters can only assume without fully knowing. Duddits simply is, without explanation, the way the dreamcatcher exists without connection to culture or tradition.

The function of the large and colorful dreamcatcher at camp seems to be as decoration, like the Navajo rug and the Micmac wall hanging. It is perhaps "rugged" and "outdoorsy," invoking thoughts of mighty hunters and a simpler, "less civilized" time. There is no reference to this dreamcatcher drawing the bad to it, away from the camp's occupants. The dreamcatcher in Jonesy's mental "office," the one he and Henry have to run along during the book's climax, has apparently caught Mr. Gray and kept him from escaping, but otherwise the original meaning of the dreamcatcher is lost. Duddits has strong associations of the one at camp tying them together in friendship, and thus they all feel the same. Duddits is not, then, an actual dreamcatcher, but the group's perversion of the word. This is, at least, personal and private instead of the commercialized dreamcatchers sold for tourists and other non–Indigenous buyers, but the use of a word with so many previously existing levels of meaning is confusing.

In the author's note, King informs his Constant Readers that the title for the book was only changed from his original idea—*Cancer*—to *Dreamcatcher* when his wife refused to call it *Cancer*.[7] He does not indicate whether the title change also resulted in an increased importance of that word throughout the book, although the theme of friendship and interconnectedness could have been represented by any number of symbols. King specifically chose and emphasized one from Indigenous culture, using it as a pseudo-explanation for how the surviving childhood friends could once again join together—in the dreamcatcher, or in Duddits' or Jonesy's head—to save the world. If Duddits himself is the dreamcatcher, this final act destroys him. Magic or mysticism is not limitless, and in spite of how extraordinary a person he was, the cancer, combined with the mental effort of slowing Mr. Gray down and then allowing Henry and Jonesy to kill him, is too much for Duddits. He dies in Henry's arms before the final byrum is destroyed, but his actions and talent allowed for two of his childhood friends to live.

The dreamcatcher, like the Wendigo in *Pet Sematary*, is meant to function as a shorthand explanation for the supernatural. Henry and Jonesy must, somehow, defeat Mr. Gray if the world is to be saved, but Mr. Gray does not have a physical form of his own. He must be attacked as an idea, somehow in Jonesy's head and running Jonesy's body, without killing Jonesy. Jonesy himself occupies only a small corner of his own mind for most of the story, and Duddits, with his special abilities, is able to first contact him there, and then show him a way out that will keep Mr. Gray from immediately killing him. How Duddits manages any of this is not explained. Again, Duddits just is.

In the epilogue, Henry and Jonesy have gathered for a Labor Day cookout and talk together about the aftermath of the previous November's adventures. Even though they spent weeks as guests of the government recalling and rehashing the events, at times under hypnosis, there seems to be no explanation for Duddits. They talk about him all the same, attempting to find meaning in the sort of power that was once used for such a small-seeming miracle as finding a lost developmentally challenged girl, and once directed out of fear to kill the bullies who had sworn revenge on the boys. Duddits' power is beyond explanation, and Duddits presumably beyond replication, although Henry tries to wax philosophical and proclaim that Duddits is the sum of the human race. The epilogue consists of two men attempting to explain the inexplicable, to wrap up the events and the plot in a neat little package, and perhaps the most helpful contribution is that Henry admits that "dreamcatcher" is not the right word—but that, for now, it "will have to do."[8] Presumably it will be in the human race's best interest to define it quickly, since Henry also believes that, although the aliens who came to the Jefferson Tract in November 2001 have all been eliminated, there will be others. Presumably the information Henry and Jonesy provided during their extended debriefings will assist Earth in any future attacks, but the term "dreamcatcher" will be meaningless to anyone who does not have their own personal references. Whatever Henry means is both confined and confused by his language use, and in the end, there is no explanation at all.

Psychopomps of American Folklore

The Dark Half is a novel that clearly references King's own experience with writing under a pseudonym. King published five novels in the 1970s and 1980s under the name "Richard Bachman" until Bachman's true identity was discovered after the publication of *Thinner*. King accepted that he had been outed and published the next would-have-been-Bachman book, *Misery*, under his own name.

In *The Dark Half*, author Thad Beaumont has also recently had his pseudonym uncovered. When the "creepazoid" who has made the discovery attempts to blackmail him, Beaumont, with his wife Elizabeth's blessing, not only reveals himself to be George Stark, but participates in a photoshoot for *People* magazine in which he and Liz are shown shaking hands over Stark's tombstone. While King's own reveal has not prevented more Bachman books from being published, Beaumont makes the decision to give up both Stark and his drinking in an attempt to be a better husband and father.

The theme of twins runs through *The Dark Half*, since Thad himself is revealed to have needed surgery as a child in order to remove what was thought to have been a tumor in his brain, but actually turned out to be pieces of the twin he had absorbed in the womb. This tidbit is of special interest to Castle Rock sheriff Alan Pangborn, considering the strange occurrences that have been happening in his town.

The fake tombstone with Stark's name on it had been placed in Castle Rock's own cemetery, although not over any of the cemetery's occupants. In spite of this, one of the caretakers discovers what looks to be an impossible story: that a man, buried alive, pushed himself up out of a six-foot-deep hole, paused at the edge of it to get to his feet, and then started walking for the road. Whoever it was is under suspicion of murdering town resident Homer Gamache and then stealing his truck, which is later discovered with fingerprints aplenty, including one cast in a piece of gum. Those fingerprints match the exemplars of one Thaddeus Beaumont, bringing Alan Pangborn to the Beaumonts' door.

Beaumont's brain surgery is more of a red herring than a help in explaining what is actually happening, since Pangborn spends his time trying to make the odd occurrences fit within expected reality. The fingerprints in the stolen truck, especially the one in gum, become a sticking point at which Pangborn wonders if Beaumont really did steal the truck and some mystical twin provided his alibi. Forget the fact that there is no record of another Beaumont son—the doctor's recollection of what was removed from Beaumont's brain, along with Thad and Liz's twin babies, continually drag Pangborn back to the idea that Beaumont himself must be a twin. He keeps laboring away at the idea that Beaumont has somehow willfully managed to double himself, especially since a voice-print comparison from a telephone conversation between Beaumont and Stark shows a near-perfect match. George Stark is somehow the same person as Thad Beaumont, while being a separate man completely.

Beaumont and his wife are the first to fully believe what has happened: that Stark, denied his voice and therefore his existence, has emerged from the ground where his fake tombstone stood with the intent of *living*. Although Stark was never truly alive before, he has somehow emerged from the dead, unable to write on his own but convinced that some sort of transition of power between Beaumont and himself might be possible. Liz and the twins become his hostages as he lures Beaumont to his lake house in order to complete this shift, presumably away from outside intervention. Alan Pangborn, underestimating Stark, manages to get himself taken prisoner, as well, and is therefore able to witness the final outcome.

Aside from Homer Gamache, whose death was hardly necessary for Stark to steal his truck, Stark has outwitted a number of police in order to commit a string of murders in his path toward revenge, choosing those who had a role in first creating the Stark pseudonym and then killing him. In spite of warnings and precautions, Stark works his way through those who were involved in publishing "his" books as well as the photographer and reporter responsible for the article in *People* magazine, along with a number of police. Stark's "final" phone call to Beaumont, recorded and witnessed by more law enforcement, has Stark claiming to have come to his senses, realizing he only imagined himself to be the pseudonym, and promising to go back home and never bother anyone ever again. Thad realizes that Stark is only performing for the other listeners, most of whom believe him, and has to put himself in various situations out of earshot of his police tail where Stark can call him on an untapped line.

One of these calculated trips involves Beaumont visiting his office on campus, ostensibly to review the applications for a creative writing course he will be teaching. Stark does call, not using Beaumont's office phone but instead that of the only other person in the department to be present that day, Rawlie DeLesseps. Stark's using Rawlie's phone to inform Thad that he has Liz and the twins and should meet him at the lake house is not the only reason the other professor makes an appearance in the novel. Although he is able to help in providing Thad's alibi for the night of Homer Gamanche's murder, his real purpose is in providing Thad with the solution to his Stark problem.

As a child, when Thad got his blinding headaches that lead to his brain tumor diagnosis, he would hear the sound of sparrows. Since Stark has emerged from his grave, Thad has begun not only hearing, but also *seeing* large flocks of sparrows. Since Rawlie teaches a course on folk myths, Beaumont takes the opportunity to ask him if there is any particular significance to that specific bird. Rawlie tells Thad he will look into it, but he suspects that sparrows are "[t]oo common to have any deep superstitious connotations."[9] Rawlie promises to consult his books, though, and later informs Beaumont that sparrows are psychopomps: outriders of the deceased whose job is to "guide lost souls back into the land of the living. They are, in other words, the harbingers of the living dead."[10] Although Stark was not previously alive and therefore could not have been dead, Thad seizes on the idea of the sparrows as psychopomps, buoyed by the fact that the birds flock to him in astounding numbers but Stark himself cannot see them.

Rawlie cites the fictional book *Folklore of America* by Barringer, no first name given, and explains further that other forms of birds are outriders of the living, meant to escort souls to the afterlife. This is the common definition of "psychopomp," from the Greek. Many traditions and beliefs include the idea of pscyhopomps, but generally large masses of birds amass outside the homes of the dying, and not the undead. The figure of the Grim Reaper is itself a psychopomp, fulfilling the same role as Charon in the ancient Greek, Anubis in ancient Egypt, and myriad animal forms. The general meaning of psychopomp, then, is directed as souls pass from this life onto the next, and not the reverse, as Rawlie says sparrows indicate. Sparrows are commonly harbingers of death, yes, but Rawlie connects them to the coming of the living dead—a description of Stark, but one unlikely to be found in any real volume of American folklore.

Psychopomps are not under human control. Although many stories exist that show men and women bargaining with death, at times relatively successfully, few are able to evade the summons of the Grim Reaper even for a short time. When death calls, souls follow and accept the guidance provided by the psychopomps. Beaumont is not guided by the sparrows, but followed by them, and through Rawlie's information and his help, he is able to call the sparrows to do his bidding: not to bring Stark back to the living, as Rawlie had described it, but to carry Stark away, presumably back to whatever death awaits a pseudonym that was never a living man in the first place.

Once again, as in *It*, although information was taken from a book, it was then passed on orally and only tangentially used in order to confront the supernatural threat. Rawlie is a strange enough man to accept Beaumont's evasive excuses for his curiosity about sparrows, as well as to be willing to let Beaumont take his less-recognizable car and even a wooden bird call that might come in handy. Although he is presented as an absentminded sort of person, perhaps not even liked by Beaumont, he is the only one Beaumont can ask for help when it comes time to evade his police tail and confront Stark at the cabin—and Rawlie himself comes through admirably, with only a few further questions. He drifts rather vaguely into the story in time to provide his telephone and the information about psychopomps, and drifts away again after he has given Beaumont the tools to call and therefore use the sparrows.

But Rawlie does not do so without a warning: "No man controls the agents of the afterlife. Not for long—and there is always a price."[11] He has just seen Beaumont urge a large flock of sparrows to fly and the birds apparently obey him, but if Beaumont called the sparrows, it was unconsciously. They were appearing again long before Rawlie provided Beaumont with the explanation of why, both around Beaumont and around Stark, and Rawlie's statements seemingly contradict each other. If sparrows are the harbingers of the living dead, then they came with Stark, transporting him out of the afterlife into the present, a mission that completely counters Beaumont's wishes. If Beaumont is fully controlling the sparrows and they are not acting on their own instincts or at the direction of an outside Other, then Beaumont would himself have wanted to call Stark back from the grave in the first place.

In the wake of so many murders, and with Stark holding his wife and babies hostage, Beaumont can see how terrible of an idea this is, although a part of him would admit it was true: he missed being Stark. When he was Stark, he could be someone else—someone Liz Beaumont did not like. Stark was not a very nice man, but he was a very successful author. If Beaumont somehow managed to call the sparrows to bring Stark back to life without understanding what he was doing, then he has to now convince them to take Stark away again in direct contradiction to his first, unconscious desire.

Even though his body has begun to decay, Stark has proven himself more than a match for men trained in ways that Beaumont himself cannot match. Stark has outwitted Beaumont, holding Liz and the twins hostage, and is clearly more dangerous physically. Beaumont cannot defeat him and has to therefore go along with Stark's plan: the men will go up to Beaumont's office, each of them with a twin in his lap, and will start writing the next George Stark book. Beaumont will hold the pencil himself first, but, as the story picks up speed, Stark will be able to continue, writing for the first time since he came back from the dead. During this process, the energy—the life force—will transfer from Beaumont to Stark until they have switched places. Beaumont will be dead, and Stark will exist fully in the real world.

Beaumont waits until Stark is distracted with his writing and then blows the birdcall Rawlie gave him, summoning the massive flutter of sparrows outside the study to burst in. Beaumont grabs both his twins to protect them, and the last anyone sees of Stark is a twisting, fighting figure being borne off into the sky. The sparrows, Rawlie's psychopomps who escort the dead back to the land of the living, carry the not-dead Stark away. Although his actual fate is uncertain, it seems that Stark will not be able to return and threaten the Beaumonts in his physical form.

The Dark Half is one of King's books that has an apparent ending, but where the actual story is completed elsewhere. In the last scene, the four Beaumonts and Sheriff Pangborn stand outside the Beaumonts' lake house as it, along with Stark's car, burns. Thad puts his face in his hands, and the story ends. Although so much has been destroyed and Stark has been carried off, many questions remain unanswered. Some of them are referenced as part of the backstory to *Needful Things* when Alan Pangborn considers the fact that he was distracted from his wife's headaches by the Beaumonts' continued troubles: their separation, Thad's drinking, and his suicide. Although the sparrows could remove George Stark's body from the world, Stark was still entangled in Beaumont's mind and his life in ways that psychopomps could not touch.

Stark's existence as a physical being is inexplicable. The closest the Beaumonts and Pangborn come is to imagine that Stark did exist as a separate identity somehow, and then possessed some unimaginable strength of will in order to create himself. The sparrows are not connected to Stark's physical manifestation as being the cause, but their return to Thad occurs around the same time Stark returns to life after his ceremonial burial. Somehow the *People* photographer's idea of creating a papier-mâché headstone must factor into Stark's return, as well, since he emerged from the cemetery ground beneath where it had been placed for the photoshoot.

Thad, personally, has no meaning to attach to the flocks of sparrows he sees. He does not know what to do with them, or even if he *should* do anything, or if they have come to him to menace or protect. Sparrows haunt his subconscious because of his childhood connections with their song and his headaches, and while his surgeon recounts the amazing flock of sparrows that took off and bashed themselves against the hospital when Thad woke up from that surgery, Beaumont himself does not seem to recall it. The first sights of the large flocks make him uneasy. If Thad has called them, it was not consciously. He needs to go outside of himself, to Rawlie, to seek some sort of explanation and meaning.

Rawlie does at least draw on American folklore instead of Indigenous or Himalayan traditions. Although the barebones Ritual of Chüd is able to guide *It*s Losers through their confrontation with the monster, Rawlie's solution is presented as homegrown. Whether or not any book on American folklore would consider sparrows to be pscyhopomps in reverse, bringing the dead back to the land of the living, within the world of *The Dark Half* this is meant to be a traditional American belief. It is not one Thad has heard before, but it is of course one he can use, especially since the information has come to him so neatly in the nick of time, not through a library book but through Rawlie.

Once again, though, King's main character deviates from the information provided in a book. Rawlie tells Thad that the sparrows conduct souls in one direction: death to life. He mentions other birds that function as traditional pscyhopomps and guide souls the opposite way, but Thad does not attempt to summon loons or whippoorwills. Neither of these birds has come to Beaumont, so he has to make do with the ones that have, and hope that they can do what he himself cannot: fully get rid of George Stark.

Beaumont, like the Losers and even Billy Halleck, does not know *how* this solution is meant to work. He just knows that it *should*, a sort of blind belief that leaves him blowing the bird call, grabbing his babies, and simply diving for cover afterward. Like the Ritual of Chüd, Rawlie's explanation of sparrows as psychopomps sets up a loose sort of expectation, but the hero—or heroes—himself has to feel his way along in the dark, being reduced largely to simply hoping that he has enough of a grasp on what he must do for the situation to turn out in his favor.

Raising Demons

These sorts of responses are not limited to King's lengthy novels. In the short story "Sometimes They Come Back" (collected in *Night Shift* 1978), high school English teacher Jim Norman finds himself with a number of inexplicable new students in his period seven Living with Literature class. Even though it was packed at the beginning of the semester, previous students conveniently die in order to make room for three new ones: one with a small strawberry birthmark on his chin, one with recognizable blonde hair, and a third who initially means nothing to Norman. In connection with the other two, however, his apparent role falls into place.

When Norman was a child, he watched his brother get attacked and murdered by four teenage boys. Three of them, with different hairstyles, now sit in his classroom, apparently not a day older even though Norman himself has grown up, gone to college, and become a high school teacher. It was not always easy—he suffered a nervous breakdown as a student teacher—and now, faced with the deaths of some of his better students and the insolent attitudes of these three new ones, he believes he might be headed for a breakdown yet again. Norman starts to piece things together as well as he can, and he assumes that the fourth boy has not joined the others because, of the four who killed his brother, only that fourth is still alive. The other three—the ones looking back at Norman during period seven—are all dead.

Apparently the boys believe that there is some unfinished business from that day back in Norman's childhood, and they want to torture him even more than the memory of his brother's murder already has. Norman's wife finds him reading a book called *Raising Demons*, but when he cautions her to take a taxi to her friend's house in spite of it only being four blocks away, he cites a made-up attempted rape. She knew he had been having bad dreams about his brother's murder, but Norman has no chance to decide whether or not to try to explain to her that his brother's murderers have all turned up, apparently ageless, in period seven. That night, she is struck by a car and killed. One of Norman's new students calls to tell him that he is next.

Rather than continue to cower, waiting for the three boys to make a move, Norman consults the chapter in his book titled "Malefic Spirits and How to Call Them." He goes to his classroom and chalks a very specific diagram on the floor, offering up a photograph of himself and his brother; blood from a stray cat Norman caught and killed; the sweatband of one of his brother's old hats; and his own index fingers, chopped off with a sharp knife. In exchange for these gifts, the unseen force Norman summons agrees to rid him of the three new additions to Living with Literature. Once this deed is done, it tells him, "I'll come back, Jim,"[12] echoing the title of the short story and indeed the boys' own reappearance. The story ends with Norman reminding himself that, yes, the book said demons could be summoned and dismissed, but that they do not always stay away forever.

Confronted with the inexplicable and supernatural, Norman does what so many of King's characters do, especially in the pre-internet age: find a book in the library. A high school teacher checking out a book on raising demons will draw less attention than the same man asking around for anyone's firsthand personal knowledge, and it saves Norman explanations he simply does not have. When he calls up the detective who worked his brother's murder case, he is only able to get the information that three of the boys involved died in the same car crash and thus could not possibly be a threat to him. When Norman refuses to tell the detective why he suddenly has such a renewed interest, the detective hangs up on him. There is no sane, acceptable explanation for what is happening, although the fact that all three boys newly added to his class are supposed to be dead somehow makes more sense than anything else. The fourth, still alive, cannot have returned from the grave to threaten him.

Presumably they chose the timing of their return to coincide with Norman's new teaching position. His interview for the job provides the backstory of his previous breakdown, presenting readers with what Norman sees as his weakness. If he believes he is hallucinating boys who can no longer be boys—and boys who have been rotting in their coffins—then the more rational explanation would be another mental break. Norman shows his clear understanding of the situation when he refuses to even try to explain it to his wife. For quite a while he simply tries to put up with the new students in his class and their disruptions and insolence as if he does not recognize them. It is only his wife's death that spurs him on to action, and he chooses to act alone.

Like so many others, Norman blindly follows the information in his book. He has no understanding of why he needs to draw the shape he does, or even why the thing he summons agrees that his brother's sweat is a worthy offering. He does not know much at all about *what* he summons, aside from the fact that it agrees to rid him of the three boys who are haunting him—and that it threatens to come back.

Norman is not shown to consider trying to murder the boys himself. Even after they kill his wife, Norman continues with his library book, which may or may not have recommended summoning a demon over direct confrontation. Perhaps he thought that the three-against-one odds would not be in his favor, or he worried about his future prospects if he were caught, although Norman seems to take the task of explaining his now-missing index fingers in stride. Without his wife, it seems he has little to live for anyway, since he is willing to risk the consequences of the demon. He has no idea of what those consequences might be but, again, like so many other King characters, Norman is satisfied that his current, most pressing issue is resolved. The future will have to take care of itself.

Flying Blind

When King's characters reach for information about other cultures to help them confront supernatural threats, they do not do so from a position of full understanding. The threat might seem mystical and magical, outside of their own mundane existence, and thus it seems necessary to then look outside of those everyday lives for a solution to the problem. They do not fully understand the threat facing them, so it might almost be comforting not to understand the power or mysticism of the rituals they perform to eliminate that threat. There is power beyond their knowledge, and they have seen it in the monster, so they seek to find that same power to use for themselves.

But this lack of understanding is a problem. Bill and Richie can feel as though they are biting into Its tongue without grasping *why* this biting is necessary. They have also been told to trade jokes back and forth until either one of them laughs and thus loses, but Bill instead speaks a tongue twister and Richie, although he laughs, does not lose. The explanation Bill got from the book was enough to get them pointed in the right direction, but either they did the Ritual wrong—which resulted in Its return in 1985 and the hint of Its continued existence in 2001 in the novel *Dreamcatcher*—or the Himalayan Ritual of Chüd itself was not in fact the solution. It was simply enough to keep the Losers moving through the tunnels to find Its lair, not exactly confident that they would be able to face It, but with enough hope in their hearts.

When Billy Halleck laid his "white men from town curse" on Lemke's group of Gypsies, he likewise had no idea what he was saying. He clearly had at least a vague notion of white privilege and the damage white supremacy has done to marginalized groups, but in the moment when he speaks these words, Halleck has no idea how he, personally, would be able to curse the people in front of him beyond the same systemic processes of which he has always played a part. His "curse" is only enacted through another man who uses his own underworld connections to obtain weapons and terrorize Lemke's family and friends into giving up. His lack of understanding of the curse Lemke put on him is clear when Halleck keeps insisting Lemke remove it, and he finally accepts the idea that it can only be transferred when Lemke goes against his own great-granddaughter's wishes and offers the surrender in the form of the means of that transfer. Halleck still fails to understand, although it is human nature—and his own wife and daughter—that once again plunges him into despair and makes him eat the rest of the pie himself.

In *Dreamcatcher*, the object itself is a recurring theme meant to symbolize friendship, or connection, or Duddits and his strange power, but no one understands how Duddits can do what he does, or how he can bring out special abilities in those around him. The dreamcatcher from the Clarendon hunting cabin becomes the shorthand to describe all of this without actually getting into a deep explanation of *how*, exactly, these connections and powers work. It is simply used by the friends, first as boys and then as grown men, as their own personal symbol, devoid of its original culture and meaning, and one of them even concludes that it is not, in fact, the right word, but will have to do until a better one is found. Duddits gave his life to save the world, and it worked, and neither the aliens nor Duddits' powers are a threat anymore, so no deeper understanding is necessary.

Finally, "Sometimes They Come Back" presents readers with an everyday high school English teacher willing to dabble in the dark arts as a solution to his current problem, and who ignores any possible future implications until after his most pressing crisis is averted. Prior to the sudden influx of new students in his seventh period class, Norman had never considered the possibility of evil returning to haunt those touched by it. He had bad dreams about his brother's murder, of course, but he had not been given the information that three out of the four boys present that day had died in a car crash. The real event haunted his subconscious, and then three apparently flesh-and-blood boys arrived in his classroom and killed his wife. The combination of terror and grief spurred Norman on to act without fully recognizing the possible consequences of his summoning. Although it apparently worked, producing the mysterious voice and removing the three threatening boys, Norman realizes that he has no idea what the consequences will now be for him, above and beyond needing to explain why he cut off his own fingers.

This lack of understanding does not necessarily impede these characters in the moment. The various evils are in fact defeated, at least for a while—but as a solution, King's white characters reaching outside of their own cultural experiences are only stopgap. It may be a momentary victory, but that moment does not necessarily last long, and winning the battle does not always mean winning the war.

II

My God Is Strong
Christianity in the Face of the Unknown

When confronted with the supernatural, it is common for King's characters to look for a similarly mystical or spiritual way to respond to the threat. In the first section, those characters chose to reach outside of their home culture in order to find something properly ritualized from a marginalized culture. In this section, we will look at King's characters who seek their spiritual response from closer to the mainstream and reach for Christianity as their chosen form of defense.

Horror films such as *Poltergeist* (1982) have solidified Christianity as a possible response to the unknown, building on what *Dracula* (1897) had already begun. Catholicism is the most common form of Christianity to be used in these situations, not only because it is older than any of the Protestant branches, but also because of the many physical trappings associated with it. Catholicism comes with saints, relics, crucifixes, and holy water, all of which are invoked frequently during the practice of the religion. Protestant services turn wafers and wine into cubes of white bread and grape juice and often engage in rites such as communion on a less frequent basis. The closest accepted American culture comes to mystic ritual lies in the Catholic church.

Although King does have a handful of characters who are themselves leaders within the church, from *'Salem's Lot's* Father Donald Callahan to *Revival's* the Rev. Charles Jacobs, Christian belief is more often found within the common man or woman. These characters have not undergone dedicated schooling or training, and frequently seem to live by following the voice of God in their hearts. Whether or not they choose to participate in organized religion seems to have little affect on their ability to call upon the Lord for help in their darkest hours. In fact, for King, organized religion is frequently just as big a menace as the supernatural threat itself.

The first essay in this section discusses the handful of King's texts in which Christianity is in fact a helpful part of the solution. Religious trappings and teachings are seized upon more frequently than they help King's characters succeed, but the few cases in which the Lord plays a major role in that success are discussed here. These are cases in which the use of religious trappings and symbolism are still clearly rooted within the Christian faith.

Chapter 4 concerns itself with the blurred line between Christianity and white magic. Dualism between good and evil in late twentieth- and early twenty-first-century America is still deeply rooted in the idea of God as the good and the White, with the figure of the devil as His opposite in the dark. At times King's characters seize upon Christian representational objects in order to use them as a magical, mystical defense against evil, relying just as much on their knowledge of Bram Stoker as of the Bible. It seems to be their belief that powers the magical white light seen to surround crucifixes and holy water, but whether that belief is in religious or secular teachings is up for debate. At times even a nod toward religion is foregone and the light inhabits an entirely secular object, even if the good versus evil fight seems to align itself with Biblical expectations.

Christianity is not, however, always a good defense or a comfort to King's characters in their trying times, as Chapter 5 explores. In some of King's stories, Christianity itself *is* the problem. It can lead to the creation of the threat itself or increase the threat exponentially even when in the hands of well-meaning interlopers. Instead of being a solution or a comfort, Christianity itself becomes a weapon, generally leading to multiple deaths. Frequently the Christianity presented in these stories is not a common variation that would be found in a church on any given Sunday, but a belief system that has been bastardized by its tiny number of practitioners and could conceivably be argued *not* to be Christianity at all, no matter what the small group calls it. They do, however, engage with their version of the religion *as* a religion and are often fanatical about their beliefs.

Finally, Chapter 6 deals with narratives in which Christianity might be mentioned, but actual belief is absent. Characters invoke the Bible and Jesus as verbal placeholders and wield them as social clubs, but without actually engaging in religious practices as a rule. They give religion lip service and frequently use the appearance of piety for their own gain, but do not in fact believe that they, too, must follow the Ten Commandments or the Golden Rule. They use religion and the idea of God, often without actually believing in Him, generally with disastrous results. It would seem that Christianity, no matter how it is used, frequently fails King's characters and leaves them worse off than when they began.

3

The Power of Prayer

*Christian Solutions
to Supernatural Problems*

There are times when God Himself is a character in a King novel, speaking to His chosen children and instructing them on what to do. When God—or at least the voice which receives that label—speaks, He cannot be disobeyed. Even unbelievers are seen to follow His divine instructions, at the urging of those who have actually heard His voice. The quiet, constant belief of a character in the Lord can be more believable to others than a supernatural threat. Those who witness miracles of a dark variety often find it easier to dismiss them than another character's quiet religious presence.

The emphasis here is indeed on "quiet." In *The Stand* and *Desperation*, the religious main characters live their faith day in and day out, not bending to the discomfort of family members or ceasing because there is no one around to see them. These are not King's preachers, shouting from the pulpit or in revival tents, or commanding that others join them in showy prayer before a meal. The faith of Mother Abigail and David Carver does not go unchallenged, but neither of them attempts to convert others through fire and brimstone. They simply pray, and sing hymns, and open themselves up to God—and then listen and obey when they hear His voice.

Perhaps one sign to the others around them, generally nonbelievers, that they actually hear God is how that voice never seems to tell them what they actually want to hear. In fact, obeying God seems to be the quickest path to more death and destruction, even if obedience is meant to provide a solution in the long term. Considering the outcome, perhaps it is not strange that few of King's characters honestly ask God for help when dealing with their troubles.

Mother Abigail and the Dark Man: *The Stand*

In *The Stand*, a man-made plague quickly kills off more than ninety percent of the human population. Those who are left, rather than remaining isolated and spread across the country, start to congregate in either Boulder, Colorado, around an old Black woman named Mother Abigail, or Las Vegas, Nevada, with someone who calls himself Randall Flagg and looks like a young white man. This mass assemblage was made possible through shared dreams. Survivors tended to feel strongly about each figure: terrible fear of Flagg and great love for Mother Abigail, or the opposite. Those who flock to Boulder are meant to be the good people, as opposed to those who willingly enter Sin City.

Those who assemble in the newly-named Boulder Free Zone come to the conclusion that, if they do nothing about Flagg, then the dark man and his people will do all they can to kill every person in the Zone. Thus they decide to strike first, initially by sending three spies west to gain more information. Unfortunately, two members of the Free Zone in actual fact belong to Flagg, and the bomb they set off effectively eliminates the Zone's leadership, first in the blast and then thanks to Mother Abigail's vision.

The woman around whom the remaining "good" men, women, and children of America have gathered is over 100 years old and regularly converses with God. During her time in Boulder, she commits the unforgivable sin of pride and goes out into the wilderness in order to make herself right with God. She is found on the same night as the bomb that is meant to kill all members of the Free Zone's leadership committee, drawing some of them out of the house before it can go off and then living just long enough to pass on God's orders to the remaining members.

Unfortunately for them, Mother Abigail herself has a strong hold over those who refuse to believe in her God. Only pregnant Fran Goldsmith is spared, but the four surviving men of the committee are supposed to start walking to Las Vegas that very day, carrying nothing and wearing the clothes they currently have on. There is no time for preparation and, if they listen to Mother Abigail—and if she has correctly passed on the Lord's message—no need to gather supplies. To lend some weight to her orders, Mother Abigail heals Frannie's back, which was badly sprained in the course of the explosion. Fran still resists, not wanting to let the men—including *her* man, Stuart Redman—simply walk into the West where they are likely to die. Mother Abigail could not see if any of them would return, although she was able to tell them that one of the four would not even make it to Vegas in the first place.

Mother Abigail's trust is, and has always been, in the Lord. Her faith for the first 108 years of her life is constant, but not miraculous. It is only after the superflu has made its away across the country that she witnesses miracles, most of them involving the people who first dream of her, and then come to her. Mother Abigail is able to converse with God at least enough to know that she has a role in all that will unfold, and that He has kept her alive when she has buried three husbands and all of her children prior to the plague because of the mission He has set for her. She is also bitter, because those 108 years of her life were spent in Nebraska but, in the summer of 1990, God bids her move to Colorado, where she knows she will die. Although she hears and obeys God's orders, even Mother Abigail does not do so without tears.

She is also imperfect and human. The fact that so many have come so far just to meet her fills her with the pride that then drives her from Boulder in her attempt to once again make things right with the Lord. If Mother Abigail cannot hear Him speak, and if she is not confident that her prayers are actually reaching Him, then she knows that there is no hope for the people who dreamed of her. She takes herself into the wilderness with little to eat or drink, and only returns after many of Boulder's residents have given up hope.

Mother Abigail's belief is in the Lord, but that is not what sets Stu, Larry Underwood, Glen Bateman, and Ralph Brentner on their journey. It is their devotion to Mother Abigail herself that makes them agree to go. Stu must do this against Frannie's wishes, and even then she harshly argues that "God can't run all of it!"[1] Fran wants Stu to promise he will do everything he can to make it back to Boulder, even though Mother Abigail was not able to tell them if anyone would. Fran, for one, cannot place all of her trust—or all of her future—in either Mother Abigail's hands or her God's.

None of the four men who set out walking for Vegas are particularly religious, either, although they gamely speak of being willing to see what, exactly, will come. Glen Bateman, a sociologist with a penchant for lectures, puts forth the idea that this strange walk, when they could have taken motorcycles or other forms of transportation, is meant to help them both empty out and recharge, like batteries. Once they are free of Boulder and their immediate responsibilities, the men focus on the apparent simplicity of their task, since they have already clearly made the decision to obey Mother Abigail's orders. What remains to be seen is whether those orders did indeed come from God, and whether this quest will allow them to save the Free Zone.

Stu is the one to suffer first bad luck and then his own miracles. When the group crosses a washout, the ground crumbles from underneath him on the far side, leaving Stu at the bottom with a badly broken leg. He sends the others on, as Mother Abigail had ordained, but the dog that had followed them from the East Coast remains with Stu and brings him wood for a fire and small game to cook over it. Later, the only surviving spy sent west comes across Stu on his trip back to Boulder and is able to nurse him back to relative health.

The other three men all die in Vegas. Glen Bateman is shot in his cell during a conversation with Flagg himself, dying with Christlike forgiveness on his lips for the man doing the shooting. Larry and Ralph are meant to be literally torn limb from limb in front of the dark man's people but, before this can happen, one of Flagg's less stable disciples drives into the crowd with a nuclear warhead. It is one of Flagg's own pseudo-miracles that sets it off, vaporizing Larry and Ralph along with the rest of them. Stu is able to make it to the top of the washout to see the mushroom-shaped cloud left behind and can therefore take this information back to Boulder when he returns. For the Free Zone, the story ends with optimism: Frannie's baby lives, giving hope for the future of the human race, and the fact that Flagg has been killed means there will be time for her baby and all the others to grow up.

The very last chapter, however, shows a man who thinks of himself as Russell Faraday—not Randall Flagg, but retaining his favored initials—waking up and meeting a new group of people. They do not yet understand each other, but they will, and the story ends with him laughing. Even though this new iteration of Flagg cannot yet make himself understood, he will begin all his old tricks again soon enough.

Mother Abigail's God is the Christian God who sent His only son to die on a cross for the sins of the world, and thus it is believable that He would ask Stu, Glen, Larry, and Ralph to give their own lives for the remaining Americans in Boulder's Free Zone. Although she is frequently seen playing her guitar and singing hymns, and although she makes it clear that she is not Catholic, Mother Abigail is not seen attending church and her particular brand of Protestantism is not identified. Of those who arrive in the Boulder Free Zone, none are identified as priests or ministers, and although the body disposal crew notes that many Boulderites gathered in churches to die, none of the post-plague citizens are shown organizing church services or even wishing for any. The group yearns for doctors and starts arguing over whether or not law enforcement should carry guns, but the religion of the Free Zone is not itself Christianity.

When Glen and Stu are initially discussing how to bring some organization to Boulder, Glen points out that any sort of government they wish to employ has to have Mother Abigail at its center. All of them dreamed of her, playing her guitar on her porch in the middle of the corn. They did not dream of Jesus or God, and if their perception of Randall Flagg lined up with the devil, it was more a reflection of late twentieth-century America's dualistic perceptions of good and evil. Even Mother Abigail herself thinks that "her" people would hardly recognize Flagg if they met him, unless he wanted them to, because evil is not physically identifiable in that way. Instead of good and bad divided into angels and devils, post-plague America has set the ends of the spectrum at Mother Abigail and Randall Flagg. Their power must come from somewhere, and Mother Abigail insists that hers comes from God, but that does not mean anyone else in the Free Zone believes it.

The Christianity of *The Stand*, then, resides fully in Mother Abigail. When Stu, Larry, Glen, and Ralph agree to go west, they do so because of Mother Abigail and her own belief in her God, but not theirs. Their belief and their love are invested in the old woman, and they are only lucky that she loves her God enough to obey Him, even when it brings harm to herself. It was certainly not in her best physical interest to go out into the wilderness, but when her God ordered her to, she obeyed—and returned with her vision of how to save her people.

It may seem to be a small distinction, but the four men only go west because they believed that Mother Abigail believed, and not because they themselves believed. In spite of the dreams they had all shared, and in spite of Mother Abigail's demonstration of God's power by healing Frannie's sprained back, it was their love for her, and not for her God, that spurred them onward, three of them to their deaths. Only one of them was able to return to Boulder and see that their possibly stupid, possibly heroic quest had been successful, although even Stu was not in a position to know whether Larry, Glen, and Ralph's presence in Vegas that day really had any effect on the outcome. Since Flagg's erstwhile follower had already been shunned and wanted to beg forgiveness by returning with a weapon in the first place, would that not have happened even without the emissaries from the Free Zone?

The belief system in *The Stand* thus centers around a woman who is herself a Christian, but whose followers are not. Mother Abigail herself is their guide, and while she sings her hymns and talks and listens to her God, there is no indication that this religious nature will be passed on. Even when Frannie begs Stu to tell her that they can be better than the people who came before the plague, he does not reference religion. The Free Zone wishes to move forward with laws and guns, not organized systems of belief and morals, although this could also be argued to be wise. Although Mother Abigail's God helped save the people in the Free Zone, it came at a high cost—as Joseph Reino observed, "few escape, and even fewer triumph"[2]—and Flagg was not defeated forever. In a time and place far distant from Boulder, Colorado, he rises again.

God is Cruel: *Desperation*

In 1996, King published two novels on the same day: *Desperation* under his own name, and its fraternal twin, *The Regulators*, as Richard Bachman. Each book shares the same basic threat, an otherworldly presence called Tak who is uncovered in a pit mine in Nevada. Each book's characters even share the same names, although they might not be similar to each other in many, if any, other ways. Not only the physical description of each character, but that character's fate, differs between the books. Because they were published on the same day, it is also difficult to differentiate between which one is the "original" character and which is the "variation." One major difference between the two, however, is that the theme of Christianity plays a major role in *Desperation*.

David Carver is an eleven-year-old boy when his family is taken prisoner by a crazy cop in the town of Desperation, Nevada. His younger sister is killed almost immediately, although he also loses his parents through the course of the book. The initial group of prisoners taken by the otherworldly Tak, currently controlling the cop's body, dwindles drastically as they confront the animals Tak controls, the totems that also wield Tak's power, and Tak itself. None of them are allowed to leave Desperation while this is happening, and the group must first discover what Tak actually is and then how to defeat it if they have any hope of surviving. David himself is their key to that survival.

The first sign that something is special about—or perhaps wrong with—David is when he kneels to pray after being locked up. It is clearly something that bothers or perhaps embarrasses his parents, although the entire reasoning behind this is not explained until later. Earlier in the year David's best friend Brian had been hit by a car and was not expected to live. After David visited a comatose Brian in the hospital, he prayed ... and his friend woke up. His friend's parents wanted to give David all of the credit but, unlike Mother Abigail, David both downplayed any influence he might have had, while at the same time keeping up his end of the bargain: if Brian lived, David would have to learn about God.

Since that time David has read the entire Bible and begun to pray multiple times a day. He also began taking private instruction with the Reverend Martin, in spite of his parents' concerns about leaving him alone with a young man. The reverend, although an alcoholic, always made sure his study door was open during these sessions, which have become the foundation for David's survival.

During the events in Desperation and especially after rounds of prayer, David performs a number of miracles. He first manages to escape the holding cell by soaping himself up and slipping through the bars while the others distract the coyote Tak had left standing guard. Although God assisted enough to make sure David's head made it through, a physical impossibility, He did not also muzzle the coyote. The other prisoners were able to take care of that. Everyone who has assembled in Desperation that day was brought not by the cop Tak was controlling, but by God, and they also have to play their parts.

David manages to send some of Tak's animals away; to multiply Ritz crackers and sardines like loaves and fishes; and to descend into a meditative state of prayer in which his guide—not God but sent by God—allows him to come to a greater understanding of what Tak is and how to defeat it. Throughout all of this the eleven year old is subjected to physical and mental horrors, almost being throttled by one of Tak's helpers and having to confront the fact that Tak has taken over his mother's body and killed her. Still David persists, quietly standing by his faith and insisting that they should all stand together and fight.

In the end it comes down to convincing one of the other members of the group, Johnny Marinville, that God is real and honestly has a plan. Marinville has spent much of the book dismissing David's prayers and struggling with his own self-image and place in the world. If Marinville leaves Desperation and the rest of the group behind, David knows that Tak will win and the rest of them will die. While David is the one to show the way, Marinville is the true key to success.

It is revealed that David's tour guide through the land of the dead, the man who told him the story of how Tak originally came into the world and how Tak had remained trapped for so many years, is actually Marinville. Even though the author has been with the living throughout the book, he is revealed to have died, at least spiritually, decades previously. Marinville ends up falling to his knees and praying to God—David's God, the Christian God—before the final battle begins. This is the battle in which David loses the remaining member of his family, and he fully expects to be the one to make the final sacrifice necessary to trap Tak once again. However, as David's the Reverend Martin taught him over and over again, God can be cruel.

It is Marinville who makes the final deadly descent into the mine shaft, and Marinville who causes the explosion to plug up the small gap between our world and Tak's. Before he does so, dying in the collapse of the old mine, he tells David that, while the boy might repeat "God is cruel," he does so without fully understanding. God *is* cruel, Marinville agrees, but the ultimate cruelty is that "sometimes he makes us live."[3] Even though God brought the Carver family to Desperation and killed David's little sister and his parents, God means David himself to live and to have to carry the weight of their deaths.

David is God's voice just as Mother Abigail was in *The Stand*, except he manages a full conversion of at least one of the people who has been brought to him. Marinville personally hears the voice of God and understands what he has to do, which includes standing up to David when the rest of the group has been convinced to blindly follow. David *wants* to be the one to die during the mine's collapse, even if it goes against God's will, because his emotional pain is so great. Marinville follows God's orders and challenges David, getting the boy to admit the truth: that he is not, in fact, the one who is meant to do this.

It is difficult to judge the success of Marinville's sacrifice since Tak itself makes another appearance—once again threatening David Carver, Johnny Marinville, and the others—in the Bachman novel *The Regulators*. In that one, the Bachman version of David dies, while the alternate Marinville lives. In *Desperation*, though, it seems that the old China Pit has once again been sealed by the end of the book, although this may or may not be permanent. The Pit had already been a thing of legend, having caved in decades earlier, and was stumbled across accidentally during this new round of mining. What was uncovered twice before by accident could easily be uncovered again, since the small group of survivors can hardly tell the story of what *actually* happened to them in Desperation.

Childhood Belief, Adult Apathy

King's characters do not often turn to Christianity as a solution to their problems. The Losers in *It*, for example, at times ponder their own religions but do not consider using any of their own beliefs in their confrontation with the monster. Eddie especially is haunted by the idea that taking the Eucharist and throwing it in the toilet would turn the water to blood—a powerful image he knows he could ban by actually trying the experiment himself, but he never quite dares. The act of taking communion has a strong effect on him ever since he heard that story in Sunday school, causing his asthma to act up, but this power is not the kind they seek to confront It. Even though their religious upbringing is enough to prevent some of the boys from eating meat on Friday with a sort of internal reaction they realize they cannot properly justify, Christianity—and Stan Uris' Jewish heritage—are not considered as being useful solutions.

Perhaps the only other time when Christian practices are used as a relatively successful balm is in the short story "Mute" (collected in *Just After Sunset* 2008). The events of the story are unsettling, but not entirely supernatural. The situation is told in flashbacks as lapsed Catholic Mr. Monette—never given a first name—enters into the confessional for the first time in years.

Monette tells the priest of how he picked up a hitchhiker whose sign proclaimed him to be a deaf mute and how, during the course of their ride together, he found himself ranting about his wife's infidelity and her embezzlement of funds. Up until the time of that ride, neither of these issues had been made public. Monette worked as a traveling salesman and was frequently on the road, as he was at the time of this one-sided conversation, and he was then supposed to return to his empty home and face the discovery of the embezzlement and, likely, her affair. He is most worried about how their college-age daughter will respond, as well as how he will continue to pay for her schooling.

At a rest stop, the hitchhiker disappears, taking Monette's St. Christopher medal with him. Later Monette is informed that his wife and her lover have been murdered in their hotel—one he named while ranting to his supposedly deaf hitchhiker. When he returned from the funeral home, the St. Christopher medal had been returned, along with a short note: "Thank you for the ride."[4] Monette feels guilty about so freely telling the story to a stranger, even if he believed his passenger could not hear him and lies when the priest asks if he honestly wants the police to catch the other man. Even though he has lapsed in his belief and religious practices, Monette assigns himself further penance for this lie.

Even though Monette has already told the story to law enforcement and helped them with a tentative ID of the hitchhiker, the incident has still shaken him enough to make him enter a church and make a confession to a priest he has never met before, returning to a ritual he has long since stopped enacting. At a time when his world seems to be turned upside down—first his wife's confession of the embezzlement and the affair, and now her murder and the investigation—Monette returns to the practices of his childhood. All the same, he does lie in the confessional once his story has been told and he just wants to escape, so the return is not complete. He is comforted by being able to remove his wife's murder from his own soul, but also relieved by the fact that she has been murdered. It is a moral and spiritual conundrum that sends him back to the spiritual roots of his life, which provide him at least momentary relief, but there is nothing supernatural about the situation.

According to his books, King is not a strong believer in the power of Christianity to solve problems. More often, as seen in Chapter 5, Christianity causes threats or makes them worse. Even the solutions offered by the Christian faith or God are incomplete or temporary, and "[b]elief and adherence to a faith in God is not an infallible means of survival in King's fiction."[5] Although following Mother Abigail's advice leads to a nuclear explosion in Las Vegas that means the continued existence of the "good" people in Boulder, three of the four men sent to Vegas to curry God's favor ended up dying, two of the three spies sent by the Free Zone were likewise caught and killed, and it was an explosion and death that caused the four to be sent to Vegas in the first place. Boulder lost a number of good people in this God-quest to secure their own future without any real assurance that those deaths would secure them protection. Then, in the epilogue, Randall Flagg rises again in a new time and place. The protection was not for everyone, everywhere, but for Mother Abigail's people directly after the plague.

In *Desperation*, young David Carver frequently repeats the mantra that God is cruel before having to learn firsthand exactly how cruel He can be. Although David was the one to bring God to Desperation, and the only one of the assembled to have undergone a true conversion and regularly both speak to and listen to the Lord, he is not the one chosen to complete the destruction of Tak. God saved David's best friend after a car accident, but He has taken David's little sister and both his parents and sent him on from Desperation in order to live his life. The honor of sacrificing himself to destroy the evil and conform to God's will goes to Johnny Marinville, who has spent much of the book ridiculing David's faith and generally being annoying. Marinville even almost abandons the group before David manages to convince him otherwise and bring him to his own conversion. In the end Marinville gets the glory of completing suicide in the explosion that seals Tak off from the rest of the world, while David has the punishment of continued life. Tak, though, is also present in the concurrently published *The Regulators*, so once again the question of destruction is one of possible temporality.

When it comes to supernatural threats, God might bring groups of people together to confront them, but the cost is always high. The death toll in *The Stand* is higher because of the number of characters present in the story, but many of those trapped in Desperation do not live to see how everything turns out. Even when God leads characters to do His bidding, His will does not always mean protection, or permanent success. Christianity in King as a solution to a threat is rare, and Christianity as true religious belief is also rare. More often Christian objects or rituals are used as a form of white magic in order to counteract the dark.

4

Was It a Miracle?

Light, Power and Belief

    Because dominant American culture lacks legends from which to draw explanations, twentieth- and twenty-first-century Americans commonly associate miracles with Christianity instead of looking for other explanations. Jesus performed marvels from walking on water, to healing sickness and blindness, to casting out demons. Many of those demons might now be understood as mental illness, but there is still the sense of taking the foreign *something* and physically removing it from where it trespasses in a body or a town. After Jesus' death and resurrection, His disciples were able to perform similar miracles in His name, healing people and pointing them in the right direction: toward God, and toward good.

    Miracles in late twentieth- and early twenty-first-century America, therefore, are inexorably tied to those performed by Jesus Christ. Christianity has permeated popular culture to the point where God is invoked on money and in the Pledge of Allegiance, and any explanation of a different belief system frequently compares it to common Christian tenets. Good is associated with God, who is associated with light—whether or not the Holy Spirit accompanies said light in the form of a dove—and stands in counterpoint to Evil. When one of King's characters invokes the light or what King calls "the White" against a threat, the most common association is to compare the resulting miracle to one performed by Jesus Christ or his disciples.

    At times the link is made explicit within the context of the story, either because the item imbued with power and light is itself a Christian symbol, or because the character involved is written in such a way that he is clearly meant to be associated with Christ. In other instances the light comes and helps repel a figure who seems to be from the Bible—Death and his pale horse—but that light comes to a non-religious person and centers itself on a non-religious object. The battle of good and evil, especially when clearly over the souls of the people from town, is still marked as being largely religious in the Christian tradition.

These miraculous occurrences in the face of supernatural evil also tend to stand independently of organized religion or a firm foundation in religious teachings and practice. The basic knowledge and recognition is present, but, for example, those holding up a crucifix in order to ward off a vampire are often not themselves Catholic. There might be the belief in some nameless, formless power for good, or just the helpless hope that *something* will arise in order to help combat the evil during a final confrontation, but religious belief is often divorced from this kind of last-ditch heroic practice in King.

Cross-Shaped Defenses and the Town of *'Salem's Lot*

Christianity is a traditional repellent for vampires, so of course it plays a major role in *'Salem's Lot* and the accompanying short stories located nearby. King's core group of characters come to realize that the new shop in town is just a front for a vampire and his apparently human familiar, although this is a difficult conclusion for rational people of the 1970s to reach. High school teacher Matt Burke is the first to hit on the idea that the strange occurrences around town, including the death of one of the local gravediggers in Matt's own house, can be explained if they accept the premise that vampires are real. Townspeople are shown growing weak from a mysterious illness that apparently makes them anemic and overly sensitive to sunlight. Some seem to disappear, while others are discovered dead without a single mark on them. Matt puts the pieces together and starts to study up on vampire lore from his hospital bed where he is stuck after a heart attack brought on by the stress of the reanimated dead lurking not just in his town, but in his own house.

Young Mark Petrie, a boy who loves all things horror, utilizes one of the book's first instances of Christianity's magical powers. When another boy, already turned, hovers outside his bedroom window and demands entry, Mark grabs for a figure from his monster collection and holds out a plastic cross. Although he tells the other boy to come in, the cross lights up with a strange glow and repels the vampire. It is not a holy relic and is in fact a cheap prop, but the cross itself is somehow imbued with the power to protect Mark. So many schlock horror movies have taught Mark the usefulness of the cross against vampires, and so therefore this one protects him.

In another example, after Ben Mears has enlisted physician Jimmy

Cody to help him figure out what disease is plaguing the Lot, Ben and Jimmy wait in a funeral home to see if a woman will rise at sunset. They have been sitting around aimlessly for a while when Jimmy suddenly asks if Ben has remembered to bring a crucifix. With none present, Jimmy uses medical tape to bind two tongue depressors together and then orders Ben, the writer, to speak a blessing on it. After protesting that he is not himself religious, Ben's awkward beginning develops into the twenty-third psalm, and the tongue depressor cross begins to glow just as the woman's body starts to move. In spite of being a hastily created object, blessed by someone who has no personal ties to the Catholic church, the cross is able to cause damage to the newly risen vampire's body and to confirm that Jimmy has managed to save himself from her bite through a quick application of disinfectant and a tetanus shot. When Ben lays the cross against his skin after this treatment, it no longer glows, even though it clearly held enough power to save them both and then send the vampire on her way.

Later the small group grows to include Catholic priest Donald Callahan, who is both disenchanted with his religion and searching for an honest spiritual battle rather than the day-in, day-out mundane rituals of the confessional and everyday sins. He has, in fact, been looking for just the sort of situation that happens to be unfolding in the Lot, although Callahan initially resists both the idea of vampires and the suggestion that his religion might be weaponized. When the others approach him, it is not as his parishioners, or even as Christians. They are simply looking for ways to repel the vampires so they can live long enough to proceed with staking them through the heart.

Callahan is thus torn. He wants to be able to lead such a religious charge, but he understands that using the trappings of his religion—a borrowed crucifix, for example—does not translate to using the *power* of religion. Mark has already successfully used his toy cross, and non–Catholic Matt has been comforted by the presence of a crucifix, but Callahan warns the brave little band that using these symbols only as symbols, without the deeper belief and understanding, could be more dangerous than confronting a vampire without a cross at all. He is in the minority when it comes to King's characters by considering this at all and suggesting that any magic or miracles inherent in an object or a ceremony might not function if simply picked up and parroted by outsiders.

The priest is himself given a chance to confront Barlow, the Lot's head vampire, and at first it seems Callahan's faith will triumph. Barlow has come for Mark in an act of personal revenge, since Mark was responsible for the death of his partner, and he kills Mark's parents in front of him. Callahan manages to secure Mark's freedom by holding up his crucifix and commanding Barlow to let the boy go, but then he falters. The vampire tells Callahan to cast the symbol aside and to face him with his faith alone. Callahan gives verbal consent, but then hesitates. The mysterious light and power that have imbued his mother's crucifix, making it glow the way Mark's own plastic cross did, suddenly fade. Barlow is able to pluck it from the priest's hand and break the arms off the cross before forcing Callahan to drink his blood, thus marking and cursing him. Callahan learns that he cannot even enter his church anymore, and a Greyhound bus takes him out of the story.

Callahan's failure is explored more deeply when he arises as a character in the fifth book of the Dark Tower and meets his ultimate death at the start of the final book of the series. In the intervening years he has been accepted back into the Church, at least on a temporary basis, and is able to carry a cross and enter holy buildings once more. His death scene therefore mirrors his final confrontation with Barlow, except for one small change: when the approaching vampires challenge Callahan to cast his crucifix aside, he does so without hesitation.

It is almost an inverse of Callahan's initial argument against joining the small band of intrepid vampire hunters. Then, he argued that taking the symbol without belief would lead to failure. Here, at the end of his life, he realizes that all of the power is in the belief. The symbol, in this case a crucifix, might allow him to focus that belief, but Callahan himself had crossed the line into believing in the symbol itself. That is why his initial attempt to defeat the vampire failed and Barlow was able to first take his crucifix and then snap the arms off. Mark Petrie's plastic scenery graveyard cross was able to repel a vampire because the boy believed it would work. Callahan's belief initially centered around the crucifix itself, but in the intervening, uncountable years between leaving *'Salem's Lot* and appearing again in the Dark Tower series, he learned this small but vital difference in belief.

While Callahan's crucifix—and his faith—fails in the face of the head vampire, other religious objects are shown to be useful against the vampires Barlow made, if not Barlow himself. The follow-up short story, "One for the Road," has two locals venturing toward the Lot in a snowstorm in an attempt to help a man from Boston rescue his wife and daughter from where their car got stuck. "Most folks who live near the Lot wear something"[1] Catholic, like a crucifix or a saint's medal, one of them explains, clarifying why a Congregationalist would have a crucifix on under his shirt just as a matter of course. The other man takes his family Bible, which he later throws at a vampire, causing it to startle and flee.

4. Was It a Miracle?

These religious objects, even in the hands of non-believers or different believers, really do seem to work, at least to an extent. The man who was entranced by the child vampire was not protected by his crucifix, which was still inside his shirt and apparently needed a direct sightline in order to be useful, but the thrown Bible was enough to make the child start and break the hypnosis. The religious object, even when treated in a way that believers are taught would normally be considered blasphemous, has an impact on the vampire that any other thrown object would not.

The main character relates the fact that the word "vampire" is actually not used in connection with whatever happened over in the Lot two years ago and continues to happen when outsiders accidentally stray too close. In all that time he only recalls hearing it once, and that the speaker was laughed out of the bar for saying it. That speaker was also convinced that anyone who thought the problem *was* vampires was crazy, and personally argued for the presence of a wild dog pack. This man was in the minority, however, and thus the unspoken conclusion was that the threat in the Lot is indeed vampires, and that religious tokens will work to repel them if necessary. For the most part the people choose avoidance over confrontation, and certainly over a direct attack on the vampires. Even though they believe they know what is lurking in the Lot, they will not act as exterminators.

Those who remain in the towns surrounding the Lot, at least at the time of the short story, approximately two years since Barlow's initial arrival and one year after Ben and Mark set the fire meant to eradicate the vampires completely, are content to wear their religious objects and wave—or throw—them if necessary. Otherwise they avoid the town, since presumably the vampires don't have much of a hunting range, and go about their lives. They are confident that, in their moment of need, their tokens will save them.

And, within the short story, this protection is shown to be relatively successful. Although the main character's crucifix does not prevent the child vampire from asking him for a hug, and presumably would not harm her if it remained behind his shirt, the Bible—and his friend's presence of mind—is enough to save him. The religious tokens seem to work, at least against the vampires Barlow created, but then, cultural consciousness seems to agree that religious artifacts will repel or harm vampires, as shown in so many media representations.

Father Callahan, who has studied the Bible and become a recognized leader of the holy Catholic church, has a greater crisis of faith than either Mark Petrie or the two men from "One for the Road." Mark's belief in the power of the cross to repel a vampire, as well as the two men's constant carrying of a crucifix and a Bible for just these moments, allow them to escape. None of them attempt to directly confront Barlow or another head vampire, however, although Mark witnesses Barlow's murder of his parents prior to Callahan's stand. As a boy who has already had to escape Barlow's manservant and who has failed to convince his parents of the danger, thereby leading to their murder, Mark is therefore in no position to summon the emotional and spiritual strength for such a confrontation. And, because the others in their group managed to stake Barlow through the heart, the men from the surrounding towns likewise do not have to face a head vampire.

That, then, would be the ultimate test to determine what, exactly, King has to say about the power of belief. Within the Dark Tower books Callahan explains about three different kinds of vampires, a distinction that is not made within *'Salem's Lot*, and only Callahan is seen using a crucifix in confrontation with head vampires. The others—the ones created by Barlow and seen in "One for the Road"—are categorized as Type Two vampires, much more feral and far less intelligent than Type Ones like Barlow. It would seem that a thrown Bible would do nothing against Barlow, who is able to handle religious artifacts when they are not imbued with the proper level of belief. Mark's glowing plastic cross likewise might not be enough to make Barlow pause. Even at the end of Callahan's life, when he is confronted by numerous Type One vampires and throws his crucifix aside, his triumph comes in defeating the vampires not by killing them, but by killing himself and preventing them from turning him. His solution is in fact a mortal sin as dictated by his faith and, by dint of King's supernatural storytelling, Callahan's second such suicide.

The shape of the cross is thus seen in multiple forms throughout these confrontations with vampires, and with varying levels of success. Mark's plastic figurine and Ben and Jimmy's quickly-made, hastily-blessed tongue depressors both fill with light and cause damage to the vampires they touch, while Callahan's first crucifix—his mother's crucifix—ends up failing him when he cannot bring himself to throw it aside. Callahan has, as shown by the resolution of his story in the Dark Tower series, imbued the object itself with too much meaning rather than relying on the belief and the power *behind* the object. Somehow Ben and Jimmy, neither one a religious man, managed to construct and bless a working magical cross using the items at hand and without a true sense of what they were up against, much less with a conviction that such an object would in fact work in their defense. Tony Magistrale argues that "Mears, unlike Father Callahan, keeps his faith in himself"[2] and thus this faith translates to the energy seen in the cross. Power and belief, it seems, are complicated and perhaps even fickle forces within the world of King's novels.

Jesus Christ, John Coffey and Miracle Healings

When *The Green Mile* was initially published in 1996, it was done so in six parts, as a serial novel. King wanted to experiment with the form for a change, which forced him to tell six arcs of the story to build toward the climax in a way that he had not done before. In novels, information can be planted or revealed in various places throughout the book and issues can be resolved in the same way. With a serial novel, he needed to make sure that each section carried the proper amount of tension and reveal while carrying the story all the way through to the end. It also meant having part one more or less set in stone—or at least in print—while he was still working toward the end, so he was unable to go back and change something in the beginning if he realized that it no longer fit the ending.

The main character, Paul Edgecombe, is now an old man in a nursing home in 1996, writing down the events at Cold Mountain Penitentiary that occurred in 1932. He wants to share this manuscript and his long-kept secret with his special friend Elaine, since no one else is left alive to remember. Paul himself has outlived anyone else involved at the time and eventually reveals that he is in fact 104 years old and shows little sign of reaching the end of his life anytime soon. The side effects of miracles can themselves be curses.

Paul writes about death row inmate John Coffey, a very tall Black man who has been sentenced to the chair for murdering two young white girls. Coffey actually occupies a position far back in Paul's concerns since other inmates are louder and more violent, and even one of the guards, Percy Wetmore, is far more of a problem than John. Their new prisoner is a giant of a man, yes, who was found holding the battered bodies of two little girls, but he is also quiet and kind in a way that is quickly revealed to be extraordinary. When Percy stomps on another prisoner's pet mouse, Mr. Jingles, John is able to breathe life back into him. Mr. Jingles, like Paul himself, has slowed down by 1996 but is still alive right up until the end of Paul's story.

There are other problems that take attention away from John Coffey. Another distraction in Paul's life is his urinary tract infection, which John cures, inadvertently leading to Paul's incredible lifespan. Percy further complicates Paul's life by accepting a job transfer, but only if he can supervise one execution first. This turns into a horrific experience as Percy forgoes wetting the sponge that goes under the cap placed on the condemned man's head in order to help the electricity flow and provide a quicker death. By the time Paul is able to focus on John Coffey and his amazing abilities, he already has so much else on his mind and so many other issues to confront, although at least his urinary tract infection is no longer one of them.

A bigger problem is looming, one for which Paul realizes he might have a solution. The Warden's wife is slowly dying of an inoperable brain tumor. If John could bring a mouse back from the brink of death and heal Paul's own infection, then perhaps, if he and some of the "good" guards can sneak John out to the Warden's house and back, then the brain tumor might be removed. The other guards, who have witnessed much of what John has done and also question whether or not the guilty verdict was true, agree to help, getting Percy out of the way for long enough that he will not notice John's empty cell.

After every other healing, John expelled a black cloud of something the others take to be the disease, but he does not do so after removing the sickness from the Warden's wife. Instead he carries it with him, back to death row, and breathes it into Percy. This is the one instance where Paul and the others witness John Coffey using his powers to harm people: Percy immediately shoots one of the other death row inmates and then collapses, insane. Considering Percy's sadistic streak, Paul is not bothered all that much by the guard's condition, but he wonders about the other prisoner. John later confesses that, in a prior incident with that prisoner, he had the vision that this man was the real rapist and murderer of the two little girls for whom John was sentenced to death. He purposefully held onto the sickness in order to inflict revenge on the worst guard and the worst prisoner he knew.

To Paul and his fellow guards, John Coffey is simply a six-foot-eight-inch Black Jesus Christ, with the monogram to match. They see his power to heal the medically incurable and overlook the fact that his supernatural empathy leaves him constantly in pain. John even tells Paul that he in fact *wants* to die so he will no longer have to keep feeling all the pain people inflict on each other. And, unlike Jesus, John does not undergo a resurrection. When John is executed, he remains dead and his miraculous power is gone.

Paul continues to quantify what John can do as a largely good sort of miracle, rather than a curse. When the examination of John's powers puts other people first, this seems to be true: other people can be healed by John when they cannot be healed by anyone else, and John's sensitivity allows him to ensure that, if he directs the sickness at others, he will only pick those who are deserving. John is, after all, capable of taking illness and injury away from a living creature and simply breathing it into the air. If he could heal Mr. Jingles, Paul, and the Warden's wife, just imagine how many more worthy people he could touch!

But John's special abilities are what landed him on death row in the first place. He was found holding the dead bodies of the two girls, crying that he could not "take it back," and this was interpreted to mean that he had killed them. What John meant, inexplicable to those who do not know about or believe in supernatural powers, was that he found the girls already dead and could not remove the pain and injuries someone else had inflicted on them. What John does when he inhales the illness or injury, then, is to "take it back" and then give it either to the air, where it presumably disperses, or to those more deserving of illness and pain. Even then he has his limits: Jesus could call Lazarus back from the dead, but John can do nothing for the girls.

Paul and his fellow guards are especially moved at John's execution, and it is the last one Paul himself oversees before getting transferred. He is upset at having to execute someone who was not only innocent, but able to help people in mysterious ways that cannot be replicated by others. He glimpsed the miracles that Christlike Coffey could perform and wanted more for the other man than simply death, when death—and release—was what John desired all along. Although Paul sees incredible potential in John, he does at least accept John's wish and does not try to figure out how he can prevent the execution from proceeding.

By the time Paul is writing this down to share it with Elaine, he has had more than sixty years to think about the series of events and to reframe them in his mind. In that time he has also lost his wife in an accident, during which he thought he saw John watching them, and has observed how Mr. Jingles has also continued to live far past the normal mouse lifespan. Trying to calculate Paul's life expectancy from Mr. Jingles' lifetime is depressing because it seems the price for having been healed by John all those years ago is another span of years, these empty and lonely because so many people Paul knew die in their own time and he is the only one left. The miracle has become a curse, and John is not around for Paul to confront about it.

It seems unlikely that John knew about this long-term side effect of his gift. He is presented as being slow and possibly mentally impaired, a gentle giant who cannot read, write, or properly tie his own shoes. Paul also has no way of knowing exactly how many people John healed before encountering the two murdered girls, although John was clearly aware of his powers prior to that moment. He knew that he *could* usually take it back, and was mourning the fact that, this time, he was too late. John was young enough that he would not have been able to study such long-term effects, anyway, even if his life had not been so itinerant.

What John knew was that he could fix problems in the moment and take away the most immediate threat.

There is no overt connection drawn between John Coffey and Christianity the way other King characters are shown to actually be practicing the religion or engaging with the Christian God. He is not a revivalist calling upon God to heal people, and certainly not an exhibitionist of his powers. John is simply a man with a strange gift that he tries to use in order to do the right thing, when all the wrongs of the world are slowly eating away at him. He does not want to fight for his life so he can continue using his gift because the evil in the world is wearing him down. Even before he came to sit on death row with other condemned men and one sadistic guard, John was getting tired.

Whatever power John possesses is not inexhaustible and, while he is seen generally directing it to heal people on the side of good, he is also able to take the illness out of them and direct it into others with clearly negative results. John can be forgiven for infecting the guard Percy, since he was clearly a cruel man, and having him kill another resident of death row because Paul believes John's explanation: that it was the other man who killed the girls. Paul has no proof outside of John's declaration, although he likely suspects that John is not smart enough to come up with the story as a lie. In the hands of a more cunning individual, John's power might have been used for evil, in spite of the cost, as the wielder negotiated the physical drain against the possible gain.

But such power cannot last forever, and in such a kindhearted, simple man as John Coffey, the strange ability leads much more quickly to destruction. Both his mental capacity and his race place him in the margins of society rather than at its privileged center, perhaps further ensuring that John would be able to use his strange gift without undue outside influence, but also positioning him without a safety net. John, like Jesus Christ, is executed while still fairly young, and John asks not to be saved because he cannot go on living in a world where people are so cruel to each other and he feels all of it so deeply. John's miraculous gift, one that he freely shares without any hope or request for reward, is his curse, and Paul likewise finds himself in the position to contemplate the downside of John's miracles as he watches so many of his loved ones die while he lives on.

Light, Shadow and a Magic Trick

In *Needful Things*, the final confrontation between good and evil is not specifically Christian, but it contains many of the elements present

4. Was It a Miracle?   79

in Father Callahan's confrontations with vampires. An everyday, man-made object, imbued with belief in the history of the man who holds it and power from some greater presence, is wielded in the name of good, in order to protect not just that man but also his community. The power of good—the power of the White, in Dark Tower terms—is momentarily granted to one person who is in direct confrontation with its binary opposite. Instead of Callahan, there is Sheriff Alan Pangborn, and instead of a vampire he makes his stand against Leland Gaunt, another supernatural threat in human form.

Although it comes at the very end of the book, Pangborn's confrontation with Gaunt is the first time these two characters have met. Gaunt has been purposefully avoiding Castle Rock's sheriff and has employed at least one person to keep an eye on Alan and warn Gaunt of his approach. Gaunt is therefore able to turn the sign of his shop from "open" to "closed" whenever the sheriff attempts to welcome his town's newest shopkeeper, while setting up traps to ensnare Alan and his loved ones in order to keep them distracted. Gaunt just needs enough time to make his escape with his weirdly bulging bag which he insists does not in fact contain the souls of anyone who made special deals with him, although Alan doubts this declaration very much.

As the two of them confront each other in the rubble-strewn street during a storm, Alan first has to regain his composure and some semblance of logical thinking. A widower, he lost his wife and younger son to a car accident not long ago, and Gaunt's trick on the sheriff was to show him a video recording purporting to show what actually happened on that day. Alan has been blinded with rage at what he saw—his long-time nemesis driving his wife's car off the road—and if he were to remain in this state he would not have been able to succeed in running Gaunt out of town. The length of the confrontation, and the interference of various other players, allow Alan enough time to calm down and realize that there is a factual error in the video and that he has been misled.

Throughout the book, Alan has been shown to be very deft with his hands, making shadow puppets and engaging in magic tricks both as a form of distraction while he is lost in thought and as a means of attempting to set other people at ease. He has also constantly come across one of his dead son's possessions, a snake-in-a-can practical joke that had been left in the family car. Alan has gotten rid of neither the car nor the can, and as he stands to face Gaunt, he makes use of them both, as well as an appearing flower trick he still has secured under his watchband from earlier in the day. When he makes shapes in front of the car's headlights, the animals he forms seem to come to life, and when Alan opens the can, a real snake emerges instead of a spring covered in tissue paper. Both of these clearly unnerve Gaunt, although he still tries to stand his ground and recover his case full of souls.

The real power, felt by Alan and seen by all as the sort of blinding white light seen on the crosses used in *'Salem's Lot*, is the tissue paper flower trick. When Alan slides it out from its hiding place and opens the catch, the nearly-broken trick unfurls into a blinding bouquet of light that causes Gaunt to first recoil and then to flee. As he does so, he and his car shift in shape and form until he is a cloaked figure riding an old-fashioned buckboard and spurring on his pale horse. Gaunt is ancient and has pulled this trick on so many people before, and will go on to do so again, but his time in Castle Rock is now over. Granted, the book is advertised as "the last Castle Rock story," so the damage has been done. Alan has simply prevented Gaunt from leaving town with the souls still in his possession.

This final confrontation presents readers with imagery firmly positioned in the good and evil binary common to American thought and storytelling. Alan, holding the brilliant light of the bouquet, is good and therefore "white." When he takes the souls back from Gaunt, they are meant to be rescued. Gaunt, represented by darkness, is inhuman and driving his pale horse of death while turning into a confidence man with a cart full of nostrums and potions meant to cure whatever ails the people he encounters. The late twentieth-century version of Gaunt offered antiques and other items that captured people's imaginations and made them feel things they were missing in their "real" lives, continuing the tradition of offering strange ointments or tinctures in order to cure illness or malaise.

Alan is only able to draw upon this mysterious bright, white, good power after he has himself seen the light and realized the video Gaunt left for him could not have been the truth. By the time Alan saw the television and the VCR in the abandoned shop, he was beyond being concerned that neither was plugged in or wondering why someone might have been standing on the side of the road filming on that fateful day when Annie and Todd died. He has been wracked with guilt about not noticing his wife's increasing headaches and not forcing her to confront the brain tumor that caused the seizure and the crash, and guilt about allowing Todd to go into town with his mother and therefore ultimately to his death. Gaunt plays on people's emotions that way, triggering anger, fear, and shame so they cannot think clearly and see the illusion. Once Alan recognizes Gaunt's trick for what it is, he is able to use tricks of his own to defend himself and his town.

Both Gaunt and Alan rely on their understanding of human nature in order to enact their tricks. Gaunt plays with feelings of jealousy and greed, while Alan's shadow puppets and close-up magic are meant to enthrall his audiences and turn them into wondering children again. He is first seen using the hand puppets to help his distracted mind focus and then, at one of his deputy's insistence, to make the other man laugh and soothe him in the face of an undesirable task. Alan uses his tricks to connect with other people and set them at ease in difficult situations, while Gaunt's tricks cause discord and make sure that problems escalate.

Alan further uses his abilities to ward off evil and protect the souls of the people who did business with Gaunt. The tissue paper flower trick, entirely secular and at this point nearly broken and in need of replacement, is brought out perhaps in a fit of divine inspiration, since Alan's gun would surely be useless against a creature who packs souls into his travelling case and whose car transforms into a pale horse that can pull a buckboard across the sky. In his fight against evil, the sheriff reaches not for a weapon but for something that is meant to bring people together and inspire wonder.

The Temporal Nature of Spiritual Power

What, then, can be gathered from these instances not necessarily of Christianity, but of the power of the White and the Light? It is generally focused on an object instead of a person, and that object displays its power with blinding light. When the power fades, the object once again turns dark and ordinary. This glowing can happen in the form of holy water, such as when Ben Mears and Mark Petrie bathe their faces and hands before going to confront Barlow; in the form of a cross, whether it is plastic, hastily made, or a crucifix; or in the form of a bouquet of tissue paper flowers. The holy water and various cross shapes take their meaning and power from a wider system of belief, while the magic tricks Alan Pangborn uses are part of his own personal rituals for calm and focus. When he needs to meditate on a problem, Alan uses his hands for shadow puppets or magic tricks as he lets his mind wander. These are not rosary beads, but their function is largely the same: the search for calmness, inner peace, and a solution to life's problems.

John Coffey does not glow, but there is a visual of the evil he draws out of others when he exhales a dark cloud afterward. Although he can clearly remove the sickness and transfer it elsewhere, usually into the air where it presumably disperses, John does not seem to actually eliminate the evil. Like Jesus transferring demons into a herd of pigs, he is not himself an object of creation or uncreation, but simply of transfer. It is a source of power enough, but John does not glow with the power of the

White. Then again, Jesus himself was not said to do so when he engaged in his own healings. Jesus had the physical appearance of a man through whom God's power flowed, and John seems to be much the same.

What, then, is the outcome of wielding such miraculous power, even for a short time? Mark Petrie and Ben Mears survive the main events of *'Salem's Lot* and return a year later to start a fire in the town with plans to then track down and stake any surviving vampires. They miss at least one, however, leading to the events related in "One for the Road" where the two main characters carry Christian artifacts with them in order to protect themselves against the Lot's vampires. Dr. Jimmy Cody, who had the idea to make his own cross out of the equipment in his doctor's bag and have Ben bless it, survived his initial encounter with a vampire only to die of more mundane means: simple trickery and multiple knife blades. The cross only activates, and is only useful, against the supernatural. None of them expect it to warn them about purely physical dangers. Father Callahan wields his mother's crucifix only to have its power fail because he has put too much faith in the object itself, although he later redeems himself by maintaining his faith and his wits long enough to commit suicide rather than be turned into a vampire. Ben Mears presumably dies of natural causes decades after leaving the Lot, and Mark's ultimate fate is unknown.

While those John Coffey healed might find themselves afflicted with unusually long lives, the man himself went willingly to the electric chair. This was not a case of the power leaving him, the way the various crosses and religious implements lost their white glow, but of John himself deciding he no longer wanted it. He could not figure out a way to surrender the power without also giving up his life, and so he chose to remain on death row and go to his execution.

Alan Pangborn's wielding of his surprisingly magical sleight-of-hand tricks managed to win him the day, since Gaunt left Castle Rock but did not take the souls of the townspeople with him. Castle Rock, though, is apparently finished. Much of it has been ruined during the final storm, thanks to the explosions set by Gaunt's helpers, and many of the survivors are ready to leave. Some, like Deputy Norris Ridgewick and Polly Chalmers, may feel they have been able to redeem themselves after making their purchases and participating in Gaunt's pranks, but others might not recover spiritually. Gaunt is also expelled from town, yes, but has merely been relocated rather than being stopped on even a temporary basis. The book ends as it began, with a monologue about a small town's ills and speculation about a new store just about to open up.

What good, then, is the power of the White in these cases? It can certainly save the life of one of King's characters in a situation that would otherwise end poorly, perhaps even in a fate worse than death, although the light always fades. It is then up to the characters to keep going in spite of the shock and battle fatigue, and to proceed even when their objects of choice are not providing them with certain power and comfort. It is a comfort to know that a force for good exists somewhere out there in order to counter the evil, but in the end the characters have to decide for themselves whether or not the battle—at times, it seems, even against the weight of that power—is worth the continued struggle.

5

CARRIE WHITE IS BURNING FOR HER SINS

Christianity as a Weapon

Christianity is meant to be a religion built around worshiping God and treating one's neighbors as one would like to be treated. Frequently, violence done in the name of Christianity—such as the Crusades—is downplayed in the light of Jesus' message of peace. He died for our sins so that we may join him in heaven, and the path to heaven is paved with good deeds and forgiveness. Christians gather to hear the word of the Lord and share fellowship, to study the Bible, and for fundraising events for the less fortunate.

There is, however, a darker side. Some gather not to lift each other up, but to put outsiders down. Religious conflict has historically been, and continues to be, bloody. Messages of peace and acceptance can be ignored in favor of other verses concerning the proper behavior of a woman and the acceptable corrections to be offered by the men in her life. People concern themselves with the business of others and make excuses for their own behavior, encouraged by the fact that they have their church group supporting them.

Christianity in King can therefore be not only useless, but destructive in and of itself. Characters, especially those who use religion in their own way instead of simply attempting to hold to conservative or outdated beliefs, end up orchestrating doom for themselves and often for others. They want to listen to their God and follow His will, but frequently the instructions He passes on are incomplete or dangerous in their own right. Attempting to adhere strictly to religious tenets or to ostracize others for not having the same beliefs is, in Stephen King, a recipe for disaster.

Signs of Sin: *Carrie*

Carrie is now famously King's first published novel, rescued from the trash can by his wife, who encouraged him to finish the story even though he, personally, had never been a teenage girl. The book opens in the girls' locker room showers after high school phys ed and the title character, not one of the popular crowd, is brought out of her daydream by the arrival of her first period. Her classmates viciously mock her for it, and Carrie is sent home for the rest of the day. The girls who teased her are given a choice between detention or being unable to go to prom. One girl, Sue Snell, feels incredible guilt about the incident and not only commits to detention but asks her boyfriend, Tommy Ross, to take Carrie to prom. Another girl, Chris Hargensen, works with her boyfriend, Billy Nolan, to plan the book's famous prom coronation scene: Carrie, having been named prom queen alongside Tommy, is covered in pigs' blood from one of two pails Nolan rigged in the rafters. Once again the butt of a joke, Carrie lashes out in rage.

The book is told through the unfolding of the narrative between Carrie's first period and her first prom, interspersed with news reports, sections from books, and other "found" evidence that supports what becomes the Carrie White case. Part of this is an attempt to unfold what, exactly, Margaret White taught her daughter about womanhood, generally as a means to determine how much blame can be laid at Margaret's feet—and whether or not the immense telekinetic power Carrie displayed on prom night could have been foreseen.

The various "outside sources" agree that telekinetic power usually presents itself around the time of a woman's first menstrual cycle, coinciding with the book's opening scene. Although a later interview suggests an angry toddler Carrie was able to use her powers to cause rocks to rain down from the sky, there seem to be no documented cases of telekinetic ability between that time and the opening of the book. Carrie then begins working to strengthen this newfound ability, first struggling to lift a hairbrush and then advancing to lifting her whole bed, with herself in it, all of this without touching the objects. Her heart rate and bodily functions go into overdrive during these exercises, but she has been honing the muscles in her mind and unleashes that power on prom night.

Having been the butt of jokes all her life, from her handmade clothes to the way she knelt to pray before lunch on the first day of school, and having now been crowned prom queen wearing a beautiful velvet gown she sewed herself, Carrie finds the pigs' blood to be the last straw. It is indeed far more than a prank, since the bucket that collided with Tommy's head killed him instantly, but his is not the only death to occur that night. Only a handful of people live through prom as Carrie turns on the sprinklers while all of the band's electrical equipment is still plugged in. The doors are shut against the bulk of would-be escapees, but Carrie does not stop there. She walks through town, causing gas stations to catch on fire, power lines to go down, and roads to open up to the pipes underneath.

She also goes home in order to kill her mother.

Margaret White raised her daughter in a home of strict religious tenets. Sex, even between husband and wife, is an unpardonable sin, and speculation presented in the "outside sources" wonders whether Margaret was even aware she was pregnant prior to Carrie's birth, or if she understood what was happening during the home birth. Margaret delivered her daughter alone, and the neighbors did not call for anyone to check on her until the baby was already born. Confronted by her blood-covered daughter after the prom disaster, Margaret tells Carrie that she knew of her powers from a very young age. Just as she contemplated killing herself each time she and her husband "slipped" and had sex, Margaret also contemplated killing Carrie multiple times, including at her birth and during her early demonstrations of power.

The White living room is watched over by portraits of Christ, and Carrie has many times been locked in the closet for being unwilling to repent of her sins. Margaret does not agree with her daughter's going to prom with a boy or wearing a dress that highlights her figure and bares the tops of her breasts. Margaret has raised her daughter to be a nun and tells Carrie that even her period is a sign of sin. Margaret White sees signs of sin everywhere and has only lately balked at punishing Carrie for them, since the rise of Carrie's powers. On prom night, Carrie uses those powers to stop her mother's heart, although Margaret stabs her and wounds her terribly before Carrie can manage this. It is difficult to tell if the knife wound was itself mortal, since the strain of using telekinesis to such a grand extent has also taken a toll on Carrie's heart. Hurt and exhausted, she wanders off, and Sue Snell—who joined in on the teasing but tried to somehow atone with the offer of a prom date—finds her before she dies.

That is not quite the end of the book. There are multiple further sources quoted, from Carrie White's autopsy report, to segments from *The White Commission*, to a sign found painted on the empty lot where the Whites' house once stood—"CARRIE WHITE IS BURNING FOR HER SINS"[1]—to the final word on the subject: an extract of a letter from a young mother to her sister, marveling that her two-year-old daughter seems to be able to move her toys without touching them. Carrie White

5. CARRIE WHITE IS BURNING FOR HER SINS   87

herself might be dead and autopsied, but there are already more, and the men of the White Commission have no idea what to do with them.

Carrie White is both the title character and the supernatural threat in this story, although it is hard to characterize her as a monster. She is able to undergo a Cinderella-like transformation in time for prom, laying off the sweets long enough for her skin to clear up and simply changing from baggy, shape-disguising clothes to a gown that shows off her figure. Her hair has apparently always been lovely, and the simple change in attire, plus Tommy's arm, is enough to literally propel her from the back of the classroom to the prom queen's crown. Sue Snell is questioned time and time again over her decision to ask her boyfriend to take Carrie instead of Sue herself, and perhaps has not confronted her own guilt in the teasing of the book's opening scene, but her request, and Tommy's agreement, allow Carrie to make the transition that will be seen in so many girls-next-door in films of the 1980s. All it takes is the ability to look at her with new eyes.

Unfortunately, Carrie lives in a more realistic world: although the girls might admire her dress, and the boys respect Tommy, they have known her most of her life. The majority of them have been classmates since kindergarten, and her sudden transformation is only possible because the others have, up until then, believed they have known her so well. Carrie White has been the butt of jokes since day one, to the point where even her teachers grow frustrated, as though she purposefully wears the "wrong" clothes and does the "wrong" things. Chris Hargensen, goading her boyfriend to the pigs' blood prank, is at least honest in her consistency. Because of all of this, including Carrie's backstory of social and physical isolation with her mother, it is perhaps surprising that Carrie did not snap earlier. It seems entirely reasonable that a girl doused with pigs' blood after being crowned prom queen would indeed lash out. It is just that Carrie happens to have more than the usual means of doing so. Heidi Strengell argues that Carrie simply "overacts when taking a moral stand,"[2] but it is important to note that the stand itself is still moral. We can understand perpetual underdog Carrie wanting to teach her classmates a lesson.

Carrie is a bullied teenager given a power that goes beyond rational thinking, at a time in her life when most people are carried away by their emotions, anyway. The men on the White Commission can make their arguments after the fact, attempting to bully survivor Sue Snell simply because she is still around to interrogate, but readers generally acknowledge that the majority of us would probably misuse telekinetic powers, if we were ourselves so cursed. The real evil in *Carrie* lies with her mother, "whose fundamental fanaticism makes her more a monster than

Carrie ever is."[3] Carrie's murderous spree on prom night is only possible because of her supernatural powers, but it was caused by outside forces: namely, a lifetime of bullying and the final pigs' blood "prank."

The teasing from her classmates was certainly part of what set Carrie off, but a lot of that teasing was based on the ways she was different from the rest of them. Margaret White kept her daughter close, not even wanting young Carrie to associate with the sunbathing neighbor girl. The reaction Margaret had to seeing Carrie speaking to the teenager in her bikini was what caused Carrie to respond with the raining rocks. Margaret has taught her daughter to be ashamed of herself. Carrie is the physical sign of her parents' sin and weakness, and her own maturing body—her breasts and her menses—are curses from God, outward signs of her inward sin. The Whites do not attend church and participate in religious fellowship. Instead, Margaret held her own services three days a week, for two to three hours at a time. All of the religious instruction Carrie received came from the Lord through her Momma, and it was laced with sin and shame.

Because Carrie's mother spoke for God, she was both parent and prophet, assuming control on many levels. Carrie is out of Margaret's reach when she is at school—and is able to make the decision to stop praying before lunch, for example—but it is only after Carrie has begun to menstruate, and to come into her power, that she is able to stand up to her mother. She has been ostracized by her classmates for her clothes and her strange old-fashioned practices, but, since Tommy has invited her to prom and Carrie believes he means it earnestly, she defies her mother. She makes herself a dress out of a material and color she has never dared before, in a new shape, and is determined to take part in one of the rites of passage for the American teenager even though Margaret White—and therefore God and Jesus—wish to deny her. In order to please her mother, Carrie must remain pure, innocent, and sexless.

There are too many variables at play to suggest that, if Carrie's mother had not been so conservatively religious, the destruction on prom night would not have happened, but it did perform a large role. Margaret's isolation of her daughter and strict punishments at perceived wrongful behavior, as well as her insistence that Carrie's bodily changes were due to sin, all worked to make Carrie different from her classmates. Just as Margaret would not go to a church because all who attended were sinners, Carrie could not associate with her fellow students because of the terrible influence they might have on her. This isolation and pressure contributed to the teasing Carrie received, all of it building to the emotional flashpoint of prom night.

Although Christianity, or at least Margaret White's interpretation

5. CARRIE WHITE IS BURNING FOR HER SINS

thereof, contributed to the bloody prom night, Margaret's proposed solution has more to do with murder than Christianity. Carrie finds her at home, waiting, knife already in hand. Margaret suggests that the two of them should pray together, and when Carrie falls to her knees—to beg her mother for help rather than to pray, but the result is the same—Margaret stabs her first and then begins the Lord's Prayer. God cursed Margaret with desire for her husband, and then cursed her with a child, but apparently God did not have a solution to her problem. Margaret had to act on that herself, leaving her grievously wounded daughter to wander only for a short while longer before she died.

Margaret White's teachings, meant to save her daughter from this sinful world and the process of developing from an apparently innocent girl into a fully sexual woman, instead positioned her daughter with no safety net. While Margaret turned to Jesus for comfort, at least of a kind, Carrie did not feel the same support from religion or her mother, and this isolated position left her with no friends. Her single emergence into the "popular" crowd was orchestrated by one of the girls who bullied her at the book's opening, and her literally crowning achievement was only one step in the plan for yet another humiliation.

After her first period, Carrie confronts her mother with the fact that Margaret should have prepared her for this. The lack of practical information Margaret passed on to her daughter meant Carrie was not only once again the butt of a joke but scared because she had no idea what was happening. Her mother then took that moment of Carrie's fear and the other girls' taunts and turned it fully into Carrie's fault, because only sinful girls are cursed with menstruation. From the very beginning of the book—and, readers learn, from Carrie's conception—her mother has been set against her, viewing her as sin incarnate. Religion is therefore a club that Margaret attempts to use to purify her daughter, who is, after all, a living reminder of her own sexual sin.

Carrie has thus not only been isolated thanks to her mother's religious obsession, but has no support during the bullying that then occurs. She has been forced to rely on herself her entire life, so when this final, incredibly public, humiliation occurs during what should have been her Cinderella moment, Carrie snaps and responds with violence. Thanks to her telekinetic powers—not entirely a secret, since Margaret knows about them but, due to her fear, refuses to speak about them—that violence is extreme. Having been taught fear her whole life, Carrie finally finds herself capable of inflicting it, lashing out against the bullies, her mother, and even the entire town who stood by knowing Margaret White was doing strange things and never stepped in to intervene.

Although Carrie is the center of the supernatural, she is not also the center for evil in this novel. In fact, evil has no center—it is dispersed throughout all of those who have harmed Carrie by their action and inaction, or who have made the mistake of associating with those who have done so. Tommy Ross, one of the few true innocents, even unwittingly plays his part in her humiliation by offering the apology his girlfriend should have given and taking Carrie to prom, positioning her for this final humiliation. Out of the girls who tormented Carrie at the beginning of the book, only Tommy's girlfriend, Sue Snell, is left alive, but she faces her own consequences all the same. The one time Carrie struck back at her abusers, she eliminated them all, and paid the price with her own death.

As the sheltered and bullied girl who died as a result of her exertions that night—and also perhaps because of the knife her own mother stuck in her back—Carrie receives more empathy than most of King's supernatural beings. She begins the story, after all, as just a kid, and the only person to know she has been handed the mental equivalent of a loaded gun—her mother—does nothing to try to teach her the safe way to carry it. Isolated, with no one to turn to, Carrie is pushed into using that power rather than facing humiliation just one more time. If God helps those who help themselves, He did not serve Carietta White until the last night of her life.

A Hasty Exorcism: "The Mangler"

King's short story "The Mangler" (collected in *Night Shift* 1978) tells the story of a possessed piece of machinery at an industrial laundry. The machine itself, nicknamed the mangler, is in fact a speed ironer and folder. At the start of the story, police officer John Hunton is confronted with an accident in which the mangler has pulled one of the workers inside of it and attempted to press and fold her. When Hunton relates the story to his friend, college professor Mark Jackson, Jackson is intrigued and asks to hear how everything turns out.

The mangler's safety bar, expected to have been found defective, is deemed to have been in perfect working order, although the mystery of the machine continues. It starts up suddenly when two men are performing maintenance on it, pulling one of them in even as the other hits the emergency stop and cuts the power. He ends up having to cut the trapped man's arm off to keep him from meeting the same fate as the woman whose death started the story, and now Hunton and Jackson are properly intrigued. It is Jackson who first hits upon the idea that the mangler might actually be the site of a demon possession, and who spends

5. CARRIE WHITE IS BURNING FOR HER SINS 91

some time with the library computer attempting to figure out which demon, exactly, they might be facing.

The men quickly go down the list of things that the mangler might have already come into contact with: the blood of a virgin, which they then confirm, and likely horses' hooves, if that can be interpreted broadly enough to include Jell-O desserts from the workers' lunches. Jackson is relieved when they conclude that the machine cannot have come into contact with "the hand of glory," since its absence means that he believes they are facing a rather minor demon. Armed with the Eucharist and some holy water, although neither is a priest, the two men go to exorcise the mangler.

Once again, neither of the men has been properly trained in the act they have chosen to confront the threat. One of them reads from a book while the other sprinkles the holy water and the Eucharist when he is told to do so. Neither of them fully knows what he is doing, a fact emphasized in the narration's reveal that the mangler has, in fact, consumed a form of the hand of glory in pills taken by its initial victim. The men have underestimated their demon foe and thus the holy water and Eucharist anger it instead of banishing it. Jackson is killed almost immediately, and although Hunton flees, he is barely able to start warning anyone else before the mangler itself escapes on an unsuspecting world.

Jackson has narrowed the type of demon summoned into the mangler to be one where "[t]he mythos centers in South America with branches in the Caribbean. Related to voodoo."[4] King does not indicate either the location of this story or the race of the two men who attempt the exorcism, but it is likely that they are two white Americans who have no personal relationship with, or connection to, voodoo in any of its forms. Even though Jackson has enough imagination to consider that the mangler is possessed, and enough research skills to single out items of summoning and have a computer sort them in order to spit out a type of demon, he has no personal knowledge concerning demons. Jackson and Hunton find themselves faced with the inexplicable and are willing to expand their minds slightly to accommodate it into their worldviews.

This explanation is also a minimization: Jackson is delighted in this result, since it shows that their adversary, for all its mechanical danger, is not in fact difficult to expel. They simply need access to the laundry, provided by Hunton, and the Gideon Bible, Eucharist, and jelly jar of holy water procured by Jackson. Even the casualness of the jelly jar and the fact that the Bible was likely free and scrounged up on short notice—it is not, for example, a family Bible, or one carried by an actual priest—shows either a lack of understanding or a sense of bravado. If the demon had been summoned in part by the hand of glory, Jackson would have been afraid, but he enters the laundry that night confident that the book of Leviticus will do it. He even gives Hunton his instructions directly prior to entering the building, showing another layer of a lack of preparation. Hunton has done none of his own research and is simply along for the ride.

Jackson even believes that they have almost succeeded in driving out the demon before the mangler starts to move, change, and kills him. Unlike Hunton, Jackson stumbled in his attempt to flee, leaving him lying on the floor of the laundry, defenseless. It is unclear whether shouting some previously-memorized Bible verses might have helped him at that point, but Jackson does not even try, and it is unclear if he knows any by heart.

In this way, Jackson and Hunton are much like the Losers attempting the Ritual of Chüd at the end of *It*. Although the Losers found a ritual meant for "Himalayan holy-men" and Jackson and Hunton have found one based in Christianity, Jackson and Hunton seem no more Christian than the Losers are Himalayan. Even though they are much more likely to have access to a Christian priest than the Losers were to a Himalayan holy man, they do not try to find someone to help them. Jackson honestly believes that the two of them can handle the demon, since he thinks a reading from the Bible and judicious application of Eucharist and holy water will be enough.

It would have likely been less horrific but perhaps more interesting had the demon been the exact one Jackson had determined. *Would* the mindless following of these directions have been enough, or is a deeper belief in the meaning behind the actions necessary for a true exorcism? Was the mangler enraged because the two men had attempted to remove it at all, or especially because they had done such a sloppy job of it?

The two men treat both their identification of the demon and their choice of exorcism as though such things can be plucked from the wealth of tradition that formed them and simply plopped down as necessary where they seem to fit. It might be possible to take a screwdriver from a toolbox and force it to work even when it is not entirely the correct size, or to try a flathead on a Phillips head screw, but even then, just because a tool *does* work does not make it the best one for the job. An exorcism is not a screwdriver. It is far more complicated and would have to come with an instruction manual and years of training prior to certification. Jackson does not mention how he came by the Eucharist and holy water, but neither does he mention actually asking a priest for help. He might have been afraid the priest would laugh and not believe, but it is also likely that a priest would have refused to move ahead with the exorcism for valid reasons having to do with the practice itself.

Like many of King's characters, Jackson and Hunton cannot wait and simply must charge right in. As soon as they believe they have properly identified the problem and thus the solution, they gather their tools and arrive at the laundry so quickly that Hunton needs to be told his role in the proceedings directly before they begin. In spite of the fact that a woman has lost her life and a man has lost his arm, they believe the items in Jackson's paper bag will protect them. In short, they want Christianity to function as white magic, not understood by those who wield it but able to be pressed into service like a simple screwdriver.

Jackson chooses an exorcism and the talismans of Christianity without fully understanding his choice or his tools. The computer has simply spat out the fact that, given the items the men believe were used to summon the demon, an exorcism is necessary to get rid of it. This demon is so minor league that even amateurs such as themselves should have no problems. Not only is this untrue, but the mangler, which had previously been stuck in place at the laundry, pulls itself up from the concrete, changing shape, and starts to give chase. The attempt to eradicate the problem has in fact made it worse and set it loose so that entering the laundry itself is no longer necessary in order for people to put themselves in danger. Christianity, barely grasped and used as a talismanic weapon, is more dangerous than the original threat it was meant to quell.

A Little Child Shall Lead Them: "Children of the Corn"

"Children of the Corn," likewise collected in *Night Shift*, also deals with issues surrounding perverted Christianity. In "The Mangler," the Christian act was meant to be a solution enacted by the main characters against an outside threat. "Children of the Corn" sees the main characters as the threatening outsiders, although their attackers do believe themselves to be following the word of the Lord—and they have a deeper understanding of their God than Jackson and Hunton did.

Unhappily married couple Burt and Vicky are driving through Nebraska on a long road trip meant to help them rekindle their relationship when someone suddenly stumbles out of the corn and in front of their car. Although Vicky shrieks that her husband is now a murderer, it turns out that the child's throat was cut, and Burt insists that they need to take the boy's body to the police. This good deed gets them into trouble when they reach the small and apparently abandoned town of Gatlin. The only sign of recent activity is the title listed on the church's sermon board with the date of the previous Sunday, although the letters actually naming the church have been taken down and tossed into a pile. The Grace Baptist Church is still used for services, although not of the Baptist variety any longer.

Inside the church, reading the records of deaths and births, Burt discovers a strange pattern with a large gap in 1964. Anyone who had reached adulthood prior to 1964 was killed, and any of the children who lived through 1964, along with any born since then, have death dates listed exactly on their nineteenth birthdays. Something strange is happening in the isolated town of Gatlin, involving a strange confluence of religion and the corn. Even then Burt finds it difficult to understand how this could keep happening and continue to go unnoticed "unless the God in question approved."[5]

Aside from asking his followers to commit suicide at nineteen, He Who Walks Behind the Rows also has strict rules for defectors or outsiders. Burt's wife is taken away when a group of children find her alone in the car and, after a long time spent running through the corn himself, Burt finds Vicky again. Her body has been left as an apparent offering alongside those of a man who was likely the minister of Grace Baptist while it was still Grace Baptist, and a body in police uniform. Burt himself is sacrificed, and young Isaac, the Seer, passes on the message that the Lord is not pleased with the children. The Age of Favor has been lowered to eighteen, and the two young men who have already passed that birthday immediately turn and walk into the corn.

The religion and therefore the lifestyle that the children of Gatlin follow has clear roots in Christianity. Even though the church is no longer Baptist, it is still used. Burt sees that the keys have been removed from the organ, accompanied by a written admonition that no music should be made except with the mouth. This, combined with the Biblical names Burt reads in the birth and death records, makes it seem as though the children have adopted a more old-fashioned form of Christianity that might make them more akin to Quakers than twentieth-century churchgoers, but Burt also finds a Bible still at the pulpit. Certain sections have been cut or torn out, but the New Testament has not been removed completely, and a portrait of Jesus graces the wall behind the pulpit.

This Jesus, though, seems to be more of a mix of man and corn than a mix of man and God. So much of Gatlin's new religion, from its Christ to its artifacts to its admonitions, has to do with the corn. When the children reach the Age of Favor, they walk into the corn. *Something* is alive in the corn, but that power is obeyed instead of questioned. As soon as the children were convinced to rise up and kill any adults over the Age of Favor, they became slaves to whatever their Lord instructs them through their Seer. One of these edicts ensures that none of the children will leave, and no strangers who discover them will live to tell the tale.

This works, both within the world of the story and as the story within the genre of horror, because Gatlin itself is so isolated. There is no electricity and there are no telephone lines, so any travelers would be unable to call for help, and any curious relatives have been taken care of long before Burt and Vicky stumble into town. The mysterious power that lurks in the corn has masqueraded itself as He Who Walks Behind the Rows, perverting the religion already present within the town in order to ensure the children perpetuate the cycle of life and death in service to it.

It takes Burt longer than Vicky to realize that something is drastically wrong with Gatlin, but it is not the strange religious aspect that cues her in. Vicky laughs at both what they hear on the radio and what she reads on the roadside signs, but she believes that these are simply proof of their presence in the Bible belt. Religious fervor is nothing out of the ordinary in Nebraska, and neither is corn. They have simply had the bad luck to stumble into the one town where the two have combined due to some unseen outside force. God is cruel, yes, but the Children of the Corn do not hesitate to obey.

A House Divided: *Needful Things*

Religion does not need to be complicated—or perverted—by corn in order to cause trouble. In *Needful Things*, Castle Rock Sheriff Alan Pangborn is faced with a number of issues in his usually sleepy town. The central problem resides in the Rock's newest business and its owner, Leland Gaunt, but Gaunt is only able to wreak such havoc because of relationships already present when he enters the town. "He may have an unfair advantage because of his supernatural powers,"[6] but Gaunt still needs to use the everyday citizens of the town in order to make his plan work.

Gaunt, who claims to have come to Maine from Akron, Ohio, sets up what seems to be a sort of curio shop in which the most intriguing items do not come with price tags. Castle Rock's residents of all ages come to marvel at items both sacred—a petrified sliver of wood that gives anyone who touches it the illusion of being on Noah's ark—and mundane: the perfect comic books to complete a young boy's collection, or a rare baseball card that has long been sought. It seems that Gaunt has managed to stock his fabulous store with just the sorts of things his customers have dreamed of buying—or realize at first sight that they must possess immediately. When someone wishes to make such a special purchase, they must speak to Gaunt in private, paying partly with money and partly with a promise.

The promises amount to pranks, and Gaunt's first customer, Brian Rusk, quickly realizes that he should have been more specific in his dealings with this stranger when he is forced to play not one, but two. Gaunt's cunning and supernatural understanding of the Rock's citizens means that he knows who is already in conflict with whom. Wilma Jerzyck and Nettie Cobb, for example, are two such feuding parties, and Gaunt sends young Brian Rusk to play his pranks on Wilma while another goes after Nettie. None of Gaunt's customers sent on such errands fully understand what they are doing. They simply know that, should they refuse, they will lose their apparently priceless treasures.

Many of the tensions Gaunt seeks to escalate are between individuals, but one introduced early on in the novel is that between the Rock's two main churches. The Baptists and the Catholics have been heating up over the proposed Casino Nite, which the Baptists decry as being sinful gambling, while the Catholics argue that it will simply be an evening of fun with all proceeds going to charity. The Reverend Rose even goes to meet with Pangborn in an attempt to have Casino Nite cancelled from a legal perspective, only to have the sheriff warn him about how far his own parishioners might go in their protests. Clearly each church has strong feelings about the event, and it allows Gaunt to draw two large groups of people into conflict.

Again using customers who themselves have no connection to either group, Gaunt first applies pressure through the delivery of anonymous messages threatening group leaders. Each church then agrees to meet en masse on the same night, the Catholics to continue to plan for their fundraiser and to discuss security measures that now seem essential, and the Baptists to figure out their own next move to prevent Casino Nite from happening. Others doing Gaunt's bidding have planted timed stink bombs that go off during those meetings, and some even have orders to shout something before making sure all the building's doors are locked.

Like many of Gaunt's so-called pranks, these stench machines stretch the meaning of the word. The smoke is vile enough to cause spontaneous, and in some cases continuous, vomiting. Because the main doors to the buildings have been blocked, people need to escape through windows or force themselves closer to the machines in order to get to the open doors. At least one person is killed in the initial frantic reaction, breaking her neck—although she herself "had not bought a single thing from Mr. Gaunt or participated in any of his little games."[7] There was no personal grudge against her, but she, like the others around her, was swept up: first by the holy grudge match over Casino Nite, and then by the call to battle issued with the stink bombs.

Gaunt's method would not function without the underlying tensions already present in the town. He had not yet set up shop when Casino Nite was announced, and Pangborn warns the Reverend Rose against escalation before Needful Things opens to the public. The local paper had to expand its letters-to-the-editor section in order to properly accommodate all of them sent about Casino Nite, and the Baptists had even begun wearing anti-gambling badges. Through the anonymous angry personal letters, Gaunt initiated these group meetings, and the stench bombs were timed to make sure that both groups would emerge at the same time, stinking, coughing, covered in vomit, and ready to throttle the other side.

The two groups begin to march toward each other, loudly singing hymns, and start to brawl in the middle of a storm. When a state trooper attempts to stop them, he is shot by someone who bought one of Gaunt's special guns. Even if the trauma itself was not enough to kill him, the poison on the bullets would be. The brawl continues as members are knocked out—King does not indicate if any of those who have bowed out of the fight are in fact dead—and simply redoubles when the town is shaken as dynamite starts to go off. Only the last and most violent explosion, the one that erases Castle Rock's Municipal Building, is enough to startle those still standing out of their bloodlust. When the town is all but destroyed, Father Brigham helps the Reverend Rose to his feet. The fight that began with two healthy congregations and well over a hundred people brawling in the street is now over.

This is also the last time either the Catholics or the Baptists appear in the novel. All of the dynamite has exploded, the storm is abating, and the only thing left is for Sheriff Alan Pangborn to face off against Leland Gaunt. Pangborn relieves Gaunt of his travelling case—and, presumably, the souls of those who made special purchases at Needful Things—but the shop's proprietor makes his escape. He has been foiled, but not killed, and the book ends as it began: with a folksy monologue informing the reader of hurts and ills in the town, finishing by mentioning the name of a new store about to open. He may have been chased out of Castle Rock, but Leland Gaunt has found a new town.

Religion here functions to unite these large groups of people within the town and to set them against each other. The lines of Us and Them have already been established prior to Gaunt's arrival and, indeed, had been in place since Luther left Catholicism. Gaunt likely thrives on small towns with multiple churches, especially when one group has been taught that the other is hell-bound. Along with these feelings of animosity and superiority-cum-herd mentality and the congregation's tendency to respond predictably when their respected leader is threatened. Although he has no use for religion, Gaunt can rely on its organization to help him rope large groups of people together and set them on each other.

As with Carrie and the pigs' blood on prom night, it is difficult to say what would have happened if there had been no outside influence. If Gaunt had never come to Castle Rock, how far would the religious battle over Casino Nite have gone? Clearly one side felt they would be blessed by the Lord for the charity performed, while the other believed the Lord would have condemned it as sinful gambling. The posters, badges, and letters to the editor would likely still have all been made. The angry and inciteful letters were not actually sent by members of the other religion, but perhaps only because Gaunt was rushing the natural pace. Without the concurrent meetings and the carefully-timed stench machines, the Baptists and Catholics would not have marched toward each other for a brawl at that exact moment, but the seeds of violence had already been planted.

In the other examples where Gaunt used his special customers to escalate conflict, he needed one customer per person involved. Brian Rusk had to be set on Wilma Jerzyck, for example, but someone else had to go after Nettie Cobb—who herself had been set to play a prank on yet another citizen of Castle Rock. For many of these cases, Gaunt needed to use two customers in order to anger each member of the feud, and he also was careful to make sure that the customer had no relationship with the person in question. They were then willing to plant a letter, or rip up flowers, or throw rocks through windows, or kill someone's dog. At times this was because they were not aware of the contents of the message but others—either Gaunt's "hardened" customers or those he could threaten more efficiently, like the children—broke windows and stabbed dogs simply because the alternative was losing their treasure.

By tapping into the religious tension that was already dividing Castle Rock, Gaunt was able to manipulate two large groups of people into feeding his need for violence and death without having to attend to each member of the congregation personally. Through threatening religious leaders and then planting his stench bombs at meetings of each groups' leaders, he was able to stir up the emotions of the most devoted followers and bring them to a head. Through his planning and careful timing, Gaunt was able to cause this to happen at the same time as so much further chaos. He may have even been able to call in the storm just for that night.

Religion is a unifying force, but it does not offer solace or protection to the citizens of Castle Rock. Even those who personally had nothing to do with Gaunt or his store were pulled into the fray, and at least one was killed without ever having spoken to Gaunt. The cohesive groupthink inherent in these congregations allowed Gaunt to reach further and harm even more people, blinding them to what they were doing by making them think their actions had a deeper spiritual meaning. Since they were already arguing over the souls of the people who dared to plan Casino Nite, the brawl in the street was an easy continuation. The question of whether Casino Nite was acceptable or sinful was easily escalated by Gaunt and his helpers, none of whom were members of either church themselves, and thus the congregations were manipulated until their respective leaders were brawling in the middle of the mobs.

These are the only groups in town that King set against each other. Castle Rock is not large enough to have rival high schools, for example, around which similar animosity could be formed, and the idea of Protestants against Catholics is an established real-world conflict that can be easily transplanted into one of his fictional towns. Religion can unite people, yes, but it can also divide, and it is this division that King finds more useful for his novels. After all, an unholy demon like Gaunt could hardly pass up the chance to test the way Christ's followers would cling to the Golden Rule of treating others the way they want to be treated.

JESUS OF FIRE COMING: *Under the Dome*

Under the Dome (2009) presents readers with a small-town, multiple-church situation similar to *Needful Things*, except Chester's Mill is not troubled by a new shopkeeper and his obsession with souls. Rather, The Mill has been sealed in a clear Dome that perfectly conforms to the town line, extending high enough into the air to interfere with airplane flight paths and deep enough into the ground that tunneling in is impossible. The Dome appeared in an instant, cutting anything that happened to be straddling the town line at the time and causing numerous wrecks and crashes as people drove various vehicles into its transparent, but unyielding, side. Further chaos is caused when the chief of police discovers that the Dome has a disastrous effect on electronics, as well, since his pacemaker explodes in his chest as he approaches it. Citizens of Chester's Mill are stuck in town with no one to depend on but each other.

Religion is a major theme of *Under the Dome*, and the vast array of characters leads to numerous different approaches to religion. Certain citizens, such as Lester Coggins, minister at Christ the Holy Redeemer Church, seem to actually hear God's voice speaking to them in prophecy. Others, such as Phil Bushey, now known as "Chef," may or may not possess the same direct pipeline to the Almighty. If Coggins is anything to go by, being able to listen to the Lord is not actually a saving grace.

Coggins, along with Chef and the town's Second Selectman Jim Rennie, among others, has been participating in what might be the largest meth lab in New England. Income from this illegal business has funded the new church building, the massively powerful radio station-cum-meth lab, local businesses of the men who have been participating, and other religious endeavors for the less fortunate. Thanks to Rennie, at the time the Dome came down there had not been enough evidence for police to have moved on any of them involved in the manufacture of so much meth, but now all of those involved are stuck inside town with the meth lab and a large shipment now just sitting there. After a long session of prayer and self-flagellation, Coggins hears the voice of God telling him to keep his mouth shut until God sends him a sign.

Unfortunately for Coggins, that sign comes quickly. He sets up a time to meet with Rennie and tells him that the Dome is punishment for their sins, and they must come clean immediately. Rennie, who has absolutely no intention of doing so, murders Coggins, whose God did not warn him of any such thing. The Lord spoke to Coggins enough to tell him to hold his tongue until a sign came, and Coggins obeyed. By being told to eventually speak, Coggins was sent to his own death by his God. Unless, of course, God thought Coggins would be smart enough to realize that he should not speak to Rennie alone or that he should be able to keep himself safe. Perhaps God even meant Coggins to bypass Rennie and simply confess his—and therefore their—sin to the town immediately, and it was Coggins' misinterpretation that got him killed.

God continues to be cruel to the people of The Mill through the character of the Chef, who has been enjoying his own product for months now and has sunk deeper into his own religious mania. Living alone next to the radio station that pumps out religious music at all hours of the day, he believes that the Dome is but one of the signs of the Apocalypse. A commercial airliner that strikes the Dome because someone forgot to modify its flight path is, to Chef, Star Wormwood. Chef will stand and protect the radio station, and therefore his meth, because God has warned him that "bitter men" are coming. Part of this defense happens to be a brick of plastic explosives, placed near the lab where the chemicals and much of the town's propane are stored. When the police come, meaning to take some of the propane for the town, Chef and his brother-in-arms—and in Christ—deploy the explosive, as God told Chef he should.

The fact that the explosion takes place near the chemical ingredients for meth production and the propane storage is bad enough, but the Dome is largely impermeable. Even air has trouble passing through it, and after the trigger is pushed, the resulting fire quickly eats up much of the good air within the Dome. The fire itself kills most of the town members in its single rush across the available ground. Worse, most of these people are lined up at the Dome for Visitor's Day, trapped against the unseen barrier and about to die in front of their loved ones and on camera for a worldwide viewing audience. Those who do not die as a result of the flames are left trying to breathe air devoid of oxygen but filled with chemicals and char.

The numbers are stark and dispensed with in two quick paragraphs: The Mill began with a population of around two thousand people. Immediately following the fire, 397 are left. By nightfall, there are 106 survivors. The next morning, Chester's Mill has been reduced to only thirty-two[8]—although, before the Dome finally lifts, that number will fall further.

Phil "Chef" Bushey, warned by God that both the bitter men and the Apocalypse are approaching, rigged up his bomb and the garage door opener detonation switch. Because God spoke to him, Chef was able to ensure that he would not be the only one to die that day. Thanks to this advance notice, he was able to take most of the town with him.

While Coggins might have been expected to plan ahead a bit better and recognize the danger of confronting Rennie privately, Chef spent the last few months of his life either making meth or smoking it and was constantly high. Any ability he had once had to plan ahead was vastly curtailed by his drug use. In each case, God gave a sort of warning, but only an initial step, providing a small piece of prophecy. Coggins should not speak until he saw something come to pass—which Coggins took to mean that he *should* then speak after seeing it. Chef was informed that people would come, although he made the next interpretation himself: that he should not let them take anything away with them. The previous time men only took propane for the town, but Chef is determined not to let that happen again, even if they leave his supply alone. Chef does not, however, tell his companion that God has specifically told him to do anything about it. The Lord has simply sent Chef the vision and given him time to prepare their response.

Both of these visions are indeed presumably from God, since they each actually come to pass. Coggins witnesses the blindness that was foretold, and men—and one woman—do come to the radio station where Chef is sheltering. Granted, since some have already come to take propane and Chef prevented a second such expedition, it is possible that Chef did not need God to tell him that more would turn up, armed this time, to take what they needed by force. The Lord certainly does not tell Chef about every impending visitor to the radio station, since he was on guard and wary when two policewomen came to make sure it was evacuated, without God's voice telling him that they were harmless and had no intention of touching his drugs. But both Coggins and Chef tell others that God has spoken to them, and each plots a course of action based on what he has been told.

While God's revelations might be true, He seems to care little about whether those who listen then act intelligently afterward. Coggins winds up getting himself killed, which might be construed as no great loss—it is unclear what the Lord thinks about Coggins' participation in the meth lab—but Chef's actions amount to mass murder. He is about to die himself when he presses the button that dooms the vast majority of the town to his own fate, innocents alongside the guilty, while others slowly strangle on the atmosphere left behind. Chef sees himself as a soldier of the Lord, and apparently this is the old testament God who would destroy an entire town if He did not find enough pure souls within it.

It is possible that, even without this one specific vision, Chef would still have caused the same explosion, chemical reaction, and conflagration. He believed that making and smoking meth was indeed the Lord's work, and the fact of the Dome troubled him little. At one point Chef worries that he, personally, will run out of the drug since much of what is stored in the radio station is meant to be shipped out, showing his lack of understanding about the Dome and his current situation. Chef might think that his explosion will end his life and those of the bitter men, and that will be the end of it, but the Lord does not correct any of these misconceptions. It seems God has turned His back on The Mill and the only ones inside its borders who can hear His voice.

Organized Religion, Disorganized Chaos

These examples of Christianity increasing the issues within the story are, perhaps, extreme, but frequent within works by Stephen King. He repeatedly plays with the uniting and excluding factors of Christianity, showing how a young girl like Carrie White can be isolated from her peers through her mother's religious teachings, or how a group of children could be brought together by a corn/Jesus hybrid to the point where they willingly sacrifice their lives to the corn at the stated time.

Belief, especially group belief in superiority or protection, is dangerous to King's characters.

It is not the formation of a group, per se, that is the threat. Many of King's main characters do not act alone, forming ka-tets in which the group is stronger than any individual member. Frequently a group of people is needed to confront the supernatural if there is any hope of success. Many of these groups need slow convincing that the problem they are confronting is indeed supernatural—or alien—and the process of coming into belief strengthens their ties. These groups are segregated from outsiders and unbelievers, but instead of giving them strength in feelings of superiority, this isolation tends to be yet another threat in their fight to eliminate the supernatural danger. King's groups are working for the greater good, whether that serves just their town or presumably all of existence.

In contrast, King's most emphatic Christian believers find smugness in their sense of belonging. The larger group provides support that is often unquestioned by all involved and serves to support a simple message, such as whether or not Casino Nite is sinful. Once the group decision has been made, justification can be found, or members can charge mindlessly forward knowing that others share their belief. Instead of illuminating, such dogmatic religious belief blinds all members while binding them together under false premises.

The examples given in this essay are all those where a stated religious belief led to an increase in the threat, such as the Mangler prying itself free from the laundry to prey on the world, or physical violence and large-scale deaths. These are all cases in which some form of Christianity was actively employed as a guidance for the characters, who truly believed they were doing the right thing and, frequently, that they were hearing the voice of God. United in their belief and faith, they were indeed able to act in a way that had a large influence on the plot. The next essay addresses another kind of Christian character in King: those who do not in fact believe, but who speak of God and Jesus all the same.

6

ForJesussakeamen

The Danger of Performative Belief

Christian beliefs permeate King's books, and God Himself has even been given a voice in many of them, if not a face. The Lord is not a character, per se, although various forms of Jesus do appear, but neither is He nonexistent. Characters in previous essays have heard Him speak to them, although their reactions to what they hear bring various results, from success to increased destruction. The characters in this essay, however, outwardly proclaim themselves to be religious, although none of them in fact believe.

It is not the lie in itself—the outward representation of Christianity and inward atheism—that determines whether the characters end up being "good" or "bad." Two of them are even ministers who put on vestments and preach to various congregations, invoking Jesus' name and the Bible, but their fates are not shared. Pretending to be a minister long after one's faith has lapsed is not enough to merit divine or narrative retribution in and of itself. It is perfectly fine, in fact, for a King character to have no religious affiliation whatsoever and still to triumph when confronted with a supernatural evil, and also acceptable in many cases for his characters to lie. Most often they do this in order to reassure well-meaning but clueless loved ones before they go off to confront the evil that so many neither see nor believe in.

In the previous essay, characters who proclaimed themselves to be Christian could in fact have perverted the religion, leading to murder and destruction. The strict and apparently faithful adherence to a professed religion is not in itself enough to make a character "good," and the lack of belief is not enough to make a character "bad." It is almost as if survival depends not so much on true or professed belief as it does the quality of a character's heart and purity of intention, and even lying ministers can exist on a continuum in this matter.

Religious Battles Under the Dome

As previously mentioned, *Under the Dome* has a large focus on religious belief in the face of the problem currently confronting Chester's Mill: the invisible Dome that has cut the town off from the outside world has also forced all residents to depend on each other for the unknown duration. Since Police Chief Perkins is one of the first casualties of the Dome, leadership falls largely on The Mill's Second Selectman, Big Jim Rennie. As all astute townspeople know, Rennie might be listed as Second behind Andy Sanders, but Sanders is just the puppet on Rennie's knee.

One of the very first things revealed about Big Jim is that he gave his heart to Jesus when he was sixteen and thus does not use foul language. Thus he describes the Dome situation as a "clustermug"[1] and frequently responds to ornery constituents by talking around swear words instead of using them directly. Big Jim is also known to pray in public, loudly, and to drone on longer than many of his listeners would like. He prays before meals, or with others who have lost loved ones, Andy Sanders among them. His stock comfort is that the dead are eating roast beef and mashed potatoes with Jesus, and he staunchly stands by the fact that the meth lab that has gotten him rich has also served to help the Holy Redeemer Church and radio station WCIK, call sign Christ is King, which itself has saved who knows how many souls. When trying to talk hesitant people into risky situations, Big Jim demands to know if they are Saved and then dismisses all concerns, because at least if they die, they have that roast beef to look forward to.

In spite of being a self-professed Christian and a public supporter of Lester Coggins' Holy Redeemer Church, there is little about Rennie that could be considered Christlike. He is a used car salesman and embodies many of the worst stereotypical traits thereof, double-crossing those he does not like and going out of his way to help others so that they are in his debt. He carries this methodology into his life as a public servant, too, threatening anyone who tries to stand against him—even The Mill's Third Selectman. Rennie knows what he wants, and he is never seen listening for the still small voice of God. For one, Rennie is much better at speaking than listening. For another, even if he believes in God, he could not conceive of a Lord who would know better than he does. This is exemplified when, instead of listening to Coggins' explanation of his own conversation with the Lord and the order to confess their sins, Rennie murders his own minister.

It is not the Second Selectman's first murder. Although no one else, including his only son, could prove it, he put a pillow over his wife's face and sped up her death from cancer, telling himself he was easing her into the everlasting arms. Although Junior only suspects that his father killed his mother, he knows for certain that Big Jim failed at being true to his marriage and engaged in adultery with at least one of his secretaries.

Big Jim even uses prayer as a weapon near the end of his life when, after the fire has swept through town, he finds himself in Chester Mill's bomb shelter with his new second-in-command, Carter Thibodeau. The air outside is unbreathable, and although the shelter has an air purifier, its supply of propane is limited. Big Jim is overweight and has heart troubles and thus cannot risk letting the air quality deteriorate too far. When Carter calculates about how long he and his boss could survive down there in the dark, as opposed to how long he might be able to stretch the propane on his own, he decides to kill Big Jim. Carter's fatal mistake is forgetting how sly his boss can be.

Big Jim requests time to pray and fakes a sob, asking Carter to turn off the flashlight so he might not be seen crying. When Carter acquiesces, Rennie moves quickly and ends up gutting the boy before shooting him. He then sits in the shelter in the dark with a corpse—only one of those he has created since the Dome came down—near his feet and no one to help him. Rennie later breaks his flashlight and fails to change out the propane tank, his prayers finally coming out as the demands they had always been: "make it stop, none of it was my fault, get me out of here, I did the best I could, put everything back the way it was, I was let down by incompetents, heal my heart."[2] Even alone, Rennie continues to justify his actions to himself and apparently to his God, not bargaining for more time but demanding it. Rather than listen for a response, however, Rennie first flies into a rage and then panics, fleeing out of the shelter and dying when he takes a breath of the poisoned air and his heart finally quits on him.

Rennie's prayers are a far cry from those offered up by Mother Abigail or David Carver. The only ones he is shown to give when he is alone are those that come in the form of demands. He more often prays out loud, either trapping his audience until the end of a long monologue or quickly brushing over a mumbled, run-together jumble of words for show. Rennie does not sit in silence or listen for the still small voice to guide him. In fact, Rennie would rather tell God what to do, the same as he orders around everyone in Chester's Mill. When the Dome descended, Rennie decided to bypass becoming leader of the people and went straight for becoming their God, offering benefits to those who obey him and punishment to those who try to suggest anything different.

God and religion, to Rennie, are justifications for him to continue being himself. The meth lab has made him incredibly rich, but he pacifies his fellow investors by reassuring them the money is going to God's work both in The Mill and elsewhere. He refuses to change his diet or lifestyle in order to lose weight and help his heart because surely God would not let him die. Prayer traps others in silence until he finishes saying his piece, out of respect for his religion even if they do not themselves believe, and gives Rennie yet another platform from which to espouse his ideas. Even murder is reframed as sending someone directly into the everlasting arms and the eternal feast. What Rennie wants, he can justify through God and the Bible, and use them both as a club against anyone who attempts to stand against him.

In this way Rennie differs from his own pastor, Lester Coggins, who does indeed listen for the voice of God—even if his reaction to the message ends up with Rennie murdering him—and from The Mill's other pastor, Piper Libby. Piper leads the First Congregational Church, but when she prays, she no longer believes anyone is listening. When readers first encounter her kneeling in her empty church after the Dome has descended, she addresses "The Great Not-There." Piper does not need to listen because she expects no response.

Piper's congregation, though, has no idea that their pastor no longer believes in the positive messages she preaches. On the first Sunday under the Dome, Piper preaches not Coggins' message about how sin will always be found out, but how faith and helping their neighbors will get The Mill through this new hardship. She offers reassurance, not Biblical punishment, and even seems to find comfort of her own in the act of prayer despite her lack of belief. When Piper's temper gets the better of her and the end result is the death of her dog, she once again prays to the Great Not-There, alone in her church, and although no specific Voice of God answers, other townspeople enter the building and give her a new task and a sense of purpose. Piper thus becomes part of the newly-formed resistance against Rennie immediately following her prayer, if not clearly as a direct result of it.

Piper does not use God as a justification of her flaws, and she even sees at least one aspect of her character as actually *being* a flaw, unlike Rennie. She is aware of her temper and the fact that God put it in her so that she had to learn to control it. The greatest lesson her father ever taught her had to do with that temper and a simple, open plea for Piper to get the upper hand. After learning that some of the newly-deputized police officers committed a vicious rape that landed a woman in the hospital, Piper went to confront them with her dog at her side. She was injured and her dog was shot and, afterward, kneeling on a pew cushion to aid her bruised knees, Piper admits that she has to own at least a part of her dog's death.

Like Lester Coggins, Piper knows the feeling of guilt. Although she does not flagellate herself as Coggins did, she scourges herself mentally and emotionally, admitting that her own actions led to a less than favorable outcome. Piper and Coggins both accept their own role in a situation that turned ugly, Piper quicker than Coggins and with a much smaller footprint, but in this way they are both different from Rennie. Rennie invokes God to excuse his errors, sins, and illegal acts, while Piper prays to no one and shoulders her burden.

Although her dog does not survive to the end of the book, Piper herself does. Coggins dies when he hears the voice of God and decides on a choice of action that makes him another of Rennie's murder victims, and Rennie dies still giving God orders in the guise of a prayer, but Piper, who still kneels in her church to pray even as she grows convinced that no one is listening, serves the people of the town and manages to make it out alive. This is perhaps where King's point lies.

Coggins, like Rennie, performatively served God. He preached like a revivalist, calling others to be saved and looking down on any who did not follow him—him, not Jesus—while throwing himself in with the meth lab for the money it brought. The church was improved and the radio station built, with donations going to various religious services around the world, and Coggins felt like he was doing good work. He was doing God's will, and, unlike Rennie, he is shown to actually listen for God's voice, and then to hear it. The narrator does not in fact confirm that it was indeed *God's* voice Coggins heard, but it did seem to accurately predict at least a part of the future. Coggins put his faith in that voice, although he did hesitate, and instead of going to confess his sin to the town, he went to Rennie first. Coggins was attempting to be kind and offer his partner in crime the chance to come clean himself, but instead Rennie murdered Coggins on the spot in order to continue to keep their sins a secret.

Rennie lived his life, according to himself, for the good of the town, which was as much justification for his acts as the Bible and his God. When anyone tried to confront him, he either brought out the Bible or The Mill as his final response. Everything Rennie did was for the good of others, although it did also happen to have the side effect of lining his pockets or producing addictive drugs. Even when Coggins tried to tell Rennie that the Lord was not pleased, Rennie brought out the idea of the town and overrode what Coggins had to tell him. He did not, however, serve either the Lord or his town.

Piper is the only one shown to both listen, even though she no longer believes she will hear any sort of reply, and to actually work for the good of Chester's Mill. Even though her faith in the Lord, as well as in her religion, is failing, her good works do not. She makes herself available, and reaches out, to members of her congregation who are hurting even if the book has not necessarily presented those people as being easy sites of empathy. She does not distinguish between her own parishioners and those who attend a different church, or who do not attend at all. Piper sees the needs of others and does what she can to fill them without rationalizing that each deed will secure her a better space in heaven. With no God, there is also likely no afterlife, and nothing to look forward to as a reward. Piper acts without justification or expectation, and she owns her mistakes, setting her apart from the other main religious men of *Under the Dome*. Just as professed religion alone cannot make Rennie or Coggins good people, Piper does not need her belief in God in order to do the right thing.

That being said, Piper is not blameless as far as misleading the people of Chester's Mill religiously. Although she no longer believes in God, she continues to act as the minister of her church and shepherd her congregation through the various stations of life—lately concentrating on funeral and death rituals. She does eventually admit her lack of belief, but this only comes near the end of the book, when she is speaking to a very small handful of survivors. When confronted with the alien presence that is responsible for the Dome, Piper confesses that she was wrong in saying there was a Great Not-There, because something happened to be There, after all. It just so happens that the presence is nothing like the God of her past, and there seems to be no reward for good deeds or the promise of a life after this one. Notably, even though Piper feels shame surrounding her anger and the death of her dog, she is not part of the trio that goes to face the alien children in the last-ditch attempt for rescue. Her shame remains private, and her acts of atonement are directed toward the people around her, not toward the mysterious alien box powering the Dome.

Who Betrayed Jesus, Freddy? The Religion of Abraham Kurtz

Big Jim Rennie has a counterpart in Abraham Kurtz, and not just because Kurtz finds himself the leader in Maine's battle against extraterrestrials in *Dreamcatcher*. Kurtz does not pray in front of his "boys," but he does ask if they have read their Bible. During a particularly tense moment when Kurtz's second-in-command has betrayed them and fled, Kurtz even goes into what his new second, Freddy, recognizes as a mantra. The call-and-response asks Freddy if he loves Jesus; if he swears to be telling the truth; how *much* he loves Jesus; and whether he loves Jesus more than he loves the group.[3] These are questions Freddy knows he must answer properly but, having worked with Kurtz for a while now, he is confident in his answers.

Kurtz also invokes the Bible when he compares the now-fled Owen Underhill to Judas Iscariot. At this point the narration reveals that Freddy has in fact only read his Bible—and is thus able to follow the allusion—because Kurtz is the one who gave him the book in the first place.

This veneer of Christianity introduces the same sort of higher control over the group that Big Jim holds in Chester's Mill. Because Kurtz is apparently religious, he is therefore meant to be incapable of doing wrong. Even though their mission in the Jefferson Tract is to first kill any surviving aliens after a spaceship crash, and then to kill the humans who have come into contact with the alien fungus, Kurtz still relies on Jesus and the Bible to ground himself in front of his men. Owen Underhill defected after trying to save some of the people Kurtz and his men were meant to kill, and yet Underhill is Judas in this situation.

Freddy knows that his boss is only mouthing the words, using them to center himself without actually putting belief into them, but he will not point this out to Kurtz. None of Kurtz's inner circle would dare, especially considering how easy it is to be considered expendable on Kurtz's missions. The boss has his rules and his quirks, and he is a dangerous man who can turn on a dime—and shoot a cook's third in the foot for "use of inappropriate epithets"[4] when talking about the aliens—and therefore cannot be trusted. He must, if possible, be placated, and if this includes rituals of performative Christianity, then so be it.

The main difference between Big Jim and Kurtz is that Big Jim is not as open about his acts of violence or orders to others invoking the same. Kurtz gives his "boys" a speech before they go to kill the remaining aliens, and his inner circle knows of his plans to kill not only the hunters within the Jefferson Tract but most of the soldiers as well, and when Kurtz shoots the cook's third it is so the man can carry the message to others. These are not covert acts that can be easily denied, even if the whole truth of what was meant to happen in the Jefferson Tract would not have been truthfully made public. Kurtz is crazy, and Kurtz is a killer, and the killers who work for him—and might not be entirely sane themselves—are aware of both of these. They also, however, work to help isolate Kurtz and his actions from the rest of the world, supporting him the way some citizens of Chester's Mill begin donning blue armbands to show that they back Rennie. Where Rennie has the rebel group led by Dale Barbara and Julia Shumway, Kurtz has Owen Underhill.

Kurtz, unlike Rennie, is not shown to pray at all, either in public or in private. He might praise the Lord in his thoughts after a careful self-inventory reveals that he is not infected by the alien fungus, but it is simply a phrase that has worked its way into his speech pattern. He has to talk that way in front of his men, so casual mentions of God have worked their way into his sense of self, the way he adopted the name Abraham Kurtz. Almost nothing about the man is authentic, but his casual references to the Bible and mentions of the Lord are some of the most blatant counterfeit parts of his public self.

Neither Kurtz nor Rennie is a minister, like Piper Libby, but King did not leave his non-believing people of the cloth solely in The Mill.

Electric Miracles: Godless Faith Healings in *Revival*

The title of *Revival* (2014) refers both to the idea of a religious gathering of great fervor and healing, usually within a traveling tent sort of setting, as well as secular meanings of reviving. The main character, Jamie Morton, narrates his life largely through interactions with the man he calls his "fifth business," Charles Jacobs. At their first encounter, Jamie is six years old and his counterpart is a young minister, married and with a small child of his own. The Reverend Jacobs is new in town, and he and his family quickly become well-liked, fully accepted members of their town.

Jacobs takes Jamie under his wing in a way, encouraging his involvement in Methodist Youth Fellowship and even letting him in on a little secret. He has a model of Jesus walking across the water, the first indication of Jacobs' obsession with electricity, and Jacobs shows young Jamie how the trick is actually accomplished. Once the knowledge has been passed on, of course, it cannot be taken back, and Jamie is confronted with the first instance of where an apparent miracle actually has nothing more than a mundane explanation.

There is, however, another occurrence during this childhood encounter that brushes up against the title of "miracle" while falling under Jacobs' electricity obsession but not religion. When one of Jamie's brothers is injured on a skiing trip and loses his voice, the Reverend Jacobs invites him over for a wholly experimental treatment of his own devising. Either desperate or naïve, Jamie's brother submits himself to this entirely new device, and recovers his voice. Afterward Jacobs downplays his own role and that of electricity, saying it was all psychosomatic and the young man just needed an extra boost, but Jamie has cause to doubt this very much later on.

Tragedy strikes both the Reverend and his faith when his wife and son are killed in a car accident. The final sermon Jacobs manages to preach in the wake of his loss is deemed blasphemous, and he is all but run out of town. His parishioners appreciate that he has undergone a terrible experience, but they cannot understand that it would have destroyed his faith rather than deepened it. Young Jamie has to bid Jacobs farewell in secret because the feelings of the town have turned completely against him.

Jamie keeps encountering Jacobs at other times during his life, and he discovers that his old minister has lost neither his obsession with electricity nor his religious trappings entirely. After working for a while as a carnival showman depending entirely on his inventions, Jacobs takes up the life of a faith healer, "using religious activity to further his studies in electricity."[5] In this role he wears two rings, the one on his left hand ostensibly his wedding ring and the one on the right meant to show a similar devotion to Jesus. By placing the rings on the people who have come to him for healing, Jacobs is largely able to cure their ailments. Jamie is skeptical, of course, and notes how not everyone who lines up for healing is actually allowed up on the stage, but eventually Jamie himself is on the receiving end of Jacobs' ministrations.

After this encounter, Jamie is cured of his heroin addiction, although he initially has some strange side effects. He finds himself waking up, having apparently sleepwalked, and repeating the phrase "Something happened" while poking at his skin with various objects. This fades, though, and seems to be a mild price to pay for the fact that his addiction is utterly and completely cured. Jacobs even helps Jamie find a job, which both puts Jamie in further debt to him and keeps Jamie away as Jacobs embarks on his next occupation.

This time apart gives Jamie time to do some more research into others who have been healed by his former minister, and the results are not necessarily encouraging. A large number of people who have been touched by Jacobs' electricity, either through his sideshow act or his faith healing, have ended up with side effects of their own, and many have committed suicide. Because of his itinerant lifestyle, Jacobs has not stuck around long enough to see these side effects on his own—or, more likely, Jacobs would not have cared. All of this experimentation has been building to a final test case, and Jacobs secures Jamie as his assistant through means more foul than fair. In exchange for healing Jamie's first love, Jacobs demands Jamie's full support, including a lack of questions.

The deaths of his wife and young son have weighed on Jacobs his whole life, and with the disruption in his faith he is unable to simply believe that the two of them are in heaven. He wants to use electricity to answer the question of what awaits us all after death, thereby reassuring himself that his loved ones are safe and happy, as his former religion would have him believe. Jacobs therefore provides hospice care to a dying woman on the condition that he can use her corpse after her death in order to open up a gateway between this world and the next and answer the question once and for all.

The glimpse into the next world is nothing short of Lovecraftian and leaves Jamie mentally and emotionally scarred and Jacobs dead of a massive stroke. There is no comfort in what Jamie saw, and indeed, the side effects of Jacobs' former patients seem to increase in violence. Jamie's former girlfriend, healed by Jacobs, kills her partner and herself. Jamie's brother, even though his own medical encounter was now decades in the past, made a halfhearted attempt to kill his own partner and now lives in a psychiatric center in a state of semi-catatonia. Although Jamie himself is seeking psychiatric help and taking medication, he suffers from depression brought on by the horrific picture of the afterlife to which Jacobs treated him. Jamie tries to tell himself that what he saw might have been a lie, but the intrusive visions persist.

Jacobs touched—and therefore cursed—many people while he was on the road. Although part of this was through his work in a carnival sideshow, showing nothing more than photographic images of women done up in fancy evening dress, even the women brought up on stage for these demonstrations were not safe from side effects. Jamie tracks one who walked into a jewelry store, broke the glass case with her bare hands, and declared the diamonds she liberated truly belonged to her. Those who attended the so-called faith healings are more deeply affected and more likely to participate in the rash of murder/suicides Jamie has been tracking.

During these faith healings, Jacobs himself knows that any "God" he is selling is a lie. The revival tent is perhaps the only place he can use his two gold rings and his electricity in the way he wants to experiment, since clearly his treatments are not approved by the FDA or covered by HMOs. In order to gather participants for his experiments, Jacobs needs to lure them in with the idea of faith, and at this he succeeds admirably. These healings provide him with the funds necessary for him to continue his private experiments with "special electricity."

Jamie reflects, though, that Jacobs is not entirely a shyster. When Jacobs was still working the carnival circuit, he healed Jamie's heroin addiction without any expectation of payment. At that time Jamie had been mostly broke and unable to offer any, but Jamie reflects that this healing, as well as some of Jacobs' others, were the remnants of his Christian faith. Even though Jamie watches Jacobs, now styled as the

Rev. C. Danny, perform his revival healings, he knows that Jacobs healed his own heroin addiction at least mostly out of charity. Jamie, like those who go up on stage for their turn, was also a step along Jacobs' path to his final experiment. No matter how much gospel is sung on the healing stage, Jacobs has long since stopped believing and, as he grows older, has focused more and more tightly on his two main fascinations: electricity, and what happens to us after we die.

The side effects of Jacobs' healings are not the same as what Paul Edgecomb receives after his encounter with John Coffey. Paul finds himself cursed with a long life in which he can only watch his loved ones die. Many of those healed by Jacobs end up committing murder and then suicide, although some—like Jamie's brother—make only a weak token gesture, and Jamie himself feels a compulsion to do neither. He does suffer from random bouts of blackouts in which he continually tries to poke at his skin, although not always with a sharp object, and the idea that he will open his mouth only able to utter two words, no matter what else he means to say: "Something happened." Another of Jacobs' charity healings suffered blackouts directly after the application of electricity and then occasional visual auras, culminating in a vision that foreshadows what Jamie will see on the night of Jacobs' final experiment. But, in each case, the side effects seem to be minimal compared to the fact that Jamie is no longer addicted to heroin and the other man's deafness has not returned, and clearly Jacobs does not believe any side effects are dangerous enough for him to stop his faith healings.

By the time Jamie discovers that his old minister is now a famous faith healer, multiple websites have been devoted to attempting to prove that Jacobs is in fact a charlatan. These are countered by the numerous testimonial videos collected on Jacobs' own website and tempered by Jamie's knowledge that Jacobs can indeed induce cures with his electricity. Jamie still knows that the tent must be seeded with plants during the nights of those healings and is positive that the instances in which Jacobs removes "tumors" involve pulling goat intestines out of a secret pocket, but he cannot shake the actual miracles Jacobs seems able to induce.

Even though he has once again adopted the title of "Reverend" during these mass faith healings, Jacobs' faith is in electricity and his experiments, not in the Lord. In fact, in this world, unlike those of *The Stand* or *Desperation* or even *Under the Dome*, where God's voice can be heard, there might not even *be* a God. Jacobs' faith is shattered when his wife and son are killed in a car accident that seems to be a true honest accident, with no place to put the blame. Jamie's most religious brother pulls through his cancer diagnosis only to be felled by a stroke at fifty-one, the same age their mother was when she died of cancer. Jamie stopped believing in God after hearing Jacobs' terrible sermon on his last day in the pulpit, and his family was dealt further tragedy when the eldest child and only daughter was shot and killed by her estranged husband. There is little kindness in *Revival* and the only miracles come after applications of Jacobs' experiments.

The glimpse Jacobs, and therefore Jamie, have into the afterlife further confirms the idea that God does not in fact exist. Instead of Heaven, they see Hell as devised by Lovecraft and Bosch, where every dead person serves a creature called "Mother." There is no rest, no peace, and certainly no happiness. Jacobs, who had been clinging for so long to the idea that he might be able to see his wife and son in heaven, has his hopes dashed just before he dies and experiences the next step for himself, and Jamie lives but is haunted by what he saw. There is no God, and Jacobs' transition from young minister to old shyster was not a fall, but a maturing.

In most of King's novels that deal with the question of religion, the power of God or at least the White is revealed for at least some of his characters. They hear the still small voice—although whether their reactions to it lead to success or more suffering varies—or are able to hold up an object that has been imbued with such power that it glows too brightly to be looked at directly. In *Under the Dome*, for instance, false pretense at belief has different consequences because God does, in fact, exist. Others hear Him, and attempt to obey. There is a God, or at least alien children playing at being God, so people like Big Jim Rennie can anger Him and reap the consequences. Charles Jacobs, however, does not need to face the Lord at the end of his life and answer for no longer believing in Him, because God in *Revival* is an elaborate lie, or perhaps only a kind one. The idea of God allows people to live their lives without knowing that the monstrous "Mother" waits for them at the end.

American Christianity and King

Religion and Christianity permeate much of American life even if individuals themselves are nonpracticing, and the casual nature of religion is also evident in many of King's works. In *It*, for example, although young Eddie Kaspbrak attends church every Sunday with his mother, he does not think about using any part of his religion in order to confront the monster. Ever since a Sunday school lesson in which he was told that throwing the Host in a toilet would turn the water to blood, he has been terrified of taking communion, so clearly the religious beliefs and practices hold power over him. However, he, like the other kids, do not even consider using the weekly rituals of their religions against It. Their faith remains untested.

Other books make religious references without asking the characters to actually engage with the teaching. *Pet Sematary* contains a liberal retelling of the story of Jesus and Lazarus, interspersed between each major part of the story, although the Creed family is not seen attending church and Louis does not consciously make the connection even as he digs up his son's body to rebury it in the Micmac burying grounds. King as author makes these associations concrete, although his characters do not need to ponder them. They are literary references without the faith to support them.

These instances, though, seem like so many of the characters who live in or around *'Salem's Lot*: the use of popular stories or references without the accompanying deep faith, continued practice, or professed belief seen in these other essays. Eddie, for example, does *not* go to the others and suggest that they should all stock up on communion wafers and grape juice before their journey into the sewers, or even that they should pray. The only mentions of religion that pass between the Losers are semi-uncomfortable situations in which the group confronts the fact that one of the seven members is in fact Jewish, and thus would find no comfort or power in the Lord's Prayer, anyway. Unlike Big Jim Rennie, no one forces the others to pray or engage in religious practice in which they do not themselves believe.

It is perhaps easy for King's characters to adopt Christianity as a veneer because their position in late twentieth- or early twenty-first century America gives them easy access to Christian beliefs even if they have never attended Sunday School or regular church services. Bible stories are common secular references and many popular figures profess their Christian faith as a matter of course. Christianity, especially with roots in Europe, is a dominant force in American culture and shapes many American values.

The characters discussed in this essay give lip service to Christianity while their actions and goals generally do not align with what Jesus Christ is meant to have preached. Jim Rennie uses the Bible and his own outward religiousness to browbeat others who attempt to stand against him, and to justify his whims even to himself. For Abraham Kurtz, the Good Book is only one of his many clubs used to keep his subordinates in line. Charles Jacobs likewise preys on the belief—or desperation—of those who come to his revival tent so that he can fund his personal research and continue his experiments with electricity. Only Piper

Libby, who confesses first to herself and then to others that she does not actually believe in God anymore, continues to work largely to serve others in their best interests, and not, as Jacobs does, to further his own.

For these characters, their outcome is not so much based on their religious practice but on themselves as human beings, independent of whatever God may or may not exist in the book's world. Because Rennie uses his religion to argue in favor of his illegal and dangerous actions, he meets an end based on the actions and not on his belief. If there is a God, He does not reach down to save Rennie from himself. Piper Libby, on the other hand, finds herself in the position to join up with the resistance as a sudden arrival interrupts her at prayer, and in her desire to act honestly for the good of the town—as opposed to Rennie's definition thereof—she both escapes the fiery conflagration that follows and lives long enough to see the Dome lift. Kurtz neither asks the Lord for help nor feels the need to vary his path to actually align his practices with Christian beliefs. Charles Jacobs, funded by the money of desperate believers who are more willing to believe his lies about God than his truth about electricity, uncovers the answer he has been searching for mere moments before his own death shows it to him for eternity.

The only one of these characters to actually ask a higher power for help is Piper Libby, but she does not expect to hear an answer. If the others had ever paused to ask in their youth, they ceased long before they met their ends. Instead of looking to serve others and through these acts to serve God, they sought ways to make God and others' belief in Him work for themselves. None of these men met a good end.

But what can be left if all belief is stripped away? If the supernatural threatens and a character does not reach for spirituality or ritual either outside of his or her own experience, or through Christianity and their own personal religion, what options are left?

III
Reality Is Thin Ice
Belief and Unbelief

When confronted with—or threatened by—the supernatural, one common reaction among King's characters is the decision to fight like with like. If the danger presents itself as mystical or spiritual, then the counterattack must itself also contain these elements. The threat is not just physical, although that is dangerous enough, but comes wrapped in mystery. A previously unencountered threat has to be explained so that its weaknesses can be discovered, and the means by which those weaknesses are exploited are often through ritual either borrowed from non–European cultures or from Christianity. Characters choose to fight danger they barely understand with objects or rituals they likewise hardly comprehend in the hope that their version of something too much for a man to grasp will be able to counter the original mystery.

Such confrontations can lead to epic battles of will or intention set in dramatic venues with the stakes being measured in human souls. These can be highly theatrical, made suspenseful through the tone and speed of narration, with the outcome of the group, the town, the country, or perhaps even all of existence at stake. There are indeed fates worse than death, and the characters attempting to wield the power of the White, Christian or not, are hoping to avoid bringing those down on themselves and their loved ones.

One weakness of these scenarios, though, is how few of King's characters truly understand what, exactly, they are doing. They fail to fully explain the threat, relying on single instances and extrapolating these into hard-and-fast rules they can use in order to psych themselves up for the final confrontation, and likewise barely understand the rituals they have chosen in order to defeat the danger. Much of the tension comes from this lack of knowledge: are they doing it properly? Did they miss something? What, exactly, could happen next on either side? This further leads to confusion in the resolution as characters might believe they have fully triumphed over the evil, only for it to pop up again in the same location, or to relocate quickly and continue its work on a new, unassuming town. Once they have eradicated the immediate threat, King's characters tend to keep their mouths shut and hope that any knowledge they have amassed will never be needed again, either by them or anyone else.

    It is largely because of this belief that a threat has no precedence that King's characters choose responses that do not rely on cultural appropriation or Christian rituals. If something is perceived to be entirely outside of shared human experience, then clearly no one has ever had to come up with a response to it before, and thus no knowledge of how to counter it already exists. The characters have to come up with their own ways and means of confronting a unique threat. Some of them react by doing their best to utterly obliterate the physical form inhabited by the inexplicable, not knowing what caused the danger to appear in the first place and likewise uncertain as to whether this means of destruction will in fact cause the threat to end. Others, either pressed for time or perhaps in possession of a calmer, clearer head, go along with whatever is happening and simply bend to their new realities—likewise with mixed results.

7

Twisted, Silent Hulk
Destroying the Outer Shell

When confronted with a threat, especially an imminent one, the fight-or-flight reaction can spur some of King's characters to choose not only the first option, but also to opt for total destruction. It might not be enough to fire a single shot at the approaching threat, much less to cause it to stumble somehow and give people time to run and hide. Whatever physical form the supernatural threat takes, from man to machine, a common response is utter destruction.

It is one that makes logical sense with what we think we know about our own "real" world. If a human or animal's physical body is harmed enough, then it ceases living. A machine that is taken apart or crushed out of shape can no longer run and thus no longer pursue its prey, no matter what possesses it. Perhaps that evil spirit can jump to another creature or machine, but the initial threat can be taken care of through the destruction of the threat's physical form.

These responses do not rely on spiritual or religious beliefs, either from the characters' own childhoods or those learned from library books and quick research, because they are not spiritual reactions. The threats themselves may not even be grasped or fully understood on the level of spirits, demons, or other non-human, non-rational explanations. It is simply known that a certain something—object, ghost, or person—presents a generally physical threat to the main characters, who respond with physical violence of their own. This may or may not qualify as murder, since the violence enacted by the main characters is not directed at a human being, or at least not at someone who is *merely* human. The thought—or perhaps the hope—is that destruction of the physical body will function the same way as it would on a human all the same, and that the threat will be eliminated permanently when the physical containment fails.

Crush It: *Christine*

Christine (1983) tells the story of a possessed 1958 Plymouth Fury and the boy who loved her. That boy, Arnie Cunningham, purchased the car not only used, but as a wreck, from Roland LeBay, its—or rather, her—original owner. Arnie's obsession with the car troubles not only his parents, for whom a vehicle means the threat of independence, but his best friend since childhood, Dennis Guilder. Arnie begins choosing the car over his family, his schoolwork, and even eventually over his first girlfriend, the beautiful Leigh Cabot. In order to afford the repairs he has to make to his beloved new car, Arnie even starts working for sketchy garage owner Will Darnell.

The repairs he makes, though, trouble both Dennis and Darnell, because there seems to be no sense to them. Arnie somehow manages to replace half of Christine's bumper, and many of the renovations seem to be merely cosmetic. For all the time he spends in the garage bay tinkering, Arnie has little to show for it. He manages to get Christine ready enough to take Leigh on their first date, and eventually on errands into the city, but even then both Darnell and Dennis have to wonder where Arnie is getting the money for so many costly parts. One aspect that Arnie refuses to touch, however, is Christine's odometer, which runs backward.

The full consequences of this "glitch" are seen when Christine, always at times when Arnie has a solid alibi, leaves the garage herself in order to hunt down and kill those who have been mean to Arnie. This includes not only boys from school, but eventually Darnell himself. Each time she sustains massive amounts of damage from collisions with people and buildings but, as she drives away and the odometer runs, dents pop themselves back out and broken headlights shine again. Arnie himself is aware of this, at least on some level. After the school bullies find Christine parked in the long-term lot at the airport, they show up drunk and vandalize the car to the point where even Leigh, who does not like Christine, is taken aback. Although Arnie does not fully remember doing so, he first began pushing the car until she repaired herself enough so that he could get in and drive her to take care of the rest.

In spite of the odometer, Christine could not heal herself alone. She is a parasite, taking energy from Arnie and turning him into a parody of her first owner. Even though he is a teenager, Arnie starts wearing a back brace and using phrases common to the much-older, now-dead LeBay. LeBay's young daughter choked to death while in Christine, and his wife then used Christine to commit suicide, leaving the car as the only woman and sole focus of his life. Leigh nearly chokes to death on a hamburger while riding in Christine as well and is only saved because Arnie had stopped to pick up a hitchhiker who administered the Heimlich maneuver. Although Arnie is only uneasy and tries to keep himself from admitting it, Leigh is adamant that Christine wants to kill her—adamant enough to take her concerns to Dennis.

Arnie's best friend has been literally sidelined and taken out of much of the story at this point by a football accident, but he has seen enough to agree with Leigh. The number of murders that occur while Arnie is clearly alibied, combined with the way he is physically, emotionally, and mentally coming to resemble LeBay, added to their notions about Christine, lead them to form a plan. At a time when Arnie is scheduled to be out of town with his mother, Dennis and Leigh will lure Christine to the now-closed garage, anticipating that the car will want to kill them both. Even though Dennis is still using crutches and has little use of his legs, he takes the day off school in order to rent a large tanker truck usually employed to empty septic tanks. When Christine comes, he hopes to use this truck to smash Christine so badly that even her backward-running odometer will not be able to save her.

The plan goes imperfectly, as most do, resulting in injuries for both humans involved. When Dennis wakes up in the hospital, he learns that there is some good news and some bad. The twisted, silent hulk that was once Christine has already been through the crusher behind the garage. Arnie and his mother, on the road to visit a college, have died in a car crash that Dennis thinks occurred when the spirit that inhabited Christine—or maybe LeBay, or both—fought for control of Arnie's body, and Arnie's father, against Dennis' advice, died as a result of attempting to investigate whether Christine was honestly dangerous. The main body of the book ends with Dennis finally coming clean and telling his father the whole story because Leigh has already told it to her own. Even though Dennis doubts his father will believe it, he tells it to keep Leigh from getting in more trouble and finishes with his declaration of love for his dead best friend.

The epilogue picks up four years later, after Dennis and Leigh have gone their separate ways. Although Dennis is haunted with dreams and the experience is what eventually drove them apart, Leigh either does not remember what happened with Christine, or pretends not to. That, however, is not Dennis' concern. What has caught his eye is a newspaper article about a "BIZARRE MURDER BY CAR IN LOS ANGELES"[1] where the victim shares a name with the one bully who escaped Christine four years previously. Dennis worries that Christine might have managed to put herself back together again and will now work her way across the country, picking off the victims she missed.

Dennis and Leigh are both teenagers when they are trying to figure out what, exactly, is happening with Arnie and Christine. They cannot talk to Arnie's parents, who were already having issues with their son prior to his purchase, and even though Dennis' father, at least, knows that something is wrong, Dennis only tells the whole story at the very end of the book. In spite of his conversation with LeBay's brother, Dennis is also still unclear about what, exactly, caused Christine to become what she is: whether she rolled off the line that way, or LeBay made her that way, or if it was some sort of mutual force. If LeBay had died before passing the car on to Arnie, would Christine have been able to rebuild herself, or would she have rusted quietly?

Clearly, though, Arnie was tangled up in what was happening, but neither his best friend nor his girlfriend would contemplate murdering him and removing *that* end of the equation. Since Arnie was so frequently with his car, Christine would likely have defended him against any sort of attack, and even with the tanker truck, Dennis struggled to subdue the car. They could not imagine attacking Arnie, so they turned their attention to Christine. Arnie died anyway, which at least puts him out of Christine's reach if she really *has* risen again to make her way across the country.

Unlike many other King characters, Dennis and Leigh do not take their problems to the library in search of a way to exorcise whatever spirit lurks within Christine. They do not attempt to sprinkle the car with holy water or perform any other kind of cleansing ritual. They simply see that Christine, as an object, is having an effect on Arnie; that she can, in fact, somehow be fixed faster and cheaper than most cars, including after the beating the bullies gave her; and that they do not want Arnie to continue down this path. Because they cannot destroy him, they do their best to destroy the car—and then Leigh at least seems to destroy those memories, as well. There is no search for information on what to do in this situation, perhaps because they conclude that there has never been one like it before, and thus it will not be found in books. The two teenagers thus bait their trap, and attempt to turn the car that has bewitched their friend into nothing more than scrap metal, hoping that this will be the end of it.

Run It Over: *End of Watch*

The Bill Hodges trilogy begins entirely in the real world, with a real-world threat: Brady Hartsfield, who is a sociopathic computer-and-gadget wiz with a penchant for death. He is the title character of *Mr. Mercedes* (2014), having stolen a Mercedes and driven it into

7. Twisted, Silent Hulk   125

a crowd in order to commit mass murder. Brady is also fond of pushing people to suicide, which he accomplished with the Mercedes' owner prior to the start of the book, and which he hopes to repeat with recently retired Detective Bill Hodges. Hodges was one of the two assigned to the Mercedes case and therefore retired without ever identifying Brady. At the end of *Mr. Mercedes*, Brady is prevented from bombing a packed concert venue—not by Hodges, but by one of his new friends, a woman named Holly Gibney. Holly uses a sock filled with ball bearings in order to beat Brady's head, landing him not in the morgue but in the neurological unit of a local hospital, where he remains throughout the second book in the series.

While he is in his coma, Brady is given experimental drugs. Either they, the beating, or a combination of the two lead Brady to discover that he is mildly telekinetic, able to perform small feats such as knocking picture frames over, and that he can also jump into others' minds if they happen to enter into a hypnotic state. Using those around him, including Dr. Felix Babineau, who administered the experimental drug, Brady starts on a rather convoluted plan directed at the boyband fans he should have killed at the end of the first book. By sending them defective gaming consoles, he hopes to get them to concentrate on a certain screen known to induce hypnosis. Brady can then enter their minds and convince them that suicide is the only option, playing on teenage hormones as much as group mentality. He hopes that the initial wave of suicides, coupled with a website he has set up, will cause a wide-reaching event.

Part of this plan involves Brady's leaving his own body behind permanently. Instead of hitching a ride in someone else's head for a while, he takes over Dr. Babineau completely. His plan to induce mass suicide was difficult enough for Hodges and the others to counter, considering how senseless and ridiculous it seemed, but Brady now gives them another problem completely: Hodges has been accused of being obsessed with Brady, and especially his supposed telekinetic ability. The retired detective has also had his friends give him an intervention in the matter. Should Hodges then attempt to tell anyone that Brady Hartsfield is not in fact dead, and that he has taken over the body of his neurosurgeon, clearly no one would believe him. The tale is fantastic in its own right, and Hodges' own history works against him. He can only turn to his closest friends if he has any hope of being believed.

Hodges is unable to face Brady-as-Babineau on his own because of his recently diagnosed pancreatic cancer, but he knows that shooting Babineau will look to the world like an unmotivated murder. The dead man would clearly be Babineau. But, as Holly and their friend Jerome both now grasp, Brady is far more dangerous than this elderly, arthritic surgeon. His desired waves of suicides might not occur, but, if left alone, Brady could hop from head to head, controlling body after body, with no foreseeable end to the destruction. Although he may have changed his face, Brady Hartsfield is still the sociopath who drove a stolen Mercedes into a crowd of job-seekers and then drove the owner of that car to suicide.

The end result of an isolated and convoluted standoff is Dr. Felix Babineau's body flayed and laid open to the backbone after being chewed up by a snowmobile tread. The description is gruesome and King invokes another master of the thriller when he says that "his guts are spread out around him like the wings of a red dragon."[2] Babineau's grievously injured body weakens Brady's power, preventing him from being able to jump to any of the relatively healthy people around him. In spite of the extent of these injuries, though, they are not what kills him. With his borrowed body in pain and not dying quickly enough from the injuries, Brady commits suicide—although he uses his telekinesis to actually pull the trigger of the gun Hodges has offered and Holly has placed against his head.

Twice, then, the response to Brady Hartsfield was violent physical action. In the concert auditorium, Hodges was sidelined by a heart attack and likely would not have trusted a gun in the midst of so many teenybopper fans. Holly had Hodges' "Happy Slapper" and needed to act quickly, before Brady could set off the bomb he had brought in with him, but Holly does far more than that. After the first blow, which dents Brady's skull, she administers a second and prepares for more when Jerome grabs her arm to stop her. Their task of preventing Brady from setting off the explosive was likely completed with the first blow, which Holly dealt after calling Brady by the name of one of the bullies from her childhood. Further beating him up would, she tells Jerome, have been "therapy."[3] She is, however, denied her "therapy" and Brady is left twitching but not dead, putting him in the path of Dr. Babineau, the experimental drugs, and his future telekinetic and mind control abilities.

At the end of *End of Watch*, Jerome is the one to cause the physical damage, not prevent more of it. Although Hodges and Holly tried to keep him out of the final confrontation, he followed them all the same, borrowing the Sno-Cat with which he ran over Babineau's body. Since Brady-as-Babineau was shooting at him and Jerome was unarmed, he had little choice. All of Babineau was destroyed, although it did end with a shot to the head, the same way Holly went for Brady's head when he still looked like Brady. This is knowledge, and even technique, that Holly carries with her even after Hodges' death.

Smash It: *The Outsider* and "If It Bleeds"

Holly Gibney does not enter into *The Outsider* until nearly three hundred pages have already passed. The main crisis—the public arrest of Terry Maitland for the brutal murder of Frank Peterson, followed by Peterson's brother's murdering Maitland—has already passed. Maitland's widow, though, realizes that there can be no life for her and her girls in Flint City, Oklahoma, unless the real killer is caught and Terry's name actually cleared. Holly is contacted in order to follow up some loose ends in Ohio, where Terry had been that spring in order to visit his father.

It is during this trip that Holly realizes so many people have disparate pieces of the puzzle without even realizing it. When she comes to Flint City to meet with a whole group of people focused on clearing Terry's name, she first has all of them lay things out on the table, uncovering a strange thread: two girls were murdered in Ohio around the time Terry and his family were there, much in the same way Frank Peterson was killed; Terry received a cut on his hand during a collision with one of the aides working at the memory unit where his father lives; and, on the night of Frank Peterson's murder, another man received a cut on his own hand during a quick encounter with Terry. This, combined with testimony from the younger Maitland girl and the main detective's wife about a man who came to pass on a warning, helps Holly make her conclusion that the creature they are dealing with is in fact very similar to El Cuco, although she quickly dubs their own specific example as "The Outsider."

Based on the limited information they have, Holly concludes that the Outsider will take on a new identity and the chain will continue. Claude Bolton will become the next man framed for murder, destroying his family and that of the victims, since the Outsider lives on pain and anguish as much as the actual murder. Even though "Bolton" has apparently been in Flint City to pass on his warnings, they discover that he is currently on vacation and with his mother in Texas. The Outsider, however, knows full well that an alibi provided by an accused murderer's mother is all but worthless. Even though it is still only a short time since the Outsider's previous murder—and previous face—Holly and a number of law enforcement officials from Oklahoma go to Texas to meet Bolton and his mother.

Through some detective work and some guesswork, Holly and Detective Ralph Anderson end up tracking the Outsider to its current lair. Like many of King's supernatural monsters, the Outsider made use of a human accomplice, another Flint City detective, and not everyone who approached the cave where the Outsider was hiding even lived long enough for Holly and Ralph to enter. Holly has surmised that the Outsider prefers to spend its transition periods near where the kin of its new form lay buried, and Bolton's mother told them a story of how two young boys were lost inside a cave known as the Marysville Hole. Although numerous men went into the unexplored depths to search for them, the boys were never found, and those men—some related to Bolton—never came out of the cave.

Ralph and Holly are able to follow the Outsider's spoor to its lair, and they discover it at the bottom of a rickety metal staircase in what was once called the Chamber of Sound. Although Ralph has a gun, the Outsider points out that cave-ins have already happened, and a single shot would likely kill all three of them. Ralph still means to try it, however, if he can get Holly to leave the two of them alone. Once she gets what he deems to be a fair enough distance away, he plans on shooting the Outsider and dying for the role he played in Terry Maitland's death.

Holly, however, refuses to cooperate. She has now had personal experiences with the monstrous Brady Hartsfield who began his life as human and gained supernatural powers at least in part through her own intervention. In the auditorium during the boyband concert, Holly used the Happy Slapper that Bill Hodges had given her: a weight in the toe of a sock. Although she did not bring such a weapon to Texas, Holly managed to go shopping before visiting the cave. It is a weapon she has used before, and one that is silent enough to be unlikely to cause the cave-in expected to follow a shot from Ralph's gun.

At no point is she shown considering that, after two blows to the head, Brady Hartsfield not only survived, but became more powerful. Before Holly hit him with the Happy Slapper, Brady was a murdering sociopath, but still completely human. The blows to his skull landed him in both the hospital and the path of Felix Babineau and his experimental drug, so even if it was the drug alone that gave Brady his supernatural powers, Holly and the Happy Slapper were the reason he was there to receive it in the first place. Those blows to the head started them on the path that led, years later, to Felix Babineau's body laid open to the backbone by a Sno-Cat and Brady telepathically pulling the trigger of a gun put against his temple.

All the same, Holly is determined to end the day with as few lives lost as possible, and she knows that Ralph has both a wife and a son to return home to. The results of using the Happy Slapper on the Outsider's skull are more dramatic and apparently more final than when she used a similar one on Brady Hartsfield: after the creature's features undergo a blurred transformation through numerous of its past faces, reminiscent of what happens to Jack Torrance near the end of his life in *The Shining*, the Outsider's physical form dissolves into a number of white worms. Both Holly and Ralph are careful not to let any of those worms touch them, and they seem hardly capable of crawling across the cave floor to the rickety metal staircase, much less following them up it. When they are later asked if they are sure they killed the Outsider, their answer is a firm "Yes."

Holly did not know for sure what would happen if she used the Happy Slapper on the Outsider's face. When she and Ralph see it mid-transformation, partly still looking like Terry Maitland but also clearly well on the way to becoming Claude Bolton, they have no doubt that the Outsider is supernatural. It cannot be human. Holly has already proven herself able to swing the Happy Slapper at a human being's head when that man was ready to perform a monstrous act, so there is little struggle for her to swing it now, when she is aiming at a monster who only appears to be human on the outside.

Like Brady Hartsfield, the Outsider presents a new level of danger that cannot be allowed to escape. Both of them hold power in the fact that sensible people of the twenty-first century are not supposed to believe in the ability of one person to take over another's mind or assume his or her body, and that disbelief, as Holly points out, is just one of the Outsider's weapons. After it scratches someone, it can fully become that person's physical body, down to blood type and fingerprints. Although the Outsider still makes sure to call attention to itself after the crimes, the forensic evidence also helps it along in its deception. Such a creature cannot be allowed to continue to live, feeding on lives and anguish.

Holly's use of the Happy Slapper is still a gamble. Although their location in the cave makes it a safer option than the gun, she is only working on assumption when she guesses that the Outsider's physical body is just as susceptible to harm as any "normal" person's body. She argues that it relies on camouflage to protect it, not armor, but none of them can be sure of anything until the Outsider actually disintegrates under the blow. Perhaps if one of the worms were to touch their skin, something might have continued to happen, but all of the final pieces of the Outsider were left to rot underground.

That particular Outsider has been taken care of and only pursues Holly and Ralph in their dreams, but the novella "If It Bleeds" from the book of the same name (2020) once again has Holly facing a creature of many faces. Before the original Outsider died, it asked Holly and Ralph, "Have you seen another like me somewhere?"[4] Although neither Holly nor Ralph, nor apparently even this initial Outsider, ever had,

Holly finds another one in Pennsylvania while watching news coverage of a bombing at a school. The man who planted the bomb was clearly caught on security cameras, and something about the first reporter on the scene also catches her eye.

After Holly's experience in Oklahoma, she sought out another therapist purely for the purpose of telling him the story about the Outsider. She did not need him to help her through it or past her "delusions," but she asked him to publish and present her case to a large audience, on one condition: that any fellow psychologist who had a patient exhibiting the same delusions should contact her. Shortly after seeing the strange news reporter and being unable to completely put him out of her mind, Holly is given the information for such a patient. The elderly man and his grandson have been tracing exactly the same news reporter across the decades and during many disastrous events.

Due to the grandfather's ability to always remember a face and the grandson's skill with audio technology, the pair is able to give Holly her missing piece. This Outsider is not entirely like the one that died in the Marysville Hole, since the reporter is able to change his face at will, although he always uses variations of one of two basic forms: the reporter Holly noticed, and the man who planted the bomb. Tired of simply flocking to tragedy and reporting on it, this Outsider has grown hungry and decided to manufacture disaster of his own. He is also able to change his appearance much more quickly than the previous Outsider, in a matter of minutes, although Holly is apparently only one of a few people who might notice something odd about him during that time.

Like the previous Outsider, this one has been around for quite some time. He, too, manages to put Holly in a tight place by ensuring that the final showdown is not just the two of them, alone. He has taken a hostage, one of Holly's young friends, first terrorizing her by changing his face in front of her and then threatening both her and Holly's lives. Through more quick thinking and some helpful interference from Jerome, Holly manages to kill this Outsider by pushing him down an empty elevator shaft from the fifth floor. When she goes to the basement to pick up any remaining evidence, she only finds his clothes, but no worms. If there were any in this other kind of Outsider, they have disappeared by the time she makes it down to check.

Each method Holly employs to get rid of the Outsider would be bloody and gruesome if enacted on a human being. She had already seen the consequences of the Happy Slapper on a human skull, and any scalp wounds bleed profusely. A fall down the elevator shaft, especially when the elevator itself then descended and may have crushed whatever body was left behind, should likewise have been very messy. Had Holly done either of these things to a human man, it would have been very unlikely that she could have cleaned up the scene in a way that would realistically pass forensic inspection. Because the Outsiders are not human, though, only the clothes are left. The first Outsider was even nice enough to help them along by luring them to a place no one else would visit, and to have no actual ties to the real world. Although the reporter will be missed, the first Outsider was in fact no one, stealing identities but having none of his own and no place to call home.

In her first appearance, Holly shows her capability for overkill in her violent responses. Only Jerome's intervention keeps her from hitting Brady Hartsfield more than twice, although she says it would be "therapy" if she continued. Holly puts all of her rage and frustration against her childhood bullies into her reaction against Brady, and that same willingness to engage in a violent solution is apparent in *The Outsider* and "If It Bleeds." She might even be able to create an argument that this overkill is in fact necessary—if Holly had been allowed to keep beating Brady, he would not have survived long enough for Dr. Babineau's mystery drug to give him supernatural powers. Complete and utter destruction of the physical form, aided by the Outsiders' complete disintegration, seems to be the only solution for confronting these supernatural threats.

Destruction Is Only Part of the Plan: *'Salem's Lot* and *Bag of Bones*

At times, attempts at complete destruction are only part of the characters' approach to a problem. In *'Salem's Lot*, after trying to eliminate the vampires one by one, Ben Mears and young Mark Petrie are the only ones left in town to stand against who knows how many vampires. They have lost multiple members of their original group and the remaining pair retreat into Mexico for a while to gather themselves and figure out their next step. It is not conclusive that this plan will involve returning to Maine at all.

One of the members of Ben and Mark's original group did indeed consult the library, and much of what he found ended up being true: that vampires cannot survive in the sunlight; that a stake through the heart will get rid of them; and that, to an extent, crucifixes and holy water will repel them. The problem with the group's previous efforts was that they were forced to search out the hiding places of every single vampire, and the heart went out of them when a trap was laid in the basement they wanted to search and they lost Jimmy Cody because of it. Further, dragging vampires into the sun is not a quick end, even slower than individually staking each one through the heart, and each act takes its own emotional toll.

In their epilogue, Ben and Mark stand on the hill above *'Salem's Lot* and start what they hope will be the fire that burns the town flat. While the fire itself might not kill the vampires, it should at least eliminate all of their hiding places and leave them out in the sun. It is a risky plan, since the fire might burn out of control and spread to surrounding towns, or it might be noticed too soon and bring firefighters before it can destroy the Lot. Some vampires might even survive the burning. There is simply too much that Ben and Mark do not know, but at least, for them, it is some form of action after a long period of inaction.

'Salem's Lot itself ends with Ben and Mark walking away after setting the fire, leaving readers with a sort of Rorschach test: will it succeed, or will the vampires win? King himself answers that in the short story "One for the Road" (collected in *Night Shift*, 1978): the fire, set about a year after strange things happened in the Lot, burned for three days. "After that, for a time, things were better. And then they started again."[5] Even though both Ben and Mark were still alive at the time, as later revealed in *The Dark Tower: Wolves of the Calla* (2003), there is no indication that they tried to intervene further. The two remaining heroes of *'Salem's Lot* returned once to start the fire, but in "One for the Road" the vampires still lurk. The Lot itself is avoided if at all possible, and those who live nearby have taken to wearing crucifixes no matter what their religion and carrying Bibles.

It is impossible to explain to outsiders, as the two men in the short story well know. A man from Massachusetts enters Tookey's Bar in the middle of a snowstorm one January, finding Tookey and his friend Booth to be the only occupants. When the man explains that his car got stuck because the roads were drifted in, and *where* it got stuck, Tookey and Booth understand immediately: because the locals know to avoid the Lot, those roads are no longer plowed. The frostbitten man in front of them has been following directions that were not given by a local. By the time they make it back to the man's car, hoping to rescue his wife and young daughter, neither is still in the car. Both are seen before Booth and Tookey can make their escape, though, and both are now incredibly beautiful and able to walk on top of the snow. The vampires still rule *'Salem's Lot* in spite of the fire meant to remove all of their hiding places.

When their initial plan to attack the vampires one by one failed, Ben and Mark decided on a scorched earth Plan B. Although the fire made things better for a time, it did not entirely succeed. There is no clear explanation as for why this might be. Were Ben and Mark convinced that, having killed the head vampire and his henchman, they had eliminated the threat of creating more vampires? Surely they should have thought that, if even one vampire lived through the burning, it could then go and feed on others and create more. If Ben continued to get the Maine paper down in their little Mexican town, he would have seen that the same sorts of oddities were still being reported in that little corner of Maine. Surely he and Mark would have wanted to follow up on the results of their fire— unless perhaps the lull was long enough to convince them that they could leave the Lot behind once and for all. Unlike Dennis Guilder and Holly Gibney, they might not have happened upon the perfect news story to convince them that their second attempt did not, in fact, work.

For Ben and Mark, the idea of ultimate destruction only comes after their initial attempt to destroy the supernatural threat failed. For Mike Noonan in *Bag of Bones* (1998), ultimate destruction is almost a sidetrack in the middle of all the rest of his troubles.

Mike's problems are many. His wife died unexpectedly a few years previously, having kept her pregnancy a secret from him and also possibly having engaged in an affair. Since then he has been suffering from intense writer's block, only able to fulfill his side of the contract by digging out his old trunk novels and handing them over once a year. When he finally returns to his lake house for the first time since his wife's death, he also happens to make a quick enemy of rich, eccentric, and ailing Max Devore. Mike therefore finds himself writing for the first time since becoming a widower, while at the same time falling for Max Devore's former daughter-in-law and funding her custody battle against the old man over three-year-old Kyra Devore. The fact that Mike is also having vivid dreams or visions of turn-of-the-century blues singer Sara Tidwell seems to be as much of a distraction as the idea that his wife's ghost still lingers in their lake house.

The lake house is itself named Sara Laughs, after the singer, who was murdered not far from it. Mike eventually learns what his wife had already discovered, in spite of all the distractions that clamor for his attention: one of his own ancestors was among the group of men who raped and murdered Sara Tidwell and drowned her son. Sara has cursed all the descendants of those men, including Max Devore and therefore Kyra, to drowning at the hands of their own family members. Mike himself experiences a trance in which he sets out to drown Kyra in the bathtub, but he manages to catch hold of himself in time. In order to keep Sara from ending the lines of the men who ended her life, Mike relies on messages from his dead wife, who spent much of her final years trying to uncover the secret of the curse and how to lift it.

Although Sara was murdered decades ago, her remains still lie beneath a tree that frequently catches Mike's attention. The ultimate physical destruction here, at his wife's suggestion, is to uncover Sara's bones and dissolve them with lye. By getting rid of the last of her earthly remains, Mike seeks to eliminate the curse Sara laid on all of the white men's families.

Once Mike manages to uncover the story of what happened to Sara Tidwell, he is able to sort out the threads of the curse. He has to do some rewriting of his own family history in order to do it and to place himself properly as one of the descendants, following the trail that his wife left him. He also struggles with the fact that she kept all of this a secret, along with her own pregnancy, because of her concern that Mike would be the next father to drown his child. In order to free himself from the curse put on his ancestor, who was both a rapist and accomplice to two murders, Mike has to complete the destruction of Sara Tidwell. The young men from town had already raped and murdered her, drowning her son and burying the two of them together, keeping quiet long enough that history seemed to have forgotten what happened to either, but Mike had to dig her up and destroy her bones.

The theme has much in common with *Thinner*: a non-white woman was killed by a white man, and the justice system did not touch the murderer or his accomplices. The marginalized group, this time a traveling group of Black musicians instead of "Gypsies," had no choice but to pack up and move on, and no recourse outside of a curse. Just as Billy Halleck stands in front of the Gypsies, including the family members of the woman he killed, and invokes his daughter as he pleads for Lemke to lift the curse, Mike centers his argument around a white girl. No matter what happened in the past and what his ancestor may have done, for Mike the concern is a single life, that of Kyra Devore, and he has to end the curse in order to let her live.

Like Billy Halleck, Mike shifts the attention from himself and onto a girl. Billy has been trying to blame his wife for the vehicular manslaughter, and Mike makes the same sort of argument: that yes, his ancestor may have done something terrible, but haven't the rest of them paid enough by now? There is no need for Mike to take responsibility for something that happened far back in his bloodline, before he was born, just as Billy does not want to take responsibility for the car accident caused, at least in his mind, by his wife. The white man wants the curse to be called off for his own sake, invoking a young—presumably blameless—girl, and the curse is only lifted or transferred after further violence.

Mike is, however, confronting a woman who has been a ghost for so long that she has gone insane, if the manner of her death had not already pushed her across that line. The only way to stop the multi-family, multigenerational curse is to completely destroy the person who has cast it. This is something Mike's dead wife, herself also a ghost, tells him, while at the same time informing him that Sara is no longer entirely human. When Mike has no idea how to act or how to prevent the threat posed by Sara Tidwell, since there are plenty of other dangers directed his way by living people, she points him toward dissolving Sara's bones with lye. Ultimate destruction of the physical remnants of her body seems to eliminate whatever hold Sara still had over the living world.

Like Dennis Guilder and Leigh Cabot in *Christine*, Mike does not go to the library in an attempt to find an explanation for what is happening to him or discover a ritual that might help rid him of the spirits haunting him. This may be in part because he only wants to dismiss Sara and not his wife, but it might also be because of what popular culture has taught so many late twentieth- and early twenty-first century Americans: that ghosts remain because they have unfinished business left on Earth. Sara lingers in her continued work to torment and kill the descendants of the men who tormented and killed both her and her son, and Mike's wife stays because she discovered this threat and wants to protect Mike. If Mike destroys Sara and eliminates that threat, his wife will go, too. With Kyra, though, Mike now has someone else to live for and his root justification for the final destruction of Sara Tidwell.

Short Stories and Violent Solutions

When King's characters are faced with the supernatural in a novel, they have plenty of space to come to terms with what is happening to them before they finally confront it. If they want to go to the library to search for similar cases from either their culture or outside cultures, they certainly have the time. In short stories, though, altercations happen much more quickly and characters are pushed into reactions at times without forethought. Reactions of destruction are thus also seen in these shorter forms. While some of them—reactions against zombies leading to destruction of the walking dead's brains, for example— rely on widespread popular culture, other characters are forced to face lesser-known threats and come up with their own solutions.

In "The Moving Finger" (collected in *Nightmares and Dreamscapes* 1993), for example, Harold Mitla discovers an extra-long finger poking up from the sink drain in his apartment bathroom. The finger apparently hides when his wife is in the room, since she makes no mention of it, although its presence is haunting enough that Harold tries to figure out how, exactly, he can survive without making use of his own bathroom until the finger goes away. It seems to be very real, interacting with its outside environment by popping out the plug and emerging with his wife's toothpaste stuck to the nail, although first it clearly has more joints than any human finger, and second ... who would believe him? What sort of creature would have a finger long and thin enough to reach its way through the plumbing of an apartment building?

The next day, after his wife has left for work, Harold has an idea and goes to the store for a bottle of drain cleaner. On impulse, he adds a set of electric hedge-clippers to his purchase, although Harold doubts that he will even need a second application of the drain cleaner. It advertises its strength in dissolving organic matter, after all, and is specifically formulated to find its way down pipes and past blockages.

Harold's wife might be gone, but his neighbors certainly hear the confrontation. The drain cleaner does not dissolve the finger as neatly and finally as the lye worked on the bones of Sara Tidwell, although it *does* harm the finger. Apparently angry and in pain, it shoots out of the sink to an alarming length and begins to fight back, grabbing onto Harold and burning him in places with the drain cleaner gel that sticks to it. It turns out that he does need the electric hedge clippers, after all, and he uses them to both cut off segments of the increasingly-long finger and then to make the pieces small enough to flush down the toilet.

By the time the policeman arrives, the batteries in the clippers are dead and the bathroom is full of gore, but no parts of the finger remain. Officer O'Bannion is under the assumption that Harold has murdered his wife, although the lack of a body is disconcerting. So is Harold, crammed in the space between the bathtub and the wall, covered in vomit and gore. During their conversation the officer hears something splashing in the toilet, and Harold suggests that perhaps he should refrain from lifting the lid and having a look. After all, "there are more fingers than one on a hand,"[6] and many drains in the bathroom. The story ends with O'Bannion deciding to open the lid.

Just as a short story leaves the characters little room for investigation and research, it is also a fine medium for a lady-or-the-tiger ending. There is no explanation for the finger, which Harold had hoped to destroy before one became necessary. It simply *is*, and has to be confronted immediately, before Harold either goes fully insane or dies from a burst bladder. The more compact form of these tales leaves little room for any sort of hesitation, even such a possibly useful one as a visit to the library. The threat emerges and must be eliminated at once.

The same is true of the living dead that rise in "Home Delivery"

7. Twisted, Silent Hulk

(collected in *Nightmares and Dreamscapes*). When pregnant widow Maddie Pace is confronted with the risen corpse of her late husband, she reacts instantly, destroying the brain. Maddie has an advantage over Harold in that she, at least, had seen enough on the news before Gennesault Island became cut off from the rest of the world to even expect Jack Pace's return, but the reaction is the same: destruction, in this case specific destruction of the brain.

In "Suffer the Little Children" (collected in *Nightmares and Dreamscapes*) elementary school teacher Miss Sidley realizes that her students have begun to change into unspeakable creatures. After an extended mental battle between elderly teacher and young children, she decides to take them one by one into the mimeograph room and shoot them in the head. Perhaps, like Maddie Pace, she has fixated on the ways that the inhuman or the undead can be stopped: by destroying the brain. Miss Sidley shot twelve children—or were they monsters?—in the head before being discovered, but the madness does not end with her suicide. Her psychiatrist seems to have caught her obsession and finds himself ever so carefully watching children, waiting for them to change. Whether or not he, too, eventually reaches for a gun is not told.

"I Am the Doorway" (collected in *Night Shift*) features a paralyzed former astronaut named Arthur who seems to have picked up some sort of parasite on his trip around Venus. Strange golden eyes have started emerging on his fingers as an alien presence starts to birth itself, causing him to murder at least two people. Arthur senses the intelligence in this deformity and clearly already knows the danger, so he douses his hands in kerosene and burns them, getting rid of a part of himself for the greater good. Unfortunately, seven years later, he wakes up to find that the golden eyes have returned, this time on his chest. As soon as Arthur finishes writing his story—typing it out using the hooks that have replaced his hands—he intends to commit suicide. Clearly the alien presence is still incubating inside him, so his last hope is to remove all of the growth medium instead of just some of it. Total destruction of the self should eliminate the threat completely, although he *is* at least leaving this strange story behind, just in case.

"Gray Matter" (collected in *Night Shift*) sends three men to investigate the physical condition of a fourth, who seems to have undergone some drastic changes since drinking a can of spoiled beer. That man's son reported that his father has started preferring the darkness, drinking his beer warm, and has broken the lightbulbs not only in their apartment but in the hallway outside. The boy finally panicked when he returned home early from school to observe his father-creature removing a putrefying dead cat from a hiding spot and having a snack.

Suddenly the recent spate of missing hobos also seems to be explained. When the three men approach the fourth, they discover that he has turned into some sort of gray-jelly creature—and that he seems to be dividing in two. This tale ends with one of the men reciting his times tables up to "32,768 times two is the end of the human race"[7] and waiting to see who, exactly, will come up the street: his friend with the gun, or the dividing gray thing.

Many of these characters have fewer pages than Harold Mitla in which to confront the nonhuman threat and they, like others in King's short stories, respond instinctively with the desire to destroy. In some cases it is unclear whether the threat is real or only in one character's head, and in many the actual, final destruction of the threat is questionable. The madness might be passed on even if the threat itself does not exist, or the golden eyes might return after a lengthy dormant period. Or, perhaps most common, the story cuts off before the return of the threat is made a certainty: waiting to see if there is another finger in the toilet, or if the friend with the gun was able to take down a blob that used to be a man.

Physical Destruction, Supernatural Endurance

While the majority of King's main characters fall into the "fight" category of the fight-or-flight response, the ones in this essay specifically aim to fight for complete destruction of the physical embodiment of the threat. Whether this means destroying a machine, a non-human living creature, or a person—even the self—the aim is to either beat up or disintegrate a physical object to the point where the ghost or demon inhabiting it can no longer function. Instead of attempting to destroy the supernatural element, these characters direct their attention toward the real-world containers for it.

On the one hand, this saves them from destruction during a ritual they barely understand or an attempt to utilize a religion in which they do not fully believe. Belief here is only a question when it comes to acknowledging the danger in the first place: recognizing that there is a car that can drive itself, or a man who can switch bodies, or an Outsider who can change faces, or any number of hazards that either seem mundane or are overlooked by others. Once the main characters assure themselves that the threat is real, they set themselves to eliminating it through physical destruction.

This solution is indeed based on real world experience. If a human's body is damaged enough, then that person dies and the soul departs from it. The supernatural is not necessarily a soul, but in each case it has a connection to a physical form. In many, it is that form that enacts the destruction, so destroying the car seems like it would logically remove Christine's ability to commit further murder. She, like many of the other threats, physically harms the people she selects. Taking away Christine's ability to drive, and therefore especially her ability to heal herself through driving, logically makes sense. The one exception to this is Sara Tidwell in *Bag of Bones*, who enacts her threat by means of a curse. Her own physical remains, however, still exist, and Mike Noonan learns that her power over him is indeed tied to those remains. Destroying the physical once again removes the threat.

For Mike Noonan, the danger seems to be over, just as Brady Hartsfield and two Outsiders are likewise apparently permanently destroyed. Christine and the vampires in *'Salem's Lot*, however, rise again, and the outcome of many of the short stories is left up to the reader's imagination. The knee-jerk, immediate reaction often spurred on by the immense horror of the situation does not always completely take care of the threat—but then, sometimes King's characters do not, in fact, want the supernatural to go away. Some of his characters like to keep it around for a while, or even to use it.

8

There Are Buicks Everywhere
Living with the Supernatural

Destruction is not the only option for confronting the supernatural, although it is high on the list when the supernatural is itself a force of destruction. If the supernatural is a nonhuman serial killer, piling up a body count as time passes, then of course it needs to be stopped as soon as possible. Crushing or otherwise ruining the physical embodiment of the threat might be the only solution that occurs to King's characters in time for them to act on it. Not all agents of the supernatural are constant threats, however, and even those that are cannot always be destroyed.

It is possible, in certain cases, for King's characters to simply choose to live with the supernatural. They can expand their minds enough to allow for its continued existence alongside the previously known and mundane, without even fully understanding it. Acceptance is not a common reaction, and not even one usually shared by all of the characters who know of the occurrence, because of that constant press of not understanding.

Other characters may find themselves giving in to the power of the supernatural event, usually in a way that is detrimental to their lives or their health. Isolated and pressed for time, they might simply not find themselves with any other options. The supernatural looms, presses in, and cannot easily be defeated, so it might be surrendered to. Still others seek not to destroy the supernatural, but to use it for their own gains and in spite of their personal lack of understanding.

Not attempting to destroy the supernatural is the least common reaction among King's characters largely because the supernatural is so frequently a threat. Many of King's supernatural entities kill children, for example, and the main characters are either children themselves or adults horrified at what they have discovered. The supernatural threat cannot be left alone to continue this dark work, and the only way to be sure that no more will die is to destroy the threat completely. It is rare for the supernatural to simply exist, without this sense of directed malevolence and at least a rudimentary cunning so that it is judged to be actively dangerous. If the supernatural seems to be passive, or at least without the intelligence to pursue victims, then it might not need to be destroyed.

Let It Be: *From a Buick 8*

One of King's more frustrating books is *From a Buick 8* (2002). Instead of an unsatisfactory explanation for the supernatural occurrence, there *is* no explanation. The great dissatisfaction for young Ned Wilcox is that the officers of his late father's former barracks, Troop D, have even stopped looking for one.

The object that Ned wants explained, like his father Curtis before him, looks something like a Buick 8 without exactly being one. It was left behind at a gas station by someone who may or may not have been a man, who then disappeared. The Buick that is not in fact a Buick was taken to the barracks and, generally, left to sit there. Although it was determined that the car was not in fact a car, made of materials that might not even be found on Earth, for the most part it was simply a stationary object, like a statue. What interested Curtis was the times when it became active.

Mostly because of Curtis, the Buick was monitored for temperature changes in its small garage, because this was one of the reliable signs that it would start flashing pulses of incredibly bright light. Curtis even made sure that Troop D had both a video camera handy and a call sign on the radio to alert him to when one of these light shows was occurring. At times, the Buick took people away—simply made them disappear—while at others, creatures emerged in, or from, its trunk. Most of these were dead on arrival, but one of them was lively enough to kill the station's dog. Curtis studied up on dissection and even filmed himself investigating one of the Buick's creatures, a bat-like thing whose innards would likely have stumped a fully trained biologist. The Buick seems to be a portal between worlds, albeit one that is slowly failing and fading.

After spending the day hearing all of these stories from various members of Troop D, Ned finds himself under the Buick's spell much as his father had been. Ned, though, nearly dies by being pulled through that portal himself, although the various members of Troop D who had spent their time recalling their parts of the story for Ned return to work in time to save Ned from becoming the Buick's next victim. They manage to work together to pull him back from that other world where they glimpse evidence that yes, the men who disappeared must have been pulled in themselves. A short time-jump to the epilogue reassures readers not only that Ned has been released from his obsession, but that the Buick itself seems to be falling apart.

From a Buick 8 is also one of the more difficult King novels to summarize because the present-day action is quite simple: those who have been at Troop D for a while now sit on a bench and relate a series of interconnected incidents that themselves have little narrative. The Buick was found, and these various things happened around it, but there is no explanation for *why* those things happened. Ned feels a personal investment in the Buick since his recently-deceased father had adopted it as his own personal mystery, and he voices his frustrations for the reader: why has no one tried to learn more? Why was Curtis the only one to study up on the side for his own dissections and investigations? Was no one else in Troop D enough of a rational scientist to want to document what was happening? The possibility for discovery seemed limitless, especially since the materials that composed the car were just as unknown and inexplicable as its takings and leavings.

It is incomprehensible to young Ned that so many people might be aware of the Buick's existence and its abilities and yet have collectively decided to simply ... let it be. To avoid it as much as possible, and to keep knowledge of its existence away from anyone who is not part of their closed group already, even though bringing in scientists or other experts might answer some of these questions. Ned firmly believes that this supernatural *thing* must be documented, explained, and carefully filed in the way all real-world objects and occurrences are. He wants to quantify the Buick scientifically and make it understandable in a way that so many members of Troop D have realized simply cannot be done.

In part, their approach to the Buick is like Dennis Guilder and Leigh Cabot's assessment of Christine: there is little use in attempting to research it, since the occurrence is so singular that library books—or outside experts—would be of no help. Even if Dennis and Leigh had somehow documented their own experiences with a troublesome car, Troop D would have dismissed it as an entirely different phenomenon than the one they were facing. Their Buick, for example, does not—and possibly cannot—move under its own power, and even though Curtis formed an immediate bond with its mysteries, the Buick shows no signs of wanting to please him. Even though there was no clear explanation for what made Christine into Christine, clearly a different one would be required for their otherworldly faux automobile.

What Troop D seeks, then, is not to explain or eliminate their supernatural object, but to contain it. They put it in a garage and keep it out of

8. There Are Buicks Everywhere

sight of others, away from the public eye, and anyone who *did* see it on the day of its driver's disappearance has either agreed to remain silent or dismissed any of the oddities. They simply want to keep it away from any potential victims and out of sight for when the next plant or animal appears out of it, especially since the still-living ones have proven to be incredibly dangerous. Troopers keep an eye on the thermometer in the shed to know when they have to be more on alert for one of the light shows, but otherwise the Buick is absorbed into their daily lives and falls mostly into the background.

Ned's youth—he is still a teenager when he hears the story, stuck between his father's death and going off to college—is presented as the main explanation for why his reaction to the Buick differs so much from that of the current sergeant, troopers, and dispatch. They want to minimize Ned's fascination, dismissing it in the wake of his grief, while forgetting that they have had all of Ned's life to personally grow accustomed to the presence of the Buick. Even though many of them did not share Ned's reaction to the Buick even when it was new and completely unknown, they take the same approach they once did with his father, arguing that there are so many real-world occurrences that need his attention instead. As an infant Ned himself was invoked against his father's fascination even during the Buick's lightshow heyday.

In part it is this constant dismissal and downplay of Ned's curiosity that allows the Buick to go to work on him and call him to come into the shed. Time and again the various storytellers invoke the fact that curiosity killed the cat, but satisfaction brought him back, and their various vignettes do nothing to satisfy Ned. They have each, in their own way and their own time, come to terms with realizing that nothing will answer their questions about the Buick. Having never been as curious and caught up as either father or son Wilcox, they believe they can simply dismiss Ned's questions by telling him that they have already said all they can. They do not feel the same frustration with unanswerable questions, and although they do return to the barracks in time to save Ned's life when he attempts to satisfy his curiosity, all of them *do* have to return. They had left, thinking there was nothing left to ponder and no curiosity could remain. The Buick is inexplicable, yes, but teenage Ned Wilcox is almost just as foreign to them.

Troop D treats the Buick as an object so foreign that there can be no comparison and no possible connection to anything else that has ever existed in the world. They do not go searching for other false objects that might also function as doorways, and no library books fairly jump into their hands to help them in their search. The Buick exists, they have taken possession of it, and the most they can do is try to keep it from further interfering with their concept of the "real" world. It may make the temperature drop and emit flashing lights, but the troopers have learned from their past interactions with it and feel confident that they can handle what comes next. They understand enough to keep the danger contained, and with that, they are satisfied.

The epilogue in which Ned both observes that the Buick finally seems to be falling apart and demonstrates that his curiosity is no longer dangerous occurs only after he has been inside the Buick and glimpsed that other world. His curiosity was strong enough—and his reasons for not being suicidal much smaller than his father's had ever been— to push him that far, so he has more answers now than any of the others had before. Although satisfying that curiosity almost killed Ned and Troop D's sergeant, Ned *did* get some answers. The epilogue gives him distance from his father's death, as well as time to sort out what, exactly, happened when he entered the Buick. There has been time, too, for the other troopers to work on Ned and reassure him with their same old Buick mantra: that is all we know, and it is enough. If the paint cannot be scratched and the thing cannot be destroyed, all that is left is to wait it out. In the final pages, it seems as though Troop D will be able to manage that: not destroying it or understanding it but outlasting it.

All for Nothing: *11/22/63*

The premise of *11/22/63* (2011) revolves around a strange sort of doorway with one side existing in the pantry of Al's Diner and the other always emerging into September 9, 1958, at 11:58 a.m. Returns to 2011 occur exactly two minutes after the time traveler left, no matter how long he stayed in the past, and this strange doorway has been at the diner for well over a decade by the time Al tells high school English teacher Jake Epping about its existence. What Al wants the younger, healthier Jake to do is walk through the mysterious phenomenon, take up residence in the past, and stop the assassination of John Fitzgerald Kennedy.

Al warns Jake that this task will not be easy. The past *can* be changed, as Al has proven himself with a test case, but it does not *want* to be changed. Added to this is the fact that each trip to the past is a perfect reset. Not only has Al been able to buy the same meat over and over again and therefore keep his prices down, but Jake's first exploratory visit to 1958 has undone Al's own longer attempt to conclusively identify Lee Harvey Oswald as the lone shooter. On the plus side, any mistakes that might be made can easily be undone with another trip back in time.

8. *There Are Buicks Everywhere* 145

But, Al argues, Jake is young enough that he *could* go back and try it a second time if the obdurate past prevented him from stopping the assassination on his first attempt.

Al, after he fully grasped the implications of what he found in his diner's pantry, and then Jake, whose hand was forced by Al, both want to use the supernatural gateway in order to change the past. At first Jake only has a vague notion of what preventing JFK's assassination might mean moving past November 1963, but Al first lived through many of the events and then took time to study up on them. He embarked on his own extended stay in the past by having prepared himself a notebook full of information he knew he would find useful, and Al passes this on to Jake and forces the younger man's hand. With far less time to mentally prepare himself for spending years in the past, when his own parents were small children, Jake takes up Al's quest and does what he can to first make sure that Oswald was the man who needed to be stopped, and then to save JFK's life.

The long and the short of it comes down to the fact that, while the obdurate past *can* be changed, powers above and beyond Jake's imagining tell him that he should stop trying. Jake *does* manage to prevent the assassination, but this comes at the expense of his fiancée's life, and he is more than willing to run from Texas back to Maine in order to trigger another reset and a second chance at a happy future, in the past, with Sadie. The new guardian of the odd portal tells Jake in no uncertain terms that he needs to stop messing with the past and, when he manages to make it back to 2011, he finds that the world has changed utterly and completely—but not for the better. Absolutely nothing Jake has done has seemed to change anything for the better except perhaps to give Jackie Kennedy her husband for a while longer.

Although Jake has spent hundreds of pages living in the past, creating a life for himself and attempting to save any number of people from their less-than-desired fates, he is forced to make one last trip into the past in order to reset everything and therefore undo every action of his last five years. All of the pain and the struggle, either against the obdurate past or to simply survive as someone completely out of his depth in so many situations, has to be simply undone. He cannot save the many people he set out to rescue from death, and he cannot better Sadie's life with his presence, either. Even sparing JFK backfired and dumped him out into a post-apocalyptic 2011 that makes a clear argument to let the president stay dead. Jake's entire attempt—indeed, the entire book—ends up being pointless and erased as Jake returns to 2011 for the final time without saving anyone.

Jake Epping at the end of the book bears a strong resemblance to

Jake Epping at the beginning: a divorced man, living alone, teaching high school English and sighing over a failed relationship. In the beginning it is his divorce that plagues him, although his ex-wife is gradually replaced by his new relationship with Sadie and the trauma of knowing that his mission to stop JFK's assassination is what led to Sadie's dying in his arms. When Jake reset the timeline the final time he made sure that she would be nowhere near Oswald on the day of the assassination, but he also took himself out of her life and was therefore not around to help Sadie through the aftermath of her own failed marriage. Jake ends up going to see Sadie in the twenty-first century and sharing a dance with her in a final scene likely meant to indicate some sort of emotional closure for Jake, who could use something positive at that point in his life. His greatest quest and most fantastic adventure had to be erased completely.

As the only person on Earth to know what happened to him, and the only one still alive to know that the strange portal in Al's diner ever existed, Jake is left much in the same position as young Ned Wilcox. Ned wants to know the point and purpose of the Buick; Jake is left pondering the point and purpose of that portal to the past. Why should it exist at all if it is not meant to be used, or if every use, no matter how small, ultimately does damage? Jake understands little enough about the time period he enters when he uses the portal and even less about the actual phenomenon itself. By the time someone starts to explain it to him, Jake has spent more than five years chasing Al's quest and only recently saw his fiancée die. This is not the proper time to tell one Jake Epping that he needs to use the portal only enough to change everything back to the way it was, without making any final alterations.

This emphasizes one of Al's initial lessons—that the past does not *want* to be changed—and also makes so many of Jake's actions feel entirely futile. Even Al's short trips to the past to buy another few pounds of cheap hamburger were doing damage he did not see and would not have understood, so Jake's attempts to save numerous lives have a wider impact. Yet all of it—his heroism and suffering—is pointless. It comes to nothing. The Jake Epping at the end of the book has simply lost more than the earlier Jake, and the only knowledge he gains is that he never should have tried in the first place.

Forced to Comply: "The Things They Left Behind" and *Insomnia*

Much like *11/22/63* attempts to confront the momentous occasion of JFK's assassination, the short story "The Things They Left Behind"

8. There Are Buicks Everywhere

(collected in *Just After Sunset*) is a response to what happened on September 11, 2001. The main character, Scott Staley, was not in his office in the World Trade Center when the Towers fell, but his fellow employees were. Scott's survivor's guilt has been plaguing him but comes fully to the front of his life when he returns to his apartment in August 2002 to find some distinctive memorabilia from his dead friends. He immediately connects each item to a former coworker even in his shock at finding those things—which should have been part of the wreckage—still in perfect condition.

Scott thinks about trying to get some professional help but living in New York less than a year after 9/11 means a long wait before he could conceivably actually get an appointment. At first, simply stunned, he hangs on to the items before having a moment of awareness and questioning why he should continue to do so. His attempt to throw them out, however, results in returning to find them back in his apartment just as they had been before. The items, and the dead people they once belonged to, even seem to speak to him. When he collects them up to store them away in a closet instead of throwing them out, they do at least stay where he put them, although the whispering voices continue.

His next move is to do his best to ignore the fact that the items exist. Scott takes to escaping his own apartment as much as possible, as well as to avoiding even thinking about the trinkets of his dead friends. They haunt him, though, and in November he finally breaks down and talks about them to one of his neighbors, a woman who lives in a nearby apartment but whom he barely knows. She, at least, has the presence of mind to agree to meet with this near-stranger in a public place, especially since her husband is out of town. Even though Scott had yet to tell her how mysterious his story would be, the desperation in his eyes when he asks to talk to her is spooky enough.

Their conversation begins with discussing where they each were on 9/11, and how Scott was only able to sit across from her because he took the day off on a whim. He then tells her about the objects that appeared in his apartment and their meaning to his late coworkers and shows her one of them: a penny in a Lucite cube. The neighbor, still humoring him a bit, asks about his survivor's guilt and suggests that someone must be playing a trick on him. She even demands that he give her the Lucite cube, telling Scott she will put it in the safe in her apartment so that *this* item, at least, will not come back to him. They part ways amiably enough, and she believes she is only humoring her poor neighbor who had the luck to survive when his friends did not.

Three days later she rings his doorbell to return the Lucite cube, which has told her more about its owner than Scott himself even knew.

Utterly shaken by the experience—although at least no longer convinced Scott was simply experiencing a strange form of survivor's guilt—she gives the cube back and wishes to never see him again. Scott, however, has something new to think about: giving the cube to his neighbor had been wrong, but there might be a proper someone to receive each of the items in his closet. Slowly, he begins to pass the objects on to the families of his dead friends, confident that these will not return, but also wondering if more items might show up, in time.

Even though the assortment of items—Lolita sunglasses, conch shell, whoopee cushion—disturbed Scott, they did not frighten him the same way they did his neighbor. He rationalizes that, since he knew the people to whom they belonged, he did not himself need convincing that they had been real, or that they had died on September 11, crouching beneath their desks and simply wishing they could live long enough to be able to mow their lawns again. While Scott's neighbor had been shaken up by the terrorist attacks, she had been across the country at the time and would not have been in the buildings that day anyway. Scott, who honestly should have been, has been battling his own feelings of guilt and wonder at his premonition to take that day off for almost a year before the items appear.

The physical items ground him in his memories of his coworkers, turning a national tragedy into the personal. The whoopee cushion, for example, would be meaningless if not for the connection between it and its owner—and the fact that Scott cannot apparently throw it away. It is a cheap joke item, but it conjures up memories of his friend and concentrates that feeling of loss.

The items also give Scott a new sense of direction, once he realizes what he is supposed to do with them. He does not attempt to figure out where they might have come from or why they picked him beyond the fact that he knows enough about their former owners to be able to return them to their families, and this is a task that he actually seems to enjoy. It is not penance, exactly, for surviving when the others died, but Scott considers that there can be "compensations"[1] for things like loss and pain. Once he figures out what he is supposed to *do* with the objects that suddenly appear, Scott actually wants more of them to come to him, in spite of the whispering voices and painful memories.

Scott is forced to do what the objects—or the unknown force behind the objects—wants him to do simply because they will not leave him alone. He is forced to take action or go mad, but Scott also has to figure out for himself what that action should be. The objects appear without explanation or instruction. Ralph Roberts of *Insomnia* is likewise driven to comply with wishes of more powerful forces, in large part because he, too, does not receive a complete explanation for what is happening. Ralph and his friend Lois are forced along an increasingly tight timeline dictated by two non-humans who, though apparently working on the side of good, either do not want to explain the full importance of what is happening, or who themselves do not in fact completely understand.

After his wife's death, Ralph finds himself suffering from insomnia to the point where he seems to start hallucinating. It turns out that the two non-human guides, nicknamed Clotho and Lachesis, have been causing Ralph's sleep troubles so that he can move "up" the levels of existence enough to help them. They are working in opposition to a figure called the Crimson King and hope to prevent a death the Crimson King is attempting to cause. It takes most of the book, though, for Ralph and Lois to get this much out of their two new acquaintances, and they realize that one of them has to risk their own life in order to prevent an agent of the Crimson King from flying a small plane into the local civic center.

On one of their tangents, though, Ralph has been shown another facet of the future: not about the boy so important to Clotho and Lachesis, but about a girl important to Ralph and Lois. That girl's fate is to be hit by a car and killed a few years from now, and this is where Ralph decides to use the powers that are, in fact, attempting to use him. Ralph bargains with the two little bald men, telling them that he will save their chosen boy if he is allowed to save Natalie's life in the future. The cost will be his own life. Although Clotho and Lachesis are not able to make such a promise themselves, a power greater than they are—also likely on the side of good, or at least in opposition to the Crimson King—agrees to let this happen. Ralph does indeed stop the plane from crashing into the civic center, and for a while he forgets that he ever encountered such beings as Clotho and Lachesis. As the time of Natalie's death approaches, however, the insomnia returns, and he is able to do what he asked: save Natalie's life, even though the result is his own death.

Like Scott Staley, Ralph does not fully understand what is happening to him. He is able to research insomnia well enough, but every cure he tries fails to work. This is because his insomnia is caused not by any natural reason, but by the same power that directs Clotho and Lachesis on their mission at their own higher level. Ralph and Lois understand that their lack of sleep was necessary in order to temporarily change them enough so that they, too, could go "up" levels of reality, but they do not understand exactly what this is supposed to mean. Likewise Clotho and Lachesis resist answering any of their questions about what it is they are actually supposed to do, only giving up information about the specially chosen boy at the very end, when it seems Ralph and Lois might exercise their free will to say no. Refusal, according to the two little men, would mean the end of all existence everywhere, on every level.

Because Clotho and Lachesis—and their bosses—are so stingy with information, and because they do not have the same luxury of time Scott has in order to experiment and see what happens, the humans caught up in this battle on a level other than their own almost refuse to do what is being ordered of them. Ralph and Lois do not understand, and Clotho and Lachesis have wasted so much time, purposefully, so that they do not have to answer questions. Ralph is only convinced to go along when he sees that he, personally, has something to gain from his participation, and after he is given reassurance that his bargain will stand.

Clotho and Lachesis are not fully able to explain why the life of this one boy is so important to them, but the life of Natalie—his neighbor's daughter and his own adopted granddaughter—is important enough to Ralph for him to both risk his life on the day of the impending civic center disaster, and then to give it in exchange for hers. The boy is a stranger and his fate is not important, but Natalie is personal. Ralph needs that extra nudge in order to submit to the will of the supernatural and make full use of the strange powers he has been temporarily given, no matter how panicked Clotho and Lachesis might feel. Unlike Scott, Ralph is angered at being singled out and used in such a way, and completion of his task is far from being enough of a reward. Ralph demands more from the powers he does not understand, and, in their desperation, they grant it.

Giving In: "Trucks" and "The Raft"

Instead of resisting in even a small way, some of King's characters simply ... surrender. The short story "Trucks," collected in *Night Shift*, presents readers with a world where vehicles have come to life. From their trapped position at a truck stop, the characters see trucks, cars, and construction equipment running around the parking lot without anyone at the wheel. The few people who were either too slow to make it to the building when the cars came to life, or who attempted to escape, have been killed. At first the small group of survivors feels relatively secure in spite of the diner's plate glass windows, since supplies were recently restocked, and they hunker down for a siege. When the power goes out, their situation grows even more dire. Adding to the question of their survival is a message one of the trucks blares using Morse code informing the people that, if they come out to pump gas,

8. *There Are Buicks Everywhere* 151

their lives will be spared. The survivors' initial resistance to the idea of being their slaves is overcome when a bulldozer starts to tear the building down around them.

The main character takes the first shift, gassing up vehicles until the pumps run dry and then refilling them from a tanker truck. He ponders the helplessness of the situation, from the fact that so much of the world is paved—and there are off-road vehicles for the parts that are not—to the fact that, when he sees jets pass overhead, he cannot be sure that there are people inside them. If people *can* escape back to the caves, then eventually the trucks will run out of gas for good or be in need of repairs that they cannot give themselves, but that does not help him now in these first days of this mysterious vehicular uprising. Right now he and the other two remaining survivors have to pump gas.

The immediacy of the short story gives the characters little time to think about what they should do. Those who begin the tale in the diner either had pulled in for some lunch before the crisis began or have quickly gotten off the expressway when they saw a large truck driving deftly enough to flick smaller cars off the road without making itself turn turtle. They are all still caught in a state of disbelief, from the man who suddenly bolts from the relative safety of the truck stop only to be hit by a car and left to die in a ditch, to the teenage girl who keeps insisting, "We *made* them!"[2] as though this will stop them in their tracks. An earlier conversation about why, exactly, this is happening was cut short because there does not seem to be an explanation—or, at least, not one that will help the survivors bring a quick halt to what is going on outside. The cars are moving on their own, and they know how to kill people if the people will not help them, and that is enough. The people will likely die soon anyway without food or water but, in the meantime, they have to accept that the trucks have come to life and need fuel. If they want to survive, they will have to obey.

The situation as the main character sees it is also largely hopeless. The vehicles that patiently line up for him need fuel, yes, and will eventually need further maintenance, but they are far less fragile than a human body. He dreams of a future fifty or sixty years in the future when all of these machines are rusting hulks, but immediately follows it up with a vision of assembly lines manned by people who work until they drop. Presumably the trucks will have to negotiate the continuation of the human race, at least to an extent, if they want the manufacture of future trucks to be controlled by people and not fully mechanized, but all of that is far in the future and likely not something the main character will personally witness. He is stuck here at this truck stop with little water and food, pumping gas until he dies.

"The Raft," collected in *Skeleton Crew*, places its four main characters in a situation similar to those who were caught in the truck stop when their vehicles came to life. College students Randy and Deke, along with their girlfriends Rachel and LaVerne, decide on the spur of the moment to see if the summer raft has been left out on the lake even though fall is already progressing. They act on the idea immediately, the young men egging each other on, and pile into a car without any further preparation. When they get to the deserted beach and see the raft still out there, all four strip down to their underwear and swim out in spite of the cold.

From his position on the raft, Randy sees something strange on the water that appears to be following the girls. He and Deke pull Rachel and LaVerne up onto the platform just as the strange, perfectly circular oil slick reaches them. A round of male posturing and female hurt feelings follows until Rachel, entranced by what she sees in the strange black patch, reaches out to touch it. The thing pulls her in, dissolves her, and appears to have grown in size. Deke is its next victim as it reaches up to grab him between the cracks in the planking of the raft, slowly pulling him down through the impossibly small gap. It is only later that Randy realizes he should have swum to shore while the oil slick was distracted.

Now stuck with a panicking LaVerne, Randy knows that they cannot lie down to sleep because the thing will grab them the way it did Deke. Trapped without food, water, or even their clothes, the pair become tired, hungry, and incredibly cold. At one point, apparently giving in to instinct, they have sex, but that comes to a horrific end when Randy sees that LaVerne's hair is in the water. Rather than fight the sentient oil slick for her life, he shoves her over the side of the raft as soon as it starts working its way up toward her face. Then he is left alone, with no one to stand watch while he sleeps.

Like the people in the truck stop, Randy is utterly cut off from outside help. The beach is closed, the raft usually brought in by this time of the year, and there is no one around to hear him call for help. Even if someone *did* hear, it would be difficult for him to convey the issue: although he was able to swim out to the raft just fine, he cannot return because of an oil slick that maintains its perfectly round shape except when it is working its way under the raft to devour his friends.

There is no explanation for the thing, and thus no way to discover its weakness. Had Randy and his friends been attacked by a known supernatural entity, they might have been able to form a plan, even if caught completely unawares. Other monsters, especially pop culture movie monsters, come with built-in weaknesses that they might have been able to exploit. The strange oil slick has no name and no easy reference, and the situation quickly becomes dire. Unlike with the sentient trucks, there is no offer of

8. There Are Buicks Everywhere 153

an action any of them can take in order to prolong their lives. Randy, left alone and without food, water, or shelter, finally decides to let the thing hypnotize him and dives right into it, opting as much as he can for suicide on his own terms rather than death following exhaustion.

In both "Trucks" and "The Raft," the characters are first isolated before being forced to make their decision. There is no way to seek outside guidance. All radio stations are static in "Trucks," and the college kids in "The Raft" end up with nothing but their wet underwear in the middle of a lake that has been abandoned with the retreat of summer. None of them have the luxury of taking their problems to the library or asking questions of an expert, and similarly neither group is faced with something they think they can explain. The situations are not any they have seen before, in real life or in the movies, and they have to choose how to act based solely on their experience.

The main characters have the added stress and benefit of watching the supernatural interact with other humans before making their own decisions. The nameless main character of "Trucks" at first tries to prepare the group for a long stay inside the diner, leading a mission to get more water from the customer bathrooms, before the arrival of a bulldozer threatens their shelter and ruins any possible plan to simply hunker down. In fact, his plan and his idea to enlist others to help him Molotov cocktail some of the vehicles seem to make things worse. Although he does not come out and take responsibility for some of the others' deaths in the course of the short story, they could certainly be looming over him as he decides to be the first to obey and pump gas, thereby preserving himself and the other two remaining survivors for at least a little while longer. His hand has been forced, and even the other two will be convinced to choose life.

Randy's situation is more dire because the danger does not offer him a way out. Granted, the oil slick seems to be isolated, threatening only this one lake in Pennsylvania as opposed to being a world-wide phenomenon, but the horizons of Randy's world shrink drastically to only the raft and the people on it. The learning curve is steep: Rachel's death teaches them that they should not look at the oil slick for too long, or touch it, and Deke's provides the further information that the thing can get them through the gaps in the raft's planking. Presumably a boat would be able to rescue them, as long as no one touches the water and it has no leaks, but the lake is deserted and no one knew where the four of them were going. Rescue is out of the question, and Randy chooses between two options: death eventually when he drops his guard, or death now as he chooses it.

King frequently isolates his characters when he positions them to fight the supernatural, but the format of the short story adds another limitation: that of time. While characters in his novels have the luxury of waiting or even choosing not to make a decision, those in his short stories are confronted with the supernatural in situations that need more immediate responses. In "Trucks" and "The Raft," the final response is one of surrender: giving in to the supernatural instead of attempting to continue on with life as they previously knew it.

Try to Control It: "Fair Extension," *Pet Sematary* and *The Tommyknockers*

There are, however, other ways to accept the presence and reality of the supernatural that do not result in enslavement—and approaching death—or imminent death. David Streeter of "Fair Extension" (in *Full Dark, No Stars*) manages to use his own supernatural encounter to not only extend, but improve, his life. Although he first resists the idea that a strange man setting up a stand behind the airport could, in fact, do all he has promised, a week's free trial from George Elvid is enough to convince Streeter to make his deal with the devil.

The terms of the contract are understandable enough. Elvid demanded Streeter name the person he hates the most in the world, and that person happens to be Tom Goodhugh: rich, handsome, with an amazing wife—Streeter's own high school girlfriend, in fact—and three beautiful children. Goodhugh is supposed to be Streeter's best friend, but Streeter trades a hypertension pill and fifteen percent of his annual income to have his cancer removed at Goodhugh's expense. Streeter does not get full information on what, exactly, will happen to his best friend, but he knows his own tumors have shrunk, and that is enough for the start. Besides, the deal has been made.

Over the course of the following years the men's situations change places. Streeter returns to good health, prospers at work, and watches his children soar to amazing success in their chosen careers. Streeter's life and relationships, including his marriage, have never been better. Goodhugh, on the other hand, watches his life dissolve in front of his eyes as he and his family undergo one tragedy after another. It reaches the point where Goodhugh sobs to his "best friend" that he must have offended God and put himself on par with Job. Streeter, however, is not content, not even after all Goodhugh has suffered. When his wife points out a shooting star at the end of the story and laughs at the thought that there would be anything she would want at this point in her life, Streeter simply "wished for more."[3]

8. There Are Buicks Everywhere

Streeter is meant, in a way, to come across as another Carrie White. While Tom Goodhugh was the popular one of the pair, Streeter wrote his essays for him and made sure he kept his grades up enough to stay on the football team in high school. When Streeter's girlfriend fell in love with Goodhugh instead, the two of them even came clean to him—and went on to have a happy, fulfilling marriage. Streeter tried to get back at his "friend" by standing up for him at the bank in order to get him a loan to start his own business, which then surprised everyone—Streeter included—by being successful, at least until after Elvid interfered. Goodhugh's relationships with his children were better than Streeter's with his own, and so on and so forth, until Streeter was simply second-best in everything. No matter what he had, Goodhugh had it one step better. Apparently Streeter never heard that comparison was the thief of joy, or perhaps he was simply happier feeling as though life had shafted him, at least until he was provided with a miraculous alternative.

The life that Streeter had at the beginning of the story was the one he had personally worked for. He even admits to Elvid that he is happy in his marriage, even if Goodhugh once stole his girl, and that, other than the cancer and his envy of his best friends, things are rather good. When left to his own devices, Streeter friend that envy and cosseted it, neither showing it outwardly nor ending his friendship with Goodhugh. It is only when offered the deal with Elvid that Streeter actually does anything about his feelings, and what he does is very little: steals one of Goodhugh's pills and promises Elvid an annual payout.

Everything good that happens to Streeter and his family from there on out is presented as happening for the same reason that the Goodhugh family's fortune takes a dive: because of Elvid's deal. It is not because Elvid has inspired confidence in Streeter or because Streeter has finally decided to shed his unhelpful negative feelings. Rather, Streeter doubles down on that envy and thrives on the schadenfreude he feels at the slow destruction of everyone and everything Tom Goodhugh holds dear. Along with the rest of his flaws, Streeter is not a self-starter. Finding out that the devil hangs out on the airport extension and offers such futures for small investments is the best thing that could ever have happened to Streeter who is, after all, not a very good man.

It is worse, perhaps, that no one realizes this about Streeter. Goodhugh remains his friend throughout his own slow descent and is happy that Streeter continues to hang around long after many of his other friends have departed. Streeter is annoyed that one of Goodhugh's tragedies means he and his wife have to return from their Hawaiian trip, but Mrs. Streeter does not seem to see this side of her husband. She is simply happy, and believes that he, too, is happy, instead of forever bubbling with envy or bitter satisfaction. In this way he differs from Carrie, whose only wish was to escape unnoticed. When she discovered her telekinesis and experienced her flashpoint moment at the prom, she lashed out in hot blood and was done—and dead—hours later. Streeter is sick when Elvid makes him the offer, yes, and has been nursing his grudge against Goodhugh longer than Carrie has been alive, but he also continues to make his annual payments over the course of *years* and the continuing destruction of Goodhugh's children, who never did anything to Streeter. His reaction is cold and only continues to grow but, unlike Carrie's telekinetic power, there is no self-destruct. Streeter can, it seems, continue on indefinitely, for as long as his own health lasts.

A perhaps more understandable personal recourse to using the supernatural in spite of the less-than-optimal results comes in the form of Louis Creed in *Pet Sematary*. Unlike Streeter, Louis does not face a one-and-done sort of situation. He is first introduced to the power of the Micmac burying grounds when his neighbor Jud Crandall helps him bury his daughter's dead cat, and even though the cat returns with a drastically changed personality and always smelling like grave dirt, Louis is not convinced to let the idea go entirely. When his young son, Gage, is run down by a truck in the same road, Louis schemes to bury Gage up in the mysterious plot of land, as well. Even Jud's story about a man who did the same with his own son does not stop Louis, who attempts to apply reason to the situation: the young man in Jud's story had been dead for much longer than Gage.

Louis has the sympathetic advantage over Streeter because he is now the father of a dead child, struggling with both a grieving wife and daughter, attempting to make it through his son's funeral and the sympathy and condemnation of other mourners. His wife, Rachel, has her own phobias about death because of a terrible childhood experience, and Louis is too caught up in his own grief and feelings of responsibility—he missed his grab on Gage's jacket right before the boy was killed—to properly support them. Louis in fact sends his wife and daughter back to Chicago with Rachel's parents, promising to join them soon, ostensibly as a sign of forgiveness to his accusatory in-laws and an attempt to help Rachel and Ellie heal. Really Louis just wants the house to himself so he can go grave-robbing, first digging Gage up and then burying him again in the mysterious place beyond the deadfall.

At the time of this decision, Louis' grief is both immediate and overwhelming. He is in no position to listen to Jud or to think logically. All of his concentration focuses on how there is a way to make Gage no longer dead. He might come back as something different, the way the cat did, but at least he would *be* back. Louis, unlike Streeter, does not have

8. There Are Buicks Everywhere

time to think about this or consider the implications. Like the characters in "Trucks" or "The Raft," he has a strict timeline which is reinforced by Jud's story: the longer Gage's body is left to rot, the less likely it seems that he will be able to return as something resembling himself.

There is also the narrative's implication that Louis is not at that point entirely in control of his own decisions, grieving or not. The burying grounds, or maybe the Wendigo, has a hold on him and is working to call him back. In his current state, Louis can hardly resist. Then, after Gage returns, the grief deepens: Louis is forced to kill his daughter's cat and his own son before finding himself confronted with his wife's dead body. At this point he has lost all sanity and, presumably still in the grip of the burying grounds, immediately takes Rachel over the deadfall to bury her, as well, once again arguing that it should work *this* time because less time has passed between death and burial. Whether or not Rachel returns to cause the same sort of damage Gage did—in spite of his small physical form, he managed to murder Jud as well as his mother, and presumably would have continued his homicidal tendencies—is left to the reader's imagination, since the book ends with Rachel's return.

Louis has been haunted by death and the old Micmac burying ground for most of the book prior to Gage's being run down in the road. Between of his own work as a physician, Ellie's natural curiosity about death, Rachel's pathological aversion to the subject, and the deaths of both the family cat and Jud's wife, Louis has been confronted with the subject on numerous occasions throughout the book. He has had visions and felt the call of the burying grounds multiple times prior to Gage's death, and the sudden grief impedes his ability to fight against it any longer. Louis *has* to use the power of that place, wherever it comes from and however imperfectly it works, because his sanity is already teetering. Having to face the fact that his beloved son will never have another birthday is just too much.

Unlike Streeter, Louis is not consciously directing harm at someone in exchange for what he wants. What he wants is in fact the opposite: to stop the hurting and the destruction that has been done to his family. If the ritual means Gage returns, even if the boy comes back changed, then he can heal his family and stop Rachel and Ellie from grieving. The fact that Gage returns murderous was not something he entirely anticipated, although the cat's newfound appetite for tearing apart small animals might have been a warning. Louis did not think that he would have to sacrifice his neighbor and his wife when he brought Gage back, although it is unclear whether this knowledge would have stopped him. Certainly by the time he carries Rachel's body toward the deadfall he is past all reason.

King gives readers much more time with Louis and his family prior to Louis' attempt to harness the power of the old burying grounds. Part of this is because *Pet Sematary* is a novel and "Fair Extension" a 32-page novella, so there is not room enough to actually follow Streeter's life prior to his encounter with Elvid. Part of this is also likely due to the fact that Streeter has primarily been a man of inactivity, stewing and feeding his envy of his best friend without actually doing anything about it. From the start of his own story, Louis is positioned as trying to do the best thing for his family, taking a new job and moving them far from the big city where the four of them can spend more time together.

Louis' attempt to use the Micmac burying ground is borne of this same desire to help his family. When Streeter accepts Elvid's offer, he likewise continues something he has already started: his hatred for Tom Goodhugh. The temptation of the supernatural works on each of them in different ways, highlighting their own mortal desires. Streeter continues to be a lazy, greedy, spiteful man who hides the worst aspects of his character from his friends and family. Louis, however, was at least on some level attempting to help his family, trying to remedy the situation by bringing his son back to life, and this misguided altruistic desire is what makes his story the more tragic.

The same misguided altruism is shown in Bobbi Anderson's arguments that the spaceship she has accidently stumbled over in *The Tommyknockers* should be fully uncovered. She may or may not actually believe in what she says when she tells her friend Jim Gardener that this could be the end of his nuclear worries and the introduction of clean energy, but that is how Bobbi sells it to Gard. She wants to continue uncovering the spaceship, allowing more and more of its surface to come into contact with Earth's atmosphere so that she and the residents of Haven can continue "Becoming." This process includes physical transformation, telepathy, and a strange capacity to invent new items and objects that run off batteries.

Bobbi's first creations are used to take her house off the grid and supercharge her ailing water heater, but the new gadgets grow to help with digging up the enormous spaceship and patrolling the borders of the town in order to keep Haven safe. Those who live in the village are eventually unable to leave it, since Earth's atmosphere is now poison to them, and the visitors who cannot be kept away likewise suffer nausea and loose teeth along with their own brilliant insights. When outsiders leave, however, those ideas fade and keep them relatively safe from the influence of the Tommyknockers.

Whether or not they truly intend to use their new powers for good, the residents of Haven embrace their Becoming. It is not always a happy process—one woman manages to electrocute her husband and herself after she discovers he is having an affair—but it is a highly productive one. The villagers even keep an eye on each other, carefully disarming the inventions of one man who has gone insane before they can destroy the whole town. The frantic need to invent is, however, apparently only a phase of the Becoming, and seems to subside as time passes.

One of the larger creations is a machine that can replicate the atmosphere created by the ship. Since they are digging up the ship in order to free it—although the plans beyond that point are never specified—there will come a time when it is not sitting in Bobbi's backyard, producing the air they now breathe. This machine comes in handy at the end of the book, at least for a while, after the ship is indeed freed and removed not only from Haven, but from Earth itself. The villagers were thus at least able to use their Becoming to look out for themselves a little bit, as long as the winds remained relatively calm.

The vast majority of the residents of Haven completely gave in to their Becoming, embracing all aspects of these changes. Although some managed to slip outside the village before the changes could become too drastic—and knew death would await them if they returned—the town constable, Ruth McCausland, managed to hold on to enough of her essential self to blow up the church steeple in an apparent attempt to warn outsiders of what was happening. The construction of her bomb was similar to the other inventions her fellow Havenites were creating, and the telepathy in the town meant that Ruth was the only insider to die as a result of her bomb. Unfortunately those who came to investigate her mysterious death also met their own ends because to let them live would be to threaten Haven.

Although the town was not able to come together to stop Ruth from sending her signal, all of Haven united during the climax of the book to stop Gard from taking control of the ship. Individual concerns were forgotten as they gathered up their most dangerous inventions and headed for Bobbi's place to protect the ship and therefore their new selves. By giving themselves over completely to the Becoming, they tied their own fates to the ship and to each other, losing themselves in groupthink and condemning themselves to share whatever future awaited them.

Destruction and Survival

Even the most passive and least dangerous supernatural objects found in King's works, such as the Buick 8, are not entirely tame. The Buick sits there *most* of the time as an apparently inanimate object, but during the few moments when it *is* active, it can kill. Two men were known to be sucked into it, presumably to their deaths, while it attempted taking a third, and one of the creatures that emerged from its trunk killed a dog before the people could in turn kill it. But, because these instances of strange activity are few and far between, and the people who find themselves in possession of the Buick believe they can now track the active periods and take precautions against them, the Buick is allowed to simply sit. The question of whether or not it *could* be destroyed is laid aside because of a simple lack of desire.

Leaving a supernatural thing unchallenged in this way, however, leads to destruction—not of it, but of people. Although the Buick's apparent final attempt is thwarted, the other stories show how hungry the supernatural is. Not a single story is without death, even if that death is bargained for, such as Ralph Roberts', or the long-ago deaths that time-travelling Jake Epping is forced to allow to occur when he could undo them. Even when characters attempt to use the supernatural for their own gain, the result is death. David Streeter feels nothing but schadenfreude for the deaths that come about as a result of his deal with the devil, and Louis Creed is so caught up in the idea of overcoming death that he does not stop to wonder what sort of hold the old Micmac burying grounds actually has over him. The Havenites are so far down the road to Becoming Tommyknockers that they have no choice but to act when the spaceship is threatened. The characters who find themselves pressed for time and giving in to the supernatural see it more clearly: the immediate deaths caused by the supernatural occurrence, as well as the threat of far more in the future.

It seems that the overall message in King's works is that the supernatural really *should* be fought with the goal of eradicating it completely. Even an apparently benign object or burying ground is a blight on the natural world, causing death and destruction of minds as well as bodies. There is simply no place in the real world for the supernatural and, especially given time and resources, King's characters *should* do what they can to destroy it.

This brings us to the final question: given the myriad responses to the supernatural in the wide scope of King's works, how can his characters best ensure their success in this destruction? Some attempts work for a while, either displacing the supernatural geographically or weakening it for a long stretch of time, instead of completely destroying the supernatural. Other attempts work well for given characters in their own situations but fail for others—or even fail for a character at one point in time and succeed in other moments. Is there any overarching assessment that can be made about how King's characters should act in order to both destroy the supernatural threat and manage to secure their own survival in the process?

Conclusion
*What It All Comes Down To:
Standing and Being True*

After this review of common ways King's human characters have of defining and confronting the supernatural threats they face, the final question is: do any of these methods have a better chance of leading to success in that final battle? How could a character increase his or her chances of eliminating the monster, rather than simply sending it away for a while or perhaps making the outcome immediately worse? Given the vast array of characters and their clearly varied responses, is there even a way of categorizing such success?

The results of the characters' choices clearly differ from book to book, so that it is impossible to categorize something like Christianity as purely detrimental to a character's chances. What we can do is now sort through those narratives based on their outcome, from less desirable to apparent complete and total success. Although King's monsters always have a chance of returning, those that fall into the final category have not done so as of this writing.

Making Things Worse

Some of the ways King's characters attempt to approach the supernatural in order to eliminate the threat in fact end up making the problem worse. When Margaret White isolated her daughter and raised her in a strictly Christian fashion with hopes of keeping Carrie sinless—and eliminating her telekinetic abilities—this approach backfired and led to Carrie's explosive reaction on prom night. Between her lack of friends and the fact that she felt she had no emotional support system, when the bullying reached its peak, Carrie called upon all of her powers to take her revenge not only on her fellow students at prom that night, but on the whole town. Rather than having someone help her through her strange experience, Carrie was taught that what she could do was a bad thing, and she strengthened her telekinetic muscles in secret before unleashing her rage in a way only she could. That night also ended in Carrie's death, as a result of both letting her powers loose and her final confrontation with her mother. Even when Carrie pleaded with her momma for help, none was forthcoming.

In "The Mangler," the possessed speed ironer that had already caused one death and one amputation is greatly angered when two men attempt to exorcise its demon, killing one of them and then pulling itself free from the laundry and beginning to stalk its prey rather than remaining stationary. Bastardized Christian practices caused a mass murder of all adults in the small town of Gatlin in "Children of the Corn," while the surviving citizens—all children—likewise kill any travelers passing through, and willingly go to their own deaths at the appointed time. In the course of that short story and their encounter with two outsiders, they anger He Who Walks Behind the Rows and cause the age of favor to be lowered by an entire year.

The strange power of the Micmac burying grounds in *Pet Sematary* likewise holds sway over some of the book's human characters, first causing Jud Crandall to tell his new neighbor about the power of the place and then urging Louis Creed to bury further members of his family there. Caught up in his complicated relationship with death, Louis hopes to overcome it by using the power of the burying grounds. The return of his daughter's cat is more or less neutral, but his small son comes back from death and commits two murders, including his own mother's. What Rachel Creed will do now that she, too, has risen from that stony ground is up to the reader's imagination, but the results so far have been increasingly negative. The burying grounds, though, is stationary and needs people to come to it, much in the same way the Mangler was bolted inside the laundry prior to the botched exorcism. It is a threat through Louis' continued obsession and not because it physically stalks its next victim.

Variations in Tolerance

Within King, the supernatural usually *is* a threat, and then generally a physical one. When confronted with the supernatural, people die, and not usually a small number. Very few "normal" people can encounter the supernatural and simply adapt to its presence within King's stories. They cannot be entirely unaffected by their encounter, either having bad dreams—"The Things They Left Behind"—or only growing complacent after long years of familiarity, such as in *From a Buick 8*. The other characters' continued dismissal of a newcomer's fascination seems almost patronizing, and they argue to themselves that it is his youth that makes Ned ask all his questions without perhaps wondering if his is a healthier reaction. Long-term members of Troop D have expanded their view of the world enough to incorporate the Buick, if not enough to perform the investigations necessary to understand it. But, because the supernatural is either easy to placate or largely inactive and nonthreatening, there is no need for these characters to attempt to eradicate it. They are the lucky few.

Death is a common outcome for King's characters and, even in cases where some of the group emerge victorious against the supernatural threat, others die along the way. If every single one of the characters dies—"The Raft"—or surrenders to the situation—"Trucks"—then that would presumably be the absolute worst outcome. The supernatural threat might have been challenged initially, but the result of these first encounters, usually death, ends with the characters' resignation to their fate. This resignation itself also tends to entail death, either immediately or in the not-too-distant future, which leaves the supernatural free to continue on its path of destruction. When a group suffers the loss of one of its members, the survivors tend to double-down and consider the threat to now be personal, so it might even spur the remaining group's members on to at least temporary success.

Relocating the Threat

It is possible that the main characters' intervention may bring about an end to the immediate danger and that the characters themselves might believe that they have actually secured a victory. They can see that they have stopped the main threat, usually human-formed, and either killed him or driven him out of town, thereby saving the remaining "good" people from his evil intent. They are then left with the cleanup and the prospect that things may never return to normal, but the malevolent force has been dispatched and cannot continue to simply make things worse.

Such is the case in both *The Stand* and *Needful Things*. In *The Stand*, the end comes when an atomic bomb explodes in Las Vegas, the seat of both the Dark Man and his followers. Randall Flagg is the embodiment of evil, and he finds himself at the epicenter of the blast. It is even Flagg's own magic that sets off the radioactive warhead, killing all his gathered followers as opposed to threatening them with radiation poisoning if it is not removed posthaste. The two main "good" characters who are present likewise die, albeit in a faster, less painful way than the Dark Man's people had planned for them, so the closest witness is Stuart Redman, who observes the mushroom-shaped cloud and assumes that Vegas is no more.

When the novel skips ahead a few months, there is nothing to dissuade the Boulder Free Zone of this notion. After winter ends and the various mountain passes open up, if Flagg were still around, they would expect to be menaced by him in some way. Instead Boulder is once again flooded with incoming groups of travelers, and there is a low rumble of the fact that the threat may have moved from the external—Flagg and Vegas—to the internal as various factions rally for power and the right to carry firearms on police duty. When Stu Redman is seen in his final scene, he is unable to reassure Frannie that the evil is in fact over and the world will never become what it was before the plague hit, but Flagg is no longer their number one concern.

It seems that Stu and Frannie might be able to live out the rest of their days believing that Flagg had been destroyed in the blast. The epilogue shows Flagg coming back to consciousness in an unknown time and place, so there is no indication of how long after the blast this occurs, or even if Flagg is still in Stu and Frannie's world. He does, however, rise again, even adopting the message of the "good" side from the bulk of the book and thinking that he should make his stand.

Similarly, in *Needful Things* Sheriff Alan Pangborn manages two victories: he drives shop owner Leland Gaunt out of town, but he first takes the bag of souls Gaunt has collected and sets them free. Although the town of Castle Rock is literally in ruins, with many of its citizens killed and multiple buildings and structures removed through dynamite, the souls of the still-living are not under Gaunt's control.

Granted, Pangborn only confronts Gaunt when he is ready to leave town anyway. In the middle of a thunderstorm and the chaos his strange deals have caused, Gaunt was attempting to slip out with his case in hand and drive away. He was already finished with Castle Rock and its residents and simply hoping to make his escape before he could be confronted. Pangborn did not, in fact, need to drive Gaunt out of town until he took Gaunt's traveling case. Having relieved him of the one thing he actually wanted, Pangborn then had to force Gaunt away without his prize. What this victory really means for the people whose souls were first taken and then set free is unclear, but presumably a person's soul should not be in the possession of a figure like Gaunt, and Pangborn has done them all a favor.

Conclusion 165

Again, the epilogue informs the reader, if not the main characters, that the evil has simply relocated. *Needful Things* begins with a monologue from a nameless resident of Castle Rock, cataloguing the town's challenges and factions and ending with a remark about the new business that is set to open any day now, and the epilogue does the same in Junction City, Iowa. The itinerant salesman has moved on to a new shop in order to make new "special" deals and continue his interrupted collection of souls.

The characters in *The Stand* had reason to believe that they were experiencing an unprecedented situation, given the characteristics of the plague. Even though Mother Abigail told the main characters that Flagg was far older than his physical form indicated and that he had gone under other names in the past, none of them seemed to carry this through and wonder what it meant for their future. The trauma and tragedy of their situation in the summer and fall of the plague year, along with the rushed feeling of knowing that Flagg was gathering his troops and hoping to terrorize Boulder as soon as possible, did not allow them much time to meditate on this. Once Flagg was gone in a mushroom-shaped cloud—and since Mother Abigail had also died—the surviving characters felt that they could relax and attempt to get on with rebuilding their lives. Besides which, an atomic blast in Vegas certainly seems like it should have been able to destroy Flagg, whatever he actually was.

The character of Leland Gaunt, however, is not actually harmed when he leaves Castle Rock. He is perhaps stripped of his outer illusion as his classic car turns into a horse and cart and he reverts into a sort of con man selling potions and nostrums on the outskirts of a medieval fair, but he has not been hurt. Pangborn has simply taken his collection of souls away from him.

It is never clear what, exactly, Gaunt wanted with said souls. He seems to derive pleasure from causing people to hurt each other in a domino effect that culminated during the night of the storm in a street brawl and dynamite blasts, but even though Pangborn thinks Gaunt lies when he says he has no use for souls, there is no indication of what Gaunt would actually *do* with them. So far he has simply stowed them in his bag, but are they a sort of food? Has Pangborn just taken away Gaunt's anticipated meal and forced him to move on more quickly elsewhere in order to harvest a fresh batch? He might have done the right thing for Castle Rock right then, but what about other unsuspecting towns in the near future?

Because citizens of Castle Rock know Gaunt as an outsider who sets up a shop and preys on the people who enter it, they might easily deduce that this is not the first time Gaunt has played this game. They might further theorize that, having failed to get what he wanted in Castle Rock, he will move on to another, less suspicious town and repeat his tried-and-true methods. It would seem that, based on the book's epilogue, Pangborn and the others involved in the final confrontation with Gaunt do not attempt to track him down further or to actually stop him rather than simply drive him out.

Granted, it would be difficult to actually put out a warning about what they had experienced: a man who was not in fact a man, who knew far more than he should have about his new town of residence, and who not only provided his customers with guns and poisoned bullets but then stole their souls in exchange for trinkets that were not, in fact, the treasures they were bewitched to see. Even if Pangborn, as sheriff, were to put out an alert for Leland Gaunt or a similar man opening a new shop, said alert might not reach widely enough in order to stop Gaunt's next venture—presumably the one in Iowa—and a lack of evidence that Gaunt in fact broke the law would also work against him. The thing that called itself Gaunt is simply allowed to leave Castle Rock, without its bounty of souls, and to move on to whatever it seeks next.

Putting the Threat into Hibernation

Some of the supernatural threats are not fully beaten, and not even really expelled, but are simply absent for a while. As the short story warns, "Sometimes they come back." It might be possible for the main characters to take a breather, but the danger returns either to the same location it occupied before, or to the same people.

Christine is one such example. Although Dennis Guilder and Leigh Cabot, who worked together in an attempt to turn the car into nothing more than scrap, are no longer living in their hometown, Dennis believes their lives are once again threatened. He starts to worry when he sees a notice in the newspaper about one of the bullies who had escaped Christine years earlier, noting that the young man was killed in a recognizably mysterious hit-and-run accident. Dennis then lists the locations where the car would have to travel in order to get all of them who were left behind, including the previous owner's brother. The serial-killing car will now likely become a spree killer, working her way across the country and presumably taking Dennis last so he has the most time to anticipate his impending death.

Enough time has passed since the final confrontation with Christine that Leigh seems to have forgotten it completely. She has been *able* to forget because their plan seems to have worked: they lured the car to the garage, yes, and battered it into a wrecked hulk that was then put into a crusher. Leigh might have spent some time jumping when she caught sight of particular cars or being more aware of her surroundings, but all that has faded. Breaking up with Dennis has also allowed it to fade since she could cut all ties with anyone even remotely involved with Christine. Leigh moved out and moved on and is presumably happily living as a wife and mother who has no more than the usual belief in the supernatural.

This means Dennis is likely cut off from even discussing the situation with someone else. Although he did tell his dad the entire story, and although LeBay's brother knew that *something* had been up with the car, Leigh was the only other one to actually witness the car's menace. She lived through it alongside Dennis but, if he wanted to try to warn her, he would find himself in the same situation he is with most of the world: knowing he would not be believed. Leigh especially might have buried those memories down deep enough that she could be harmed if he tried to confront her with them again, even if he meant to do it in order to prepare her for Christine's return.

Thus the old fears and uncertainties loom, and with them, the isolation. Dennis, at least, seems to have been keeping an eye out for the return of his old nemesis, since he saw the name in the newspaper article and immediately thought of the old high school bully. Since neither he nor Leigh could entirely explain what, exactly, had been happening with Christine—why she was sentient and how she had chosen Arnie—Dennis seems to have accepted that they could therefore never be entirely sure that they had in fact destroyed her, either. Dennis could not forget, and perhaps did not let himself forget, because he worried that this exact scenario might happen. The only problem is, even though years have passed in which he could try to make sense of what occurred during his senior year of high school, Dennis has no more answers now than he did then. All he has is one report of vehicular homicide and the suspicion that, if he waits and keeps an eye out, he will find more. Christine is coming for him, and he is no more prepared to confront her than he was last time—perhaps even less, since his one idea of how to take care of her clearly did not pan out.

While Dennis might have only been considering Christine's possible return in the back of his mind, at least one member of the Losers in *It* made his concern explicit. Stan Uris, who as an adult committed suicide rather than return to Derry, cut his friends' palms and had them stand in a circle to make a blood promise to return if It ever did. The task of keeping an eye out for such a return was not Stan's but rather Mike's, since first his family remained in Derry and then, as an adult, Mike chose to stay, as well.

Like Leigh, the six members who moved away forgot about their childhood experience with the supernatural. Even Mike himself forgot about it for a few years, until shortly before his father's death. Will Hanlon was instrumental in the children's understanding of It, as well as the adults' ability to keep their promise, since it was his interest in Derry's history that allowed Mike to show the others various wood cuts, engravings, and photographs that included "their" clown throughout the centuries. Mike picked up his father's fascination with history and was able to track the clown's active cycle, even as a child, to once every twenty-seven years or so. The Losers understood that Its tragedies came in waves even before they went into the sewers in 1958.

The conversation with Will that restores the majority of Mike's memories concerns an incident that occurred during one of those active periods. Will nearly died in a racist attack during which he saw It in the same form his son would conjure years later: a giant bird. Mike recognizes both the bird and the throughline of violence that inhabits all stories about Derry, and he does not forget again. Later, in the early 1980s, he even goes into active observation instead of simply passing the time, knowing that Its cycle is about to come around again.

The problem with fighting a creature such as It is the fact that It *does* go into these long dormant periods, each easily lasting a generation. Many of the Losers' classmates married and had children by the time It returned, and adults are usually immune to Its tricks. They can be influenced into greater violence as can only happen—and be overlooked—in Derry, but their imaginations are no longer of the fertile kind that allow It to take on a single shape and invoke fear. Until all that time had passed, there was no way for the Losers to tell whether they had killed It, or only wounded It and brought a premature end to Its current cycle of violence.

The years between 1958 and 1985 did not help the Losers prepare for their next confrontation, since only one of them even remembered what had happened—and Mike himself had not been a participant in the Ritual of Chüd at the end. He, like the other six, had stood by as Bill engaged. Further, even Mike's memory was not complete, and in spite of all the memory-sharing in the library before they went into the sewers for the second time, only Bill and Beverly are shown having an epiphany of absolutely everything that happened during the first confrontation. They go to bed shortly after and are then pulled from sleep and sent down into the sewers again quickly, without any chance to plan or prepare further. Mike, the keeper of memory, is not with them. They might be better prepared than Leigh Cabot or Dennis Guilder awaiting Christine's return, but they are equipped with the same knowledge: what they tried last time did not work. At least the Losers believe they know the next step they have to take in order to eliminate It forever.

The Losers, unlike Dennis, get their second confrontation within the novel, and they also seem to emerge from the sewers victorious. When Bill struggled with the Ritual of Chüd, Richie joined him, and Eddie distracted It using his ever-present inhaler. Then Richie and Bill chased It deeper into Its lair, which they had refused to do in 1958, and Bill smashed Its heart between his hands. Ben stayed back in order to crush every single one of Its eggs and embryonic children. Only Beverly does nothing, staying back with Eddie as he dies and telling the other men that they need to go on and finish It. Between the double smashing—heart and children—It seems to be gone completely, an idea assisted by the fact that the greenish glow in Its lair fades. Even Derry falls apart, with a large section of downtown dropping into the canal. The changes under and in the city are enough to make the Losers believe that Stan's and Eddie's deaths were worth it, because It has been defeated. This time even Mike's memories fade.

There is no further promise to return in twenty-seven years because, this time, they are all sure. In spite of their strange memory loss, the Losers even get together to donate a memorial statue dedicated to those lives lost in the flood—deaths for which they might, had their memories stayed intact, wonder if they were partly to blame—and to the children. This memorial was placed sometime between 1985 and King's return to Derry in 2001 in *Dreamcatcher* and, when seen in that novel, is covered with graffiti that reads "Pennywise lives!" It might be a lie, but someone, somewhere, has come across the name It commonly used in Its clown form and written it on the base of the statue. Clearly there is supposed to be a connection between Pennywise and the lost children, which King's Constant Readers will know even if the characters involved in that scene do not. However, it would seem that the Losers' second attempt to eliminate It was similarly not successful, even if the Losers themselves are not aware of it.

Because *It* ends so soon after the final confrontation and *Dreamcatcher* does not reference the Losers, it is impossible to say whether any of them have remained vigilant, just in case. Mike Hanlon is seen in *Insomnia*, still holding his position at the library in the mid–1990s, but he is not one of the main characters of that book. Derry is still a troubled and unfriendly town where it seems many strange things can happen, but Pennywise is not a concern for Ralph Roberts, so it is unknown whether any of the Losers will eventually learn of Pennywise's apparent continued existence. Even if they did know about it, their magic circle of seven was reduced to five by the end of *It* and might have grown even smaller in the intervening years. The remaining members might not even still be capable of the creative thinking necessary for a third confrontation, much less have the resolve to try yet again after having thought they managed it twice already.

The resiliency of supernatural evil is disheartening to those who have to figure out some way to combat it, especially when there seems to be no precedent for what they are facing. There is immediate danger involved in both bashing Christine into an unrecognizable hulk and confronting It in Its lair, with or without a ritual for help, and the consequences of such attempts are left wide open. Either the Ritual or the demolition derby could end quickly with the protagonists' deaths, and long-term consequences are not part of their thought processes. The immediate danger needs to be stopped here and now, in the most final way possible. At least for Dennis, Leigh, and the Losers, the method itself is not a new threat.

Jim Norman of "Sometimes They Come Back" chose a response that could have been dangerous in and of itself, but also one that came with a warning about the future. The title refers both to three of the four teens who killed his brother—the fourth, not being dead, is unable to return decades later to haunt him—and also the demon Norman summoned in order to deal with them. The boys' arrival came with the deaths of some of his better students and led to the vehicular homicide of his wife, so Norman acted on the book he had retrieved from the library. Offering up a photograph of his dead brother, the sweat of the same, the blood of a cat he had personally caught and killed, and his own two index fingers, he secured the promise of a demon to remove the returned boys from the present. It is only after the demon has completed this duty that Norman remembers the warning that, once a demon has been summoned, it does not always stay away. Sometimes they come back.

The threat Jim Norman faced was different from what the Losers or Dennis and Leigh did. The Losers were personally in the line of fire once they had banded together in order to defend themselves and other children against It, as were Dennis and Leigh once they discovered that Christine was both sentient and vengeful. They saw the way the danger removed others around them and knew that, eventually, they would be personally targeted unless the supernatural were stopped. It preyed on children and Christine went for anyone who harmed Arnie or tried to come between the two of them, and the Losers, Dennis, and Leigh knew that they fit these descriptions.

Norman is not quite in the same position. Although the teens threatened him verbally when he was a boy and again as his students once he was an adult, it is unclear as to whether they actually mean to kill him. Instead, they continue to target people he loves. As long as they—and Norman—are around, they are a threat to his loved ones, and he has already lost his brother and now his wife because of them. It is unclear who they might target next, since the Normans were childless and he is not shown to have any specifically close friends, but Norman felt the pressure to act and get rid of the returned boys as quickly as possible.

Unlike some of King's other characters, Norman did try to reach out for some help. He called the detective who had worked his brother's murder case but ran into the same issue as every other normal character faces with the supernormal: he could not adequately explain to the old detective why he was so interested in this information. When Norman continued to protest that he could not tell the detective the reason he was calling, the detective hung up on him. Norman was left with his library book and his grief, and he decided to summon the demon in spite of the consequences because he needed the current situation rectified immediately. Perhaps he will take solace in the fact that, if the demon does indeed return and pester him in the future, it will at least be a situation he has bought and paid for. The teenagers returned with no apparent reason or provocation.

Honestly Beating the Threat

We come now to the cases where the supernatural has been completely destroyed and has not in fact returned—at least, not yet. There is no eternal reassurance when it comes to King's monsters, and at times even the characters themselves mention that the threat might indeed return, someday. There is simply so much that the characters, themselves only human, do not understand, and a handful of them are even able to admit it.

"Wear It Home, It'll Look Like a Dress": *Under the Dome*

In *Under the Dome*, the town is utterly cut off from the rest of the world by a clear Dome made of a substance that itself cannot be understood. The protagonists, who form a rebellious group against the antagonist dictatorship that arises, are able to discover that the Dome is being powered by a specific small box that King compares to an Apple TV. This box is away from the center of town, up on a high elevation, and surrounded by multiple deterrents: a number of dead animals to be seen during the day, a glowing ring of who-knows-what at night, and increasingly dangerous readings on a Geiger counter at all times. Although they are glad to have found it, these rebels are in a way dismayed: had the box been found within a Dome of its own, then its owners might have been afraid that it would be destroyed. Instead, the various deterrents also attract attention, as though asking the trapped people to find it and see what they can do about it.

Everyone is able to approach the box and even to touch it, which gives them a vision of the beings at the other end. All of them, adults and teenagers, agree that the indescribable others are themselves children. To them, the Dome is something like an ant farm: a toy with living creatures, but creatures distant and strange enough that their deaths are meaningless. The alien children do not care that so many townspeople have died, and they do not seem to be growing bored with their toys. The situation within the Dome becomes even more desperate after the meth lab explosion and the resulting fire, since even air does not pass easily through its membrane, and the surviving group dwindles very quickly. Unless the remaining people can get rid of the Dome, all of them will die.

Newspaper editor Julia Shumway is the one to seize on an idea and make one last attempt. Two others go with her, one to drive the car and Dale "Barbie" Barbara to manage their jury-rigged air supply, but it is Julia herself who grasps the box and confronts the single alien child she finds on the other side. Julia's last attempt is a bit strange: earlier, when another survivor told them about breaking a childhood friend's magnifying glass when the other boy was using it to fry ants, she wondered if perhaps he might have heard the voices of the supposedly lesser creatures and realized that they, too, had their little lives.

When Julia speaks to the lone alien child, she does not concentrate on the good that people do, but on one of her most shameful moments. As a girl, Julia had once been pantsed and spit upon by the other girls in her class as payment for being a grade-grubbing teacher's pet. When Julia told the story to Barbie earlier, she was adamant that she had in fact *earned* this treatment thanks to her own behavior. She even went so far as to consciously change that behavior afterward, no longer being a grade-grubbing teacher's pet but allowing herself to slip into a place that, while it might not have been what her parents wanted of their only child, let her classmates overlook her and leave her largely alone. Julia was ashamed of the day she was pantsed and left crying in the town common, yes, but also of her prior behavior.

And then, even though she had participated in the bullying, one of the other girls came back and offered Julia her oversized sweater, saying only, "Wear it home, it'll look like a dress."[1] When she tells Barbie, Julia emphasizes that there was no clear emotion in the other girl's gesture—no hate or anger, but also no pity. Julia adds that she has no idea why the other girl did it and that, even though they went to school together all the way through twelfth grade, they hardly ever spoke again.

Although the two men with her have not told Julia about such similar moments in their lives that make them feel ashamed and they wish they could take back, the narrator has allowed readers glimpses inside their heads. Barbie especially has a recurring memory of being present in a gym in Fallujah when a man was tortured and killed. Even though he did not pull the trigger, he also did nothing to stop what was happening. This man had actually done nothing to warrant such treatment, but the soldiers had recently lost one of their own and they, like Barbie, were angry about it and seeking revenge. The memory haunts Barbie, and Julia somehow takes it from him to show the alien child along with her own moment of deepest shame.

It works. The box powering the Dome rises up into the sky, taking the Dome with it. Although the elderly man who drove them out to the box dies, he is able to do so looking up at the sky instead of the smudged surface of the Dome, and Julia is left trying to explain to Barbie exactly *why* this worked. She is certain that the fact that the alien child was alone was a key to her success—that this never would have worked if she had been attempting to appeal to a group—and apologizes for taking his memory of what happened in the gym. She tells Barbie that the alien child repeated what the girl had said to her that long-ago day: "Wear it home, it'll look like a dress." When Barbie asks if the alien child was talking about the brown sweater, Julia responds that no—the alien child was talking about "our little lives."[2] Then the two of them walk together toward the people waiting outside what used to be the barrier.

Julia never fully gets a chance to explain why she picked this method of appeal. The others in the group had all taken their turn at the box, to demand to know why this was happening to their town or order the alien children to stop it, and none of these attempts had worked. Trapped and cut off from the rest of the world, they were able to have this small measure of communication with their tormentors, likely because it would have little effect. The alien children, as a group, could be amused but not moved by what they saw. Just as human children use magnifying glasses to kill ants without creating an empathetic connection between themselves and creatures with which they seem to have nothing in common, the children continued to play their game.

After having some time to consider their situation, Julia approaches the box not with stories of greatness and bravado, like a child trying to get in with the cool kids, but with shame and vulnerability. She had shared this story with Barbie only a handful of days before, when the two of them were alone, and after they had gone through much of the trauma the book would have them endure. It was a story she had never told her parents or anyone else, something she had buried deep inside while at the same time living it every day, considering all the changes she had made because of it. Julia was largely shaped by this awful incident she never spoke of, as well as the inexplicable kindness: "Wear it home, it'll look like a dress." When given the chance to confront a lone alien child, it is this hurt, shame, and vulnerability she offered—and it resulted in the same pitiless response. To this date in King's works, the alien children—and their Dome—have not returned.

Not So Safe Haven: *The Tommyknockers*

In *The Tommyknockers*, another small Maine town—this one Haven—is isolated and ultimately destroyed by its own alien encounter. Like Chester's Mill, Haven is not visited by living extraterrestrials but is affected by an alien artifact. The changes in Haven begin the day Bobbi Anderson trips over a mysterious object buried on her land. It has a strange hold over her and, as she uncovers more and more of the flying saucer, its surface oxidizes and those who are close to it begin undergoing changes involving telepathy, a strange desire to manically invent, and physical transformations most visible in the loss of teeth. Although those closest to Bobbi's place feel it first, eventually all of Haven is caught up in "the Becoming."

The Becoming is not entirely peaceful. Some of the inventions the Havenites construct are unintentionally dangerous, and some residents go insane during this change. Others, now able to read minds and discover secrets, set out to purposefully commit murder. One woman seeks to kill her husband based on the orders of a talking portrait of Jesus Christ, who first tells her that he has been cheating on her and then talks her through the creation of her special gadget. The only people who seem to have any sort of immunity are those with a lot of metal on their bodies, like Bobbi's sister and her mouthful of fillings or her friend, Jim "Gard" Gardener and the surgical plate in his head.

While Bobbi's sister only attempts to come for a visit and is quickly dispatched, Gard arrives in time to help Bobbi with much of the excavation of the ship. Being close enough to it to dig has a negative effect on most Havenites, who apparently have not "become" enough to withstand it the way Bobbi does, but Gard's metal plate keeps it from affecting him for quite some time, and he is therefore able to shield his thoughts from the others, as well. Even though Bobbi tries to win Gard over with the fact that so many of her wonderful gadgets only run off batteries and could solve the energy crisis immediately, Gard is quickly convinced that the power of the ship should *not* be made available to anyone, civilian or government.

Gard, like Barbie in *Under the Dome*, is haunted by specific incidents in his past. One is the skiing accident that led to his skull injury and his apparent immunity. The other involves waking up in jail and being told that, during one of his drunken blackouts, he shot his wife. Although Gard did not kill her, he also did not quit drinking after the fact. He is constantly reminded of waking up in jail and being told what he had done, but he also constantly reaches for the bottle and enters new blackouts. When Gard shows up at Bobbi's house, he is both escaping another incident and checking up on her, wracked with yet more guilt that he uses people instead of befriending them. In part he sticks it out until the end with Bobbi because of their past relationship and the fact that he cannot bring himself to bail out on her yet again, but really, Gard becomes the book's hero "more by accident than design."[3]

In the end, Gard acts as much to save the world as he does to redeem himself. The excavation had uncovered the hatchway into the ship, and Gard knows he has to beat the others inside and to the controls. The power of the ship is finally working on him, since he has been weakened by injury, a Valium overdose, and the loss of his only friend, but Gard makes it to the ship alone and sends it up and out into space. He takes it out of the reach of the government, which he believes would only use its abilities for weapons, and also protects other people from falling under the ship's influence. Although the Tommyknockers—the nonsense word used to describe the aliens—are apparently technologically advanced, they are not very peaceable, and Gard holds fast to his belief of saving people over killing them.

In the process of sending the alien ship into deep space, Gard dies. He also dooms the remaining townspeople. Although one of them has built a machine that can turn Earth's atmosphere into the sort of air the ship was giving off—the only air they can now breathe—they only have a limited number of batteries on which to run it. As Gard mentioned to Bobbi earlier, the Tommyknockers overlooked the fact that they could have bought power converters and plugged into wall sockets. The second way Gard signs the death warrant for Haven is by calling attention to the town. Thanks to a fire he ends up setting at Bobbi's place, people are drawn to the smoke and thus are present to observe the strange physical reactions of entering Haven, as well as being there to witness the ship's emergence and flight. The town that had been very closed-off and secretive, not even allowing its own members to hint to the outside world that something was wrong, became front-page news and any survivors found themselves guests of the government for as long as they could survive.

Gard's motivating factor is not heroism or bravery. He, like Barbie and Julia, constantly revisits the mistakes of his past. Gard's initial reaction is to drown the memories and give in to his alcoholism. On the day when he sets off for Bobbi's place for the final time, he was even contemplating suicide before he got the feeling that Bobbi was in a more desperate position than he was. At that point, Bobbi is his only friend left in the world, or at least the only person he has wronged who will still talk to him and be relatively glad to see him.

Most of Gard's life has been wrapped up in selfishness or choices made for the wrong reasons. He got into his skiing accident, for example, when trying to impress a girl and hoping she would have sex with him if he could manage the slopes properly in spite of never having skied before. He did not consider Alcoholics Anonymous even after the blackout in which he shot his wife in the face, and Gard was unable to hold down a steady job. During the final summer of his life he was a last resort to fill a slot on a travelling speaking gig, working for a woman he greatly disliked, and Gard made sure to mess this up, as well. After a fantastic reading in spite of his hangover from the activities of the night before, Gard allowed himself to drink too much at a party, to engage in an argument with some of the guests and their host, and to cause their host to have a fatal heart attack. Gard never learned how to be his own best friend or anyone else's, and during his time with Bobbi digging up the ship, he frequently wonders whether it would be a better option—ostensibly for her—if he just left.

In order to stop himself from going around and around with these ethical and moral questions, and to largely ignore the fact that Bobbi and her friends are both telepathic and no longer human, Gard drinks some more. He continues to try to drown out ideas of responsibility and repentance, even though—or perhaps especially because—others from Haven attempt to make their own stands. These result not only in their own deaths, but in the deaths of others. Although Gard was suicidal at the outset, discovering the ship and the strange happenings in Haven, as well as learning that Bobbi really does need him, changes his mind and encourages him to cling to life. He cannot bring himself to kill Bobbi until he knows for certain that Bobbi means to kill him, and that he is sitting across the table from a Tommyknocker and not his old friend. However, in spite of his injuries and the many obstacles the others put in his way, Gard manages to both make it to the ship in time and to take it up and away, removing the danger.

Because Gard dies in this venture—and because he knew he would even had he entered the ship in perfect health—his actions might be considered the ultimate sacrifice and therefore redemption. Julia—along with all the remaining survivors of The Mill—will die unless something changes, so their last-ditch attempt to get her to the box and speak to the alien children will save not just the few other survivors, but themselves. Gard will die either way, and he was barely able to make it out to the ship due to its influence on him and the injuries he suffered during the last stand-off against Bobbi. Rather than waiting for death from the Tommyknockers or choosing to simply kill himself after he kills Bobbi, Gard forces himself to do the noble thing and suffer physically in his final moments for the greater good.

It is difficult to theorize whether a man who had lived a good life would have been able to push himself through the effects of the Valium and his physical injuries. At least at the start of his mission Gard is helped—or goaded—along by two others the Tommyknockers have taken prisoner, and even Bobbi's ghost apparently makes a short appearance to aid him, but Gard must complete the task on his own. He does so with grit and determination, yes, but grit and determination born not of nobility, but shame. Gard has done so much harm in his life, culminating today with shooting his one remaining friend, and his refusal to let his death be as catastrophic as his life comes from being haunted by all the wrongs he has done. Gard can only relax and be at peace once he has the ship shooting up through the atmosphere, because in this, at least, he will not hurt anyone. Anyone human, that is.

Something Special: *Dreamcatcher*

The threat is once again alien in *Dreamcatcher*, although this time the danger is not an artifact and the problem involves imperfect isolation. This spaceship, much more recently landed than the Tommyknocker saucer, is destroyed, along with most of its occupants, and the fungus the alien life-forms brought with them cannot survive for long in a Maine winter. Even though a large area of woods has been cordoned off, the threat comes in the single life-form that has slipped through: "Typhoid Jonesy," who is not consumed by the alien intelligence inside of him but whose body is driven by it in order to infect, if not the world, at least the greater Boston area.

Two of those in the final fight against the alien dubbed Mr. Gray find themselves racing the clock against their own physical conditions, much like Gard: Duddits is greatly weakened by his leukemia and will die from it before the final creature is killed, and Jonesy's body has been abused by Mr. Gray, dislocating the hip that was hurt in a car accident the previous spring. The final four men battling Mr. Gray at the end—Duddits, Jonesy, Henry Devlin, and Owen Underhill—are likewise also haunted by visions of the past.

Owen Underhill's is perhaps the simplest. Although the incident that has put him in such a tight space with his current boss is one in which he actually did *not* do something—Abraham Kurtz will shoot Underhill because, in a previous maneuver, he failed to kill the children who witnessed a rescue that should have been secret—it is Mrs. Rapeloew's plate that haunts him. As a young boy Owen strolled around his neighbors' house after she had been taken away in an ambulance because of a stroke. Mr. Rapeloew had left the front door open in his hurry to go with her, and young Owen originally only meant to close it, but he was drawn inside to wander, fascinated. When he threw her beloved serving platter to the floor and it shattered, he was shocked out of his trance and left the house. No one ever asked him about the plate, so Owen never had to own up to it—or indeed, to confess it to anyone—but standing up against Kurtz and chasing down Jonesy and Mr. Gray make him think of it frequently. Owen cannot un-break the plate, but he can try to be a hero.

Henry and Jonesy, along with their now-deceased friends Beaver and Pete, continually drift away into memories of their childhood friend Duddits. Part of this has to do with Duddits' illness and the fact that he is mentally calling his old friends, and part of this shows how special and different all of them were because of their interaction with Duddits. In this case, most of the memories are good ones in which the boys acted together heroically, first saving Duddits from three bullies and then working with him to rescue a teenage girl who had gone missing. Only one of these memories is traumatizing and guilt-inducing, but at least there are mitigating circumstances: the boys believe that they, working through Duddits, somehow caused one of the bullies to get into a car crash and therefore die before he could make good on this threat to get revenge on them for stopping his "fun" with Duddits.

Unlike the story of Mrs. Rapeloew's plate, these memories of

Duddits have a direct bearing on the current situation as an explanation both for how Jonesy can be controlled by Mr. Gray without being eliminated completely, and how Henry and Duddits can hope to help stop Mr. Gray. They are meant to show why this group of four men is special, and to place Duddits securely at the center of their connection. Whatever lingering guilt they feel over the bully's death does not compare to Owen's over the plate, or to the guilt Henry feels about how they fell out of touch with Duddits and never even knew he was so sick.

Duddits' position is similar to Gard's: he will die soon anyway and does not need to put himself through the pain and suffering which makes that time simply come earlier. Duddits, however, is excited to go on an adventure with one of his old friends again, and not only gets into the car willingly, but uses his special powers first to slow Mr. Gray down and then to show Henry and Jonesy how to defeat him completely. He is also reassured that his actions can save both of his friends in the immediate future and keep the world safe for other loved ones, like his mother. Duddits, like Gard, opts for the heroic, if more painful, death.

Owen Underhill is not killed in battle with Mr. Gray, like Duddits, but rather comes to a more mundane end: after believing it when Jonesy tells him that Mr. Gray is gone, Owen starts to return to the car only to be blindsided by Kurtz. Even though the rest of Kurtz's plans have gone astray, he is still able to keep his promise to himself and kill the traitorous Owen. Owen does, at least, die a hero, having helped Henry and then Duddits get into the position to help Jonesy and stop Mr. Gray. Owen played a large role in saving the day and therefore all of humanity, driven on by his guilt about breaking Mrs. Rapeloew's plate. The never-confessed destructive act of a child was what pushed him to stick it out, even through such strangeness as telepathy and Duddits' powers, and the recurring memory and its accompanying emotions of guilt and shame mimic Gard's driving force. The awfulness he committed in his past gives him the resolve to push on in the present, in spite of the incredible personal risk.

Like Julia and Barbie in *Under the Dome* and Gard in *Tommyknockers*, the survivors at the end of *Dreamcatcher* are left not knowing for sure that the aliens have been chased away for good, but that they have rid their town of the current threat and made a clear message in doing so. They have also had a chance to spread the knowledge about the occurrence so that others, in the future, might be more prepared. This is not a scenario in King limited solely to humans confronting aliens, however. At least one other character has managed to make her own stand in such a decisive way.

Drawing on Her Past: Holly Gibney in *The Outsider*

Holly Gibney, whose story begins in the Bill Hodges trilogy, confronts a supernatural threat in *The Outsider* and manages to destroy the human-looking being utterly and completely. When she hits the apparent man in the head using ball bearings in a sweat sock, a trick learned from Bill Hodges and originally used on then-fully-human murderer Brady Hartsfield, the Outsider's skull caves in. She is left to back quickly away from a pile of writhing white worms inside the deflated set of clothes, since the man dissolves as the result of her attack. Holly and her friend Ralph note that the worms do not seem to live long outside their host, leaving the question of what would have happened if the worms had reached either of them, but they make a clean getaway.

The first time Holly used Bill's cosh, nicknamed the Happy Slapper, she had to gather her nerves and bring herself to the point where she felt she could swing it at someone's head with the intent of killing him. Her target in that case was a known mass murderer, currently sitting in an auditorium filled with people and presumably with his finger on the ignition switch of a bomb that would kill them all. Even then, Holly did not simply hit an unsuspecting Brady, but greeted him with the name of one of her bullies from the past—and then, caught up in such memories, hit Brady again until her companion physically forced her to stop.

Holly's specific memories are of junior high when she was clearly not popular, and the in-crowd kids mocked her muttering and other stims. Holly is shown to be timid and unable to stand up for herself against her mother, just as she could not take a stand against the junior high bully. Remembering those specific humiliations, however, allowed her to find the strength to attack the stranger in front of her. Then, the mental changes brought on by both these blows and the experimental medications Brady's doctor gave him gave her the past experience with the supernatural in order to believe that the man-like creature standing in front of her was in fact what she had dubbed an Outsider: a supernatural shapeshifter that lives on murdering children and framing innocent people.

When Holly stands in the cave in Texas facing the Outsider, she is able to rely on both of her encounters with Brady Hartsfield to guide her and give her the determination to follow through with her actions. She has already used a Happy Slapper on a man's head, even though in that case she started the chain reaction that imbued that man with supernatural powers. The helper with her this time is Ralph instead of Jerome, though, and likely will not try to stop her. Further, this time the first blow seems to be enough—there is nothing but those worms beneath a thin layer of skull and the Outsider goes down, facial features flickering through any number of borrowed identities before the body dissolves.

Without Holly, Ralph and the others would not have had any such chance of success because they would have completely underestimated their foe. The men, clinging to their own past experiences as well as their beliefs in science, continue to insist to themselves that no such creature as the Outsider could exist. Even though Ralph has the ever-popular recurring memory from childhood, his is of cutting open a seemingly-perfect cantaloupe to find the inside full of squirming maggots: a disgusting and terrifying experience, but not one in which he did anything wrong. There is nothing for which Ralph feels he needs to atone or to make a belated stand. Holly's belief in her past and even her continued struggle to stand up for herself are key to their success.

At the end of the book, Holly and Ralph continue to reassure each other that the Outsider is indeed gone for good, and that he must have been the only one in the world. In King, either declaration is up for debate, since even Pennywise can apparently recover from what appeared to be certain death. Holly's appearance in the short story "If It Bleeds" at least answered one of those questions: even though the initial Outsider seemed to believe he was entirely alone, Holly finds another shapeshifting creature that feeds on pain and terror. Although there are many differences between him and the original Outsider, Holly still pegs them as being the same sort of creature. This one, too, disappears soon after a physical impact that would have killed a man, so it seems that she can be firmer in her conclusions. Yes, these deaths are permanent for each individual Outsider, but there might be more Outsiders left in the world.

Prior to the events in "If It Bleeds," Holly made a unique decision in the realm of King's characters. She did not decide that the inexplicable encounter with the Outsider was a unique experience and leave things there. Perhaps the fact that she had found so many legends of El Cuco convinced her that this one could not in fact be the only one, since there were indeed all of those stories about very similar occurrences. Holly did not assume that, since "her" Outsider was gone, that would be the end of it. Like many others she realized that she could not simply tell her tale to others without having herself marked as unreliable or in need of mental help, but Holly actually found a workaround: she selected a published psychiatrist and paid him for two sessions in which she told her story about the Outsider, and she ended with a request that he share her case in print and at conferences. If anyone in his audience had a patient who shared the same "delusion," Holly wanted him to pass on her contact information.

This is an immense step for a King character because the appearance of a supernatural threat tends to function as an isolating factor, limiting the ways in which characters can reach out *for* help, much less to *give* it. Once the incident is over, many characters—like Leigh in *Christine*—prefer to forget that it ever happened, or, as seen with the Losers in *It*, forgetting is part of the process. Characters who do remember might reach out to check in on each other, but, until Holly, none have made such a bold gesture as to reach out to strangers who may or may not have even encountered the supernatural yet.

It is possible that the silence of previous survivors is a way of protecting themselves as they insist that such a thing could not happen again. Those who have not discovered legends that explain or seem to mimic what they are seeing might likewise believe that what they experienced was indeed a one-time event, since no one had recorded it in the past. This thinking leads to another dearth of records so that, should a car like Christine arise again, or should Pennywise return after Mike Hanlon has destroyed his notes, anyone facing the same problem in the future will likewise believe themselves to be first. If they wanted to leave a trail, then their names would have to in some way be attached to the documentation. By seeking out a psychiatrist just for this one situation, Holly manages to get the details of her experience disseminated in a way that means anyone who recognizes them can indeed get in touch with her, but her daily life is not impacted by the consequences of her "delusion."

Holly did not do the same after the final encounter with Brady Hartsfield, although that situation was different and might actually have been unique. She had no way of knowing what, between the brain damage and untested medications, caused Brady's emerging telekinetic powers, but the doctor who had administered the drug died before Brady did. It is also possible that the idea of using a psychiatrist to send an open letter out into the world did not even occur to her until after the events of *The Outsider*, or that, for all his negative traits, Brady Hartsfield did not scare her—or haunt her—as much as the Outsider did. Whatever the reason, Holly acknowledged the truth of her experience, admitted to herself that other cases were likely, and discovered a means by which to allow people in similar positions to also know that they were not alone.

This, too, could be Holly's way of drawing on her own past experience to confront the supernatural. She has been constantly working with a therapist since moving to Ohio at the end of *Mr. Mercedes*, although she specifically chose a different one to hear her story on the Outsider so as not to undo the work they had already done on her mother and her childhood. She knew enough about therapy, and already had it on her radar, to seek out someone she could use for her own purposes, though, and by that point had gained enough self-confidence to indeed use him in that way and not give in to his insistence that she be treated for her delusion.

Inner Strength, Outward Success

What Julia and Barbie; Gard; Duddits, Henry, Jonesy, and Owen; and Holly have in common is that they succeeded not only in forcing the supernatural threat to leave but that, so far, the specific threat they banished has not come back. Considering the vast scope of King's stories in which the human protagonist faces off against the supernatural antagonist, this small number of successes might be disheartening. It shows how difficult it is to eliminate the supernatural completely, as opposed to giving in to it; living with it; forcing it to relocate; or inducing a long hibernation. It is much more common in King's world for the supernatural to return and continue its threat of death than it is for the human protagonists to find a way to stop it completely.

The other commonality is an approach King stated outright in some of his earlier novels and then repeated mainly in his fantasy epic *The Dark Tower*: in order to confront the supernatural, these characters had to stand and be true. They did not search outside of themselves for some sort of magical fix to the problem or choose a method of physical destruction in desperation and with no prior experience. All of these characters reached into their pasts, and then frequently the less savory elements of their pasts, to find the strength and courage to appeal to the alien children, or fly the spaceship out of reach, or work together to stop an alien invasion, or deal with a shape-shifting child-killer.

It is apparently very difficult for characters to trust themselves, especially being so aware of their own faults and weaknesses, in the face of previously unthought of supernatural threats. Because the danger is something so new and so strange, clearly their own little lives could not hold the key to fighting it. When confronted with something so awe-inspiring and outside rational teachings, it seems natural for characters to reach for their own spiritual or magical counter-measures, pulling rituals from library books or attempting to engage priests with their Christian trappings. These measures involve reaching outside, rather than in, and putting on a false face rather than being true.

In the midst of fear, King's most successful characters find their strength in their own pasts, and then also in their own past mistakes. They do not always need to share these humiliations with others, the way Julia told Barbie, but they, personally, need to know them and even to be uneasy with them. These characters are forced to relive the experience and sit with the heavy emotional outcomes: pain, shame, humiliation, self-disgust. They have been shaped by these events and, if they stand true, can learn from them. Perhaps they have not been able to do so in the past—Gard, for example, was not able to give up drinking even after shooting his wife—but, in their final confrontation, they manage to use all parts of themselves to seek victory.

It is, in fact, an uplifting message from the Master of Horror who even describes himself as being the literary equivalent of a Big Mac and fries: whatever his human characters face, no matter how horrific or threatening, the power they need to defeat it is already within themselves. Their strength comes not in perfection, but in their faults and their own basic humanity, which the supernatural of course lacks. In order to succeed within the world of Stephen King, his characters must do something that is easy to say—something King writes frequently—but difficult to do: stand and be true.

Chapter Notes

Introduction

1. Stephen King, *Dreamcatcher* (New York: Pocket Books, 2001), p. 546.
2. Stephen King, *It* (New York: Scribner's, 1986), p. 839.
3. King, *It*, p. 1087.
4. Stephen King, *The Stand* (New York: Anchor Books, 1990), p. 1138.

Chapter 1

1. Stephen King, *Pet Sematary* (New York, Pocket Books, 1983), p. 175.
2. Joe Nazare, "The Horror! The Horror? The Appropriation, and Reclamation, of Native American Mythology," *Journal of the Fantastic in the Arts* 11, no. 1 (41) (2000): 24–51, p. 30.
3. King, *Pet Sematary*, p. 202.
4. Tony Magistrale, *Landscape of Fear: Stephen King's American Gothic* (Madison: Popular Press, 1988), p. 59.
5. Heidi Strengell, *Dissecting Stephen King: From the Gothic to Literary Naturalism* (Madison: University of Wisconsin Press, 2005), p. 62.
6. Tony Magistrale, *Stephen King: America's Storyteller* (Santa Barbara: Praeger, 2010), p. 105.
7. King, *It,* p. 253.
8. King, *It,* p. 709.
9. Stephen King, *Thinner* (New York: Signet Books, 1987), p. 47.
10. https://tvtropes.org/pmwiki/pmwiki.php/Literature/Thinner.
11. King, *Thinner*, pp. 148–149.
12. Stephen King, *The Outsider* (New York: Scribner's, 2018), p. 201.
13. King, *The Outsider*, p. 386.
14. King, *The Outsider*, p. 477.

Chapter 2

1. King, *It*, p. 642.
2. King, *It*, p. 635.
3. King, *It*, p. 1010. Italics in original.
4. King, *Thinner*, p. 203.
5. King, *Dreamcatcher*, p. 71.
6. King, *Dreamcatcher*, p. 790. Italics in original.
7. King, *Dreamcatcher*, p. 881.

8. King, *Dreamcatcher*, p. 878.
9. King, *The Dark Half*, p. 305.
10. King, *The Dark Half*, p. 314.
11. King, *The Dark Half*, p. 370.
12. King, "Sometimes They Come Back," *Night Shift*, p. 169.

Chapter 3

1. King, *The Stand*, p. 909.
2. Reino, *Stephen King: First Decade*, p. 56.
3. King, *Desperation*, p. 520.
4. King, "Mute," *Just After Sunset*, p. 418.
5. McAleer in McAleer and Perry, *Stephen King's Modern Macabre*, p. 176.

Chapter 4

1. King, "One for the Road," *Night Shift*, p. 302.
2. Magistrale, *Moral Voyages*, p. 113.

Chapter 5

1. King, *Carrie*, p. 250.
2. Strengell, *Dissecting Stephen King*, p. 198.
3. Mary Pharr, "Partners in the *Danse*: Women in Stephen King's Fiction," in *The Dark Descent*, p. 23.
4. King, "The Mangler," *Night Shift*, p. 87.
5. King, "Children of the Corn," *Night Shift*, p. 269.
6. Russell, *Stephen King: A Critical Companion*, p. 125.
7. King, *Needful Things*, p. 655.
8. King, *Under the Dome*, p. 997.

Chapter 6

1. King, *Under the Dome*, p. 65.
2. King, *Under the Dome*, p. 1037.
3. King, *Dreamcatcher*, p. 601.
4. King, *Dreamcatcher*, p. 430.
5. Lippert in Simpson and McAleer, *The Modern Stephen King Canon*, p. 158.

Chapter 7

1. King, *Chistine*, p. 503.
2. King, *End of Watch*, p. 415.
3. King, *Mr. Mercedes*, p. 415.
4. King, *The Outsider*, p. 523.
5. King, "One for the Road," in *Night Shift*, p. 302.
6. King, "The Moving Finger," *Nightmares and Dreamscapes*, p. 258.
7. King, "Gray Matter," *Night Shift*, p. 116.

Chapter 8

1. King, "The Things They Left Behind," *Just After Sunset*, p. 261.
2. King, "Trucks," *Night Shift*, p. 131.
3. King, "Fair Extension," *Full Dark, No Stars*, p. 280.

Conclusion

1. King, *Under the Dome*, p. 917.
2. King, *Under the Dome*, p. 1071.
3. Magistrale, *Stephen King: The Second Decade*, p. 84.

Bibliography

Alegre, Sara Martín. "Nightmares of Childhood: The Child and the Monster in Four Novels by Stephen King." *Atlantis,* vol. 23, no. 1, 2001, pp. 105–114.
Balanzategui, Jessica. "The Child and Adult Trauma in American Horror of the 1980s." In *The Uncanny Child in Transnational Cinema: Ghosts of Futurity at the Turn of the Twenty-first Century,* 35–66. Amsterdam: Amsterdam University Press, 2018. http://www.jstor.org/stable/j.ctv80cc7v.5.
Beahm, George. *The Stephen King Companion: Four Decades of Fear from the Master of Horror.* New York: Thomas Dunne Books, 2015.
Davis, Jonathan P. *Stephen King's America.* Bowling Green, OH: Bowling Green State University Popular Press, 1994.
Freeman, Brian James, editor. *Reading Stephen King.* Forest Hill, MD: Cemetery Dance Publications, 2017.
Heldreth, Leonard J. "Rising Like Old Corpses: Stephen King and the Horrors of Time-Past." *Journal of the Fantastic in the Arts,* vol. 2, no. 1, 1989, pp. 5–13.
Herrmann, Andrew F. "Ghosts, Vampires, Zombies, and Us: The Undead as Autoethnographic Bridges." *International Review of Qualitative Research* 7, no. 3 (2014): 327–41. doi:10.1525/irqr.2014.7.3.327.
Hoppenstand, Gary, and Ray B. Browne. *The Gothic World of Stephen King: Landscape of Nightmares.* Bowling Green, OH: Bowling Green State University Popular Press, 1987.
Hoppenstand, Gary, editor. *Critical Insights: Stephen King.* Pasadena: Salem Press, 2011.
Jose, Reino. *Stephen King: The First Decade, Carrie to Pet Sematary.* New York: Twayne Publishers, 1988.
King, Stephen. *Bag of Bones.* New York: Scribner's, 1998.
_____. *Carrie.* New York: Anchor, reissue edition, 2008.
_____. *Christine.* New York: Gallery Books, 1983.
_____. *Cujo.* New York: Gallery Books, 1981.
_____. *The Dark Half.* New York: Signet Books, 1989.
_____. *Desperation.* New York: Gallery Books, 1996.
_____. *Dreamcatcher.* New York: Pocket Books, 2001.
_____. *Duma Key.* New York: Pocket Books, 2008.
_____. *11/22/63.* New York: Gallery Books 2012.
_____. *End of Watch.* New York: Gallery Books, 2016.
_____. *From a Buick 8.* New York: Pocket Books, 2002.
_____. *Full Dark, No Stars.* New York: Scribner's, 2010.
_____. *The Green Mile.* New York: Pocket Books, 1996.
_____. *If It Bleeds.* New York: Scribner's, 2020.
_____. *Insomnia.* New York: Signet Books, 1994.
_____. *It.* New York: Scribner's, 1986.

———. *Just After Sunset*. New York: Pocket Books, 2008.
———. *Misery*. New York: Scribner's, 1987.
———. *Mr. Mercedes*. New York: Gallery Books, 2014.
———. *Needful Things*. New York: signet Books, 1991.
———. *Night Shift*. New York: Signet Books, 1976.
———. *Nightmares & Dreamscapes*. New York: Signet Books, 1993.
———. *The Outsider*. New York: Scribner's, 2018.
———. *Pet Sematary*. New York: Pocket Books, 1983.
———. *Revival*. New York: Gallery Books, 2015.
———. *Rose Madder*. New York: Pocket Books, 1995.
———. *'Salem's Lot*. New York: Pocket Books, 1975.
———. *Skeleton Crew*. New York: Signet Books, 1985.
———. *The Stand*. New York: Anchor Books, 1990.
———. *Thinner*. New York: Signet Books, 1984.
———. *The Tommyknockers*. New York: Signet, 1987.
———. *Under the Dome*. New York: Scribner's, 2009.
Lant, Kathleen Margaret, and Theresa Thompson. *Imagining the Worst: Stephen King and the Representation of Women*. Westport, CT: Greenwood Press, 1998.
Magistrale, Anthony. *The Moral Voyages of Stephen King*. 1989. Cabin John, MD: Wildside Press, LLC, 2006.
Magistrale, Tony. *Landscape of Fear: Stephen King's American Gothic*. Madison: Popular Press, 1988.
———. *Stephen King: America's Storyteller*. Santa Barbara: Praeger, 2010.
———. *Stephen King: The Second Decade, Danse Macabre to the Dark Half*. New York: Twayne Publishers, 1992.
Magistrale, Tony, editor. *The Dark Descent: Essays Defining Stephen King's Horrorscape*. New York: Greenwood Press, 1992.
McAleer, Patrick, and Michael A. Perry, editors. *Stephen King's Modern Macabre: Essays on the Later Works*. Jefferson, NC: McFarland, 2014.
Mustazza, Leonard. "The Power of Symbols and the Failure of Virtue: Catholicism in Stephen King's "Salem's Lot.'" *Journal of the Fantastic in the Arts* 3, no. 3/4 (11/12) (1994): 107–19. http://www.jstor.org/stable/43308202.
Nazare, Joe. "The Horror! The Horror? The Appropriation, and Reclamation, of Native American Mythology." *Journal of the Fantastic in the Arts* 11, no. 1 (41) (2000): 24–51. http://www.jstor.org/stable/43308417.
Pollin, Burton R. "Stephen King's Fiction and the Heritage of Poe." *Journal of the Fantastic in the Arts* 5, no. 4 (20) (1993): 2–25. http://www.jstor.org/stable/43308170.
Russell, Sharon A. *Revisiting Stephen King: A Critical Companion*. Westport, CT: Greenwood Press, 2002.
———. *Stephen King: A Critical Companion*. Westport, CT: Greenwood Press, 1996.
Schlobin, Roger C. "Children of a Darker God: A Taxonomy of Deep Horror Fiction and Film and Their Mass Popularity." *Journal of the Fantastic in the Arts* 1, no. 1 (1) (1988): 25–50. http://www.jstor.org/stable/43307979.
Simpson, Philip L., and Patrick McAleer, editors. *The Modern Stephen King Canon: Beyond Horror*. Lanham: Lexington Books, 2019.
———. *Stephen King's Contemporary Classics: Reflections on the Modern Master of Horror*. Lanham: Rowman & Littlefield, 2015.
Strengell, Heidi. *Dissecting Stephen King: From the Gothic to Literary Naturalism*. Madison: University of Wisconsin Press, 2005.

Index

alcoholism 64, 176
alien 1, 2, 4, 19, 21, 35, 41–2, 45, 55, 103, 109, 110–1, 115, 137, 172–4, 175, 177–8, 179, 183
Anderson, Ralph 26, 27, 28, 30, 128, 129, 180, 181
Anderson, Roberta "Bobbi" 158–9, 174, 175, 176, 177
Anubis 48
apocalypse 100, 101
Arthur ("I Am the Doorway") 137

Babineau, Dr. Felix 125–6, 128, 131
Bachman, Richard 22, 46, 64, 66
Bag of Bones 133–5, 139
Baptists 94, 96, 97, 98
Barbara, Dale "Barbie" 110, 172, 173, 174, 175, 176, 179, 183, 184
Barlow, Kurt 71–2, 73, 74, 81
the Barrens 17, 19
Bateman, Glen 61, 62–3
Beaumont, Liz 46, 47, 48, 49
Beaumont, Thad 46–51
Bible 5, 58, 64, 69, 72, 73–4, 84, 91, 92, 94, 104, 107, 108, 109–10, 111, 116, 132
Blackwood, Algernon 12
Bolton, Claude 28, 29, 127, 128, 129
Bolton, Lovey 128
Booth ("One for the Road") 132
Bosch, Hieronymus 115
Boston, MA 42, 72, 178
Bouchard, Stanny 12
Boulder, CO 60, 62, 63, 64, 68, 164, 165
Boulder Free Zone 61, 63, 68, 164
Brentner, Ralph 61, 62, 63
Brigham, Father 97
Buick 8 3, 159, 160, 163
bully 19, 36, 45, 87–8, 89, 90, 122, 123, 124, 126, 131, 161, 166, 167, 173, 178, 179, 180
Bundy, Ted 30
Burke, Matt 70, 71
Burt ("Children of the Corn") 93–5
Bushey, Phil "Chef" 100, 101, 102

Cabot, Leigh 122–4, 135, 142, 166–7, 168, 169, 170, 182

Callahan, Donald 57, 71–2, 73–4, 79, 82
cancer 27, 42, 44–5, 106, 114–5, 125, 154, 155
cannibalism 11, 12, 13, 14
Cap City, OK 26
Carrie (novel) 85–90
Carver, David 3, 4, 59, 64–6, 68, 106
Castle Rock, ME 46, 79, 80, 82, 95, 97, 98, 99, 164, 165, 166
Catholicism 3, 57, 62, 67, 70, 71, 72, 73, 96, 97, 98, 99
Cavell, Douglas "Duddits" 41–4, 45, 55, 178–9, 183
Chalmers, Polly 82
Charon 48
Chasse, Lois 149, 150
Chef *see* Bushey, Phil
Chester's Mill, ME 99, 101, 102, 105, 106, 107, 108, 109, 110, 110, 174, 177
Chicago, IL 13, 156
"Children of the Corn" 93–5, 162
Christine (car) 3, 122–4, 139, 142, 166–7, 169, 170, 182
Christine (novel) 2, 3, 122–4, 135, 166–7, 182
Church 10, 11, 13, 30
Churchill, Winston (cat) *see* Church
Cinderella 87, 89
Clarendon, Joe "Beaver" 42, 43, 44, 178
Clotho 149, 150
Cobb, Nettie 96, 98
Coben, Harlan 26
Cody, Jimmy 70–1, 82, 132
Coffey, John 3, 75–8, 81, 82, 114
Coggins, Rev. Lester 100, 101, 102, 105, 107, 108, 109
Cold Mountain Penitentiary 75
Colorado 60, 61, 64
communion 57, 66, 116
confession 67, 71
Connelly, Elaine 75, 77
Corcoran, Dorsey 16
Corcoran, Eddie 15–6
Crandall, Jud 10, 11, 12, 13, 14, 15, 18, 28, 156, 157, 162

191

Index

Creed, Ellie 10, 11, 13, 156, 157
Creed, Gage 13, 14–5, 30, 156, 157
Creed, Louis 10–2, 13, 14–5, 17, 18, 20, 28, 30, 32, 116, 156–8, 160, 162
Creed, Rachel 11, 15, 30, 156, 157, 162
the Crimson King 149
crucifix 70, 71, 72, 73, 74, 81, 82, 131
Crusades 84
Cuco, El 26, 28–30, 31, 32, 127, 181
Cujo 1
cultural appropriation 3, 5, 7, 9, 18, 21, 120
Cunningham, Arnie 122–4, 167, 170

The Dark Half 32, 46–51
Dark Man *see* Flagg, Randall
The Dark Tower 4, 7, 72, 74, 79, 183
Dark Tower: Wolves of the Calla 132
Darnell, Will 122
Dayton, OH 27, 29
Deepnau, Natalie 149, 150
Deke ("The Raft") 152, 153
DeLesseps, Rawlie 48–9, 50, 51
demon 32, 51–3, 69, 81, 86, 90–1, 92, 93, 99, 121, 138, 162, 170, 171
Denbrough, Bill 16, 18, 20, 33, 34, 35, 36–7, 54, 168, 169
Denbrough, Georgie 20, 34, 35–6
Derry, ME 1, 15, 16, 19, 20, 31, 33, 34, 35, 167, 168, 169
Deschain, Roland 4
Desperation 2, 3, 59, 64–6, 68, 114
Devlin, Henry 42, 43, 44, 45–6, 178–9, 183
Devore, Kyra 133, 134, 135
Devore, Max 133
Disney 8
Dracula 57
Dreamcatcher 1, 32, 41–6, 54, 109–11, 169, 177–9
Dunhill, Sadie 145, 146

Edgecombe, Paul 75–8, 114
11/22/1963 144–6
Elvid, George 154–6, 158
End of Watch 27, 124–6
Epping, Jake 144–6, 160
Eucharist 57, 91, 92, 115, 116
exorcism 90–3, 162

"A Fair Extension" 154–6, 158
fairy tales 7, 9, 29
Fallujah 173
Farraday, Russell *see* Flagg, Randall
Flagg, Randall 2, 4, 60, 62, 63, 64, 68, 163, 164, 165
Flint City, OK 26, 28, 29, 31, 127
Freemantle, Abigail 59, 60–3, 64, 65, 68, 106, 165
From a Buick 8 3, 141–4, 163
Full Dark, No Stars 154

Gamache, Homer 46, 47
Gardener, Jim "Gard" – 158–9, 174, 175–7, 178, 179, 183, 184
Gatlin, NE 93, 94, 162
Gaunt, Leland 2, 79–81, 82, 95–9, 164–6
Gennesault Island 137
Gibney, Holly 27, 28–30, 31, 32, 125, 126, 127–31, 133, 180–3
Ginelli, Richie 24, 25, 38, 40
God 59, 60, 61, 62, 63, 64, 65, 68, 69, 78, 82, 84, 88, 90, 93, 98, 100, 101, 103, 104, 106, 107, 108, 109, 111, 113, 114–5, 117, 154
Goldsmith, Frannie 60, 61, 62, 63, 164
"A Good Marriage" 1
Goodhugh, Tom 154–6, 158
"Gray Matter" 137–8
The Green Mile 3, 75–8
Grim Reaper 48
Guilder, Dennis 3, 122–4, 133, 135, 142, 166–7, 169, 170
Gypsy 22–5, 31, 37–9

Halleck, Billy 12, 22, 23, 24, 25, 31, 37–41, 54, 134
Halleck, Linda 39–40, 41
Hanlon, Mike 16, 19, 20, 35, 167–8, 169, 182
Hanlon, Will 168
Hanscom, Ben 2, 17, 18, 19, 20, 33, 169
Happy Slapper 126, 128, 129
Hargensen, Chris 85, 87
Hartsfield, Brady 27, 124–6, 128, 129, 131, 139, 180, 182
Haven, ME 159, 174, 176
He Who Walks Behind the Rows 94–5, 162
Hodges, Kermit William "Bill" 27, 124–6, 128, 180
Hollywood 8
holy water 57, 58, 81, 91, 92, 124, 131
"Home Delivery" 136–7
the Host *see* Eucharist
Hunton, John 90–3

"I Am the Doorway" 137
"If It Bleeds" 129–31, 181–2
Insomnia 148–50, 169
Iscariot, Judas 110
It (creature) 1, 16, 17, 19, 20, 21, 33–7, 54, 116, 167, 168, 169, 170, 181, 182
It (novel) 1, 2, 4, 15–21, 31, 32, 33–7, 49, 51, 66, 92, 167–8, 170, 182

Jackson, Mark 90–3
Jacobs, the Rev. Charles 57, 111–5, 116, 117
Jefferson Tract, ME 42, 45, 110
"Jerusalem's Lot" 2
Jerzyck, Wilma 96, 98
Jesus Christ 14, 58, 62, 63, 69, 76, 77, 78, 81, 82, 84, 86, 88, 89, 94, 99, 101, 102, 103, 104, 108, 110, 111, 112, 116, 174
Jewish 67, 116

Job 156
Johnson, Freddy 109–10
Jones, Gary "Jonesy" 42–3, 44–5, 178–9, 183
Junction City, IA 165
Just After Sunset 67

Kaspbrak, Eddie 35, 66, 115, 116, 169
Kennedy, John Fitzgerald 144–6
Kenney, Jackie 145
Kurtz, Abraham 41, 42, 109–11, 116, 117, 179

Lachesis 149, 150
Las Vegas, NV 60, 61, 68, 163, 164
LaVerne ("The Raft") 152
Lazarus 11, 77, 116
LeBay, Roland 123
Lemke, Angelina 22–3, 24, 38–9
Lemke, Susannah 39
Lemke, Taduz 22, 23, 24, 25, 31, 38, 39–40, 41, 54, 134
Libby, Piper 107–9, 111, 116–7
Lord's Prayer 89, 116
the Losers 2, 15, 16, 17, 18, 19, 20, 21, 29, 31, 33–7, 51, 54, 66, 92, 116, 167, 168, 169, 170, 182
Lovecraft, H.P. 115

Magistrale, Tony 15, 74
Maine 7, 11, 15, 18, 41, 95, 131, 133, 145, 174, 177
Maitland, Gracie 29, 127
Maitland, Marcy 26, 28, 127
Maitland, Terry 26, 27, 28, 29, 127, 128, 129
"The Mangler" 3, 90–3, 103, 162
Marinville, John 65–6, 68
Marsh, Beverly 16, 17, 18, 168, 169
Martin, Reverend 64, 65
Marysville Hole 128, 130
Massachusetts 132
McCausland, Ruth 159
Mears, Ben 70–1, 73, 74, 81, 82, 131–2, 133
menses 85, 86, 88, 89
Mexico 131, 133
Micmac 11, 12, 13, 14, 15, 18, 20, 32, 43, 44, 116, 156, 157, 158, 160, 162
The Mill *see* Chester's Mill, ME
miracle 3, 5, 14, 18, 45, 59, 61, 62, 65, 69, 71, 75–8, 111, 114, 115
Misery 1, 46
Mr. Gray 42, 43, 44, 45, 178–9
Mr. Jingles 75, 77
Mr. Mercedes 27, 124, 125, 180, 182
Mitla, Harold 135–6, 137, 138
Monette ("Mute") 67
Moore, Pete 42, 178
Morton, Jamie 111, 113–4
Mother Abigail *see* Freemantle, Abigail
"The Moving Finger" 135–6

murder 15–16, 26–9, 35–6, 46, 47, 48, 49, 50, 52–3, 55, 67, 74, 75, 76, 77, 87, 89, 93, 100, 102, 104, 105, 107, 108, 113, 114, 121, 123, 124, 125, 127, 128, 133–4, 136, 137, 139, 157, 162, 171, 174, 180
"Mute" 67

Navajo 43, 44
Nebraska 61, 93, 95
Needful Things 2, 50, 78–81, 95–9, 163, 164–5
Night Shift 2, 3, 51, 90, 93, 132, 150
Nightmares & Dreamscapes 135, 137
9/11 147–8
Nolan, Billy 85
Noonan, Mike 133–5, 139
Norman, Jim 51–3, 55, 170–1

O'Bannion, Officer 136
Ohio 95, 127, 182
Oklahoma 127, 130
old Indian burial ground 10, 12, 14, 21
"One for the Road" 2, 72–5, 82, 132–3
Oswald, Lee Harvey 144, 145, 246
Outsider (creature) 127, 128, 131, 139, 180–3
The Outsider (novel) 1, 26–30, 32, 127–9, 131, 180–3

Pace, Jack 137
Pace, Maddie 137
Pangborn, Alan 46–7, 50, 79–81, 82, 95, 96, 97, 164–6
Pangborn, Annie 80
Pangborn, Todd 79, 80
Pennsylvania 130, 153
Pennywise *see* It (creature)
Perkins, Chief Howard "Duke" 105
Pet Sematary 10–5, 18, 32, 45, 116, 156–8
Peterson, Frankie 26, 28, 29, 127
Petrie, Mark 70, 71, 73–4, 81, 82, 131–2, 133
Poltergeist (film) 57
prayer 5, 59, 61, 64–5, 85, 88, 89, 100, 105–8, 109, 110, 116, 117
Protestantism 57, 62, 99
psychopomps 48–9, 50

Rachel ("The Raft") 152, 153
"The Raft" 3, 152–3, 154, 157, 163
Randy ("The Raft") 152–3
Rapeloew, Mrs. 179, 179
Redman, Stuart 60, 61–2, 63, 164
The Regulators 2, 64, 66, 68
Reino, Joseph 63
Rennie, Big Jim 3, 100, 105–7, 108, 109, 110, 115, 116, 117
Rennie, Junior 106
Revival 57, 111–5
Ridgewick, Norris 82
Ritual of Chüd 5, 33–7, 51, 54, 92, 168, 169

Roberts, Ralph 148–50, 160, 169, 170
Robinson, Jerome 27, 125, 126, 130, 131, 180
Rose, the Rev. William 96, 97
Ross, Brian 64
Ross, Tommy 85, 86, 87, 88, 90
Rusk, Brian 96, 98

Sablo, Yune 28
'Salem's Lot 1, 3, 57, 70–5, 80, 82, 116, 131–3, 139
Samuels, Bill 26
Sanders, Andy 105
The Shining 129
Shumway, Julia 110, 172–4, 176, 177, 179, 183, 184
Sidley, Miss 137
sin 60, 74, 86, 88, 89, 100, 107, 108
Skeleton Crew 3, 152
Smoke-Hole Ceremony 18, 19, 33, 37
Snell, Sue 85, 86, 87, 90
"Sometimes They Come Back" 32, 51–3, 55, 170
soul 48, 51, 67, 70, 79, 80–1, 82, 97, 99, 102, 105, 119, 138–9, 164–6
Staley, Scott 147–8, 149
The Stand 2, 4, 59, 60–6, 68, 114, 163–4, 165
Stark, George 46–51
Stoker, Bram 58
Streeter, David 154–6, 157, 158, 160
Strengell, Heidi 14, 87
"Suffer the Little Children" 137
suicide 27, 34, 37, 38, 50, 68, 74, 82, 94, 112, 113, 114, 122, 125, 126, 137, 144, 153, 167, 176

Tak 64, 65, 66, 68
telekinesis 85, 86, 87, 89, 125, 126, 156, 161, 162, 182

telepathy 41, 42, 43, 44, 128, 158, 159, 174, 176, 179
Templeton, Al 144–5, 146
Texas 127, 128, 145, 180
Thibodeau, Carter 106
"The Things They Left Behind" 146–8, 163
Thinner 12, 22–5, 32, 37–41, 134
Tidwell, Sara 133–5, 136, 139
The Tommyknockers 158–9, 160, 174–7, 179
Tooklander, Herb "Tookey" 132
Torrance, Jack 129
Tozier, Richie 16, 17, 19, 35, 36, 54, 169
Troop D 141, 142, 143, 144, 163
"Trucks" 3, 150–1, 152, 153, 154, 157, 163
the Turtle 18, 33, 34, 35

Under the Dome 3, 99–102, 105–9, 114, 115, 171–4, 175, 179
Underhill, Owen 41, 42, 43, 110, 178–9, 183
Underwood, Larry 61, 62, 63
Uris, Stan 16, 35, 67, 167, 169

vampire 34, 70, 71, 72, 73, 79, 82, 131, 133, 139
Venus 137
Vicky ("Children of the Corn") 93–5
voodoo 91

Wendigo 5, 11, 12, 13, 14–5, 18, 20, 28, 32, 45, 157
werewolf 17, 10, 34
Whetmore, Percy 75, 76, 78
the White (power) 79, 80, 81, 82, 115, 119
White, Carrie 85–90, 98, 102, 155, 156, 161–2
White, Margaret 86, 87, 88, 89, 90, 161–2
Wilcox, Curtis 141, 142, 143
Wilcox, Ned 141–4, 146, 163
World Trade Center 147

www.ingramcontent.com/pod-product-compliance
Ingram Content Group UK Ltd.
Pitfield, Milton Keynes, MK11 3LW, UK
UKHW042010140426
5217IPUK00015B/1085

9 781476 684734